The Appliqué Book

The Appliqué Book

Rose Verney

FRANCES LINCOLN

To my parents

Frances Lincoln Limited
Apollo Works, 5 Charlton Kings Road
London NW5 2SB

Copyright © Frances Lincoln Limited 1990
Text, designs, patterns and illustrations
© Rose Verney 1990
Photographs © Michael Dunne and Tim Imrie

British Library Cataloguing in Publication Data:
The Appliqué Book
Verney, Rose
1. Appliqué
I. Title
746.445

ISBN 0–7112–0637–6

Set in 9pt Caxton light by Bookworm Typesetting, Manchester
Originated in Hong Kong
Printed and bound in Italy

First Frances Lincoln Edition: October 1990

1 3 5 7 9 8 6 4 2

Contents

Introduction

The appliqué pieces I have chosen to illustrate this Introduction are just a few of my own personal favourites. They give an idea not only of the attractive results that can be achieved when working in this medium, but also of the wide range of objects on which appliqué can be worked.

Even before fabrics were woven, people embellished matted cloths, such as felt or beaten bark, or leather, with applied decorations as diverse as fish scales, leaves and beads. Colourful macaw feathers were stitched to the Peruvian tabard illustrated here; it dates from between AD 700 and 1000, and is made of natural undyed cotton.

Far more sumptuous and complex in its working is the fifteenth-century funeral pall from Freiburg in the Upper Rhine. It is composed of fifteen squares of black woollen cloth, worked separately and then sewn together. Each square is different, but they all have intricate and closely interlocking designs based on plant forms, applied with white woollen twill and edged with leather strips.

I am particularly fond of the Greenfield Hill coverlet made by Sarah Furman Warner of Greenfield Hill, Connecticut, because it has such a lively feeling to it. A town scene in the centre is surrounded by a richly patterned border of leaves and flowers. In several places she has sewn on printed flowers cut from a chintz, a technique known as *broderie perse*. I have used a similar technique, cutting round floral or leafy borders and applying them in my 'Home Sweet Home' wall hanging and in the Provençal Garden bag.

Below left *A bold design of applied feathers on an ancient Peruvian tabard.*

Below *Intricate appliqué on a fifteenth-century German funeral pall.*

The Greenfield Hill coverlet is a delightful and highly individual piece of early nineteenth-century North American appliqué. A floral border, with broderie perse, *surrounds a busy town square.*

Two further examples of nineteenth-century appliqué have a curiously modern appeal. Beads have long been used in applied decoration, and the combination of beads, shiny satin and stuffed and puffed effects on the English quilt shown here is typically Victorian. The colours are unusually sophisticated: a blue-green scheme with quite a lot of grey, white and black is enlivened by the occasional splash of vivid red.

An object entirely after my own heart, and an inspiration for my own Trompe l'Oeil table cover, is this one, made by a member of the Schwenkfelder religious sect of Pennsylvania Germans. I love both the idea and the way it has been executed. The bright colours, the bold floral pattern embroidered on the plates, the elegant cutlery and the generous assortment of cut-pile embroidered fruits all contribute to the humour and charm of the finished article.

The lovely appliqué panel entitled *The Magic Garden* was worked in 1937 in England by Rebecca Crompton. It has an airy, unlaborious freshness about it – the design and the embroidery are engagingly simple and complement each other perfectly.

Appliqué, both figurative and abstract, has been used over the centuries to decorate every kind of stitchable artefact, using any available materials. Native American Indians, as well as the Maoris of New Zealand, cut appliqué designs from the soft part of animal skins and applied them to the tough hide which made up the main part of a garment. And in addition to familiar objects – quilts, coverlets, clothes, hangings – appliqué has been used in a variety of more unusual situations. Saddle covers, tents and carpets with appliqué embellishments have been found in the graves of nomadic tribes who travelled in Asia between 200BC and AD220. Earlier still, in ancient Egypt, appliquéd cloths were used to wrap mummified animals and an appliqué linen collar was found in the tomb of King Tutenkhamun. The designs on such early examples usually had symbolic religious or ceremonial significance, and universal symbols, such as the spiral and the cross, are often found.

I hope in this Introduction to have whetted readers' appetites, so that they will go on to explore further this wonderfully multifarious tradition. Those who do so will be richly rewarded, for not only will they find the history of appliqué fascinating in itself, they will greatly expand their own creative vocabulary.

My final two choices – both in a popular, modern colourful idiom – come from the South American continent. The stuffed toys are an unusual application of mola work, an appliqué style developed by the Cuna women of the San Blas Islands, off the coast of Panama. They make a multi-layered reverse appliqué, cutting away patterns in each layer to reveal different colours beneath. The designs are often symbolic. Traditionally

Below left This imaginative and witty piece of trompe l'oeil appliqué was made in Pennsylvania in the nineteenth century.

Below A detail of a nineteenth-century English quilt gives some idea of the attractive eccentricity of its design.

Right In The Magic Garden, 1937, Rebecca Crompton has achieved an enviable impression of improvisation.

used to make molas or women's blouses, this form of appliqué has, by extension, become known as mola work.

In Chile, appliqué pictures such as the one shown here are made from scrap materials. Some represent scenes from family life, others may have a political message.

These, then, are a few of my own sources of inspiration. Do remember, when you turn to the various projects in this book, that you are free to adapt any of the designs you come across or to use them in different situations from those I have chosen. The cat on the tea cosy, for example, would look equally contented on a cushion cover. Appliqué is an ancient decorative art: you can enjoy making your contribution to a long tradition.

Right *Unusual examples of reverse appliqué mola work from the island of Mamitupu, San Blas, Panama*

Below *Bits of shiny leather and small shells represent fish and shellfish on the stalls in this Chilean appliqué market scene*

General Techniques

Only two basic sewing stitches, plus a few simple embroidery stitches, are needed to work all the projects in this book.

The following pages offer some easy-to-follow guidelines and explain basic techniques that will enable you to get the best results. They range from choosing appropriate fabrics to finishing off your work in a way that enhances its beauty and will double your pleasure in it. Instructions are given, too, for making up cushions and curtains.

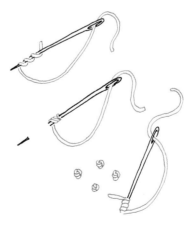

General Techniques

CHOOSING FABRICS

All fabrics used for appliqué, except felt, should be turned in and slipstitched to cover the raw edges, unless you want to create a special effect by deliberately fraying the edge, for example, or cutting it with pinking shears. Fabrics made of natural fibres, such as dress- or shirt-weight pure cotton, silk, and fine wool, are the best to use, as they can easily be creased and folded under at the edges, and they stay looking lovely. Polyester and other synthetics are, in my view, to be avoided.

Lighter weight furnishing cotton can be used, but it will be harder work turning in the edges and sewing. The backing fabric must be at least as heavy as the appliqué, so if you do use a furnishing cotton, be sure to choose a correspondingly heavy base fabric.

You may have scraps left over from dressmaking, curtain-making, etc., that can be used in some projects – thus saving shopping time and money. It is fun to be able to identify familiar bits of fabric in a piece of appliqué or patchwork, and any pieces may be used, so long as they are the right weight. To find out if the scraps are large enough, enlarge the pattern pieces and position them on the fabric (see below), observing the direction of the fabric grain.

PREPARING FABRICS

Normally I would dry-clean any of the objects in this book at a specialist dry-cleaner, but if you are likely to want to wash something by hand – such as a cot or crib quilt – then make sure that all the fabrics you use are colour-fast and pre-shrunk. Sewing and embroidery thread must also be colour-fast. If in doubt about a fabric, rinse it first in hand-hot water to be sure.

Straightening fabric Sometimes fabric is pulled 'off grain', so that the warp and weft threads do not cross at right angles. If you are cutting a large piece – for curtains, for example – where it is important that the fabric hang straight, you must make sure the grain is straight.

To do this, first straighten the ends. Cut a small snip in the selvedge on one side. Take hold of one of the crossways (weft) threads and pull it. On a loosely woven fabric you can pull quite a long length, causing the fabric to gather up fully; on other fabrics you will get only a slight puckering. Pull out as much thread as you can, then cut along the space left, or along the line of puckers. Repeat across the entire width. Measure off the required length and cut along the grain as described above.

Now fold the fabric in half

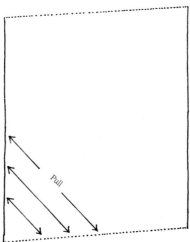

a

b *Pull*

crossways. If the corners meet exactly, or nearly exactly, you can proceed with the project. If, however, they meet at an angle, as shown in **fig. a**, you must straighten the fabric. Pull it on the bias, starting at one sharply angled corner (**fig. b**) and working along the length to the other end. You may need to get someone to help you if the fabric is wide.

Note Some fabrics, such as polished chintz, should not be straightened in this way, as it would spoil the finish. When cutting, say, a curtain panel, simply mark and cut straight lines irrespective of the grain. However, it is wise, when buying such fabric, to examine it closely. If the weft threads meet the selvedge at a noticeably acute angle it is best not to buy it, as it will tend to sag and be difficult to handle.

CUTTING OUT
Enlarging the pattern pieces

Most of the patterns in this book need to be enlarged before they can be used; a few can be traced directly from the page. The degree of enlargement is given with each set of pattern pieces, and if you have access to a photocopier that makes enlargements, this can be done quite quickly.

If you do not have access to such a machine, you will need to scale the patterns up, using graph paper. The grid printed over the patterns is based on 5cm/2in (dark lines) and 2.5cm/1in (fainter lines) so that it can be used with graph paper ruled in either centimetres or inches. If your paper uses centimetres, you should use the 5cm/2in grid as a guide when enlarging; however, if a pattern is relatively small and complex, so that the 5cm/2in grid is not much help, you may wish to draw intermediate lines at 2.5cm/1in intervals as additional guides.

The scaling-up method is essentially simple, if somewhat time-consuming. You copy the pattern lines onto your graph paper, positioning the lines in the same relation to the larger grid as they are to the smaller one (**fig. c**).

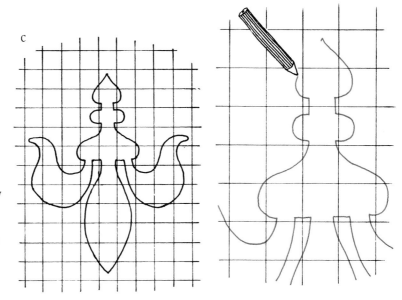

Positioning the pieces Arrows are printed on the pattern pieces to show you how to position them on the fabric when cutting out. The arrows should always be pointing along the direction of the straight grain of the fabric – that is, either the lengthways or crossways direction of the weave (**fig. d**).

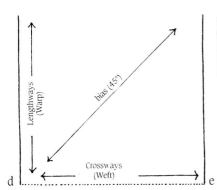

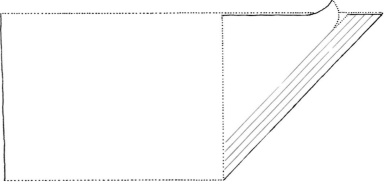

An exact alignment is not so important as in dressmaking, where the hang of a garment is determined by it. In appliqué you can cheat slightly, but you should position the pieces more or less as indicated.

Cutting bias strips and duplicate shapes. As a rule, all curved shapes are cut on the bias, and straight-sided ones are cut straight. However, there are some exceptions, such as straight strips of bias-cut fabric for piping or edging. Fold the fabric as shown in **fig. e,** press along the fold, then cut additional strips parallel to the first line, measuring and drawing pencil lines on the wrong side of the fabric if you like.

Cutting straight strips for edging, etc., is easier if you use the selvedge as a straight line to work from. Measure in from the selvedge, and cut one strip; then cut any others parallel to the first, again measuring from the edge (**fig. f**).

In some cases you will need two or more of a particular piece cut from the same pattern – sometimes quite a few, as in the Swags and Diamonds quilt. It will be quicker if you fold the fabric and cut two at a time (**fig. g**). Bear in mind, when using fabrics with a right and wrong side, that this method will produce shapes that are a mirror image of each other, unless the shape is completely symmetrical.

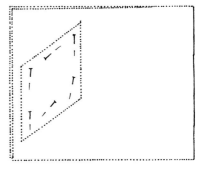

To cut circles, make a pencil line on the wrong side of the fabric, using a compass or drawing round a coffee cup, plate, pastry cutter, roll of Sellotape, cotton reel or any round object of the right diameter (including 3mm/¹⁄₈in for turning under). Cut round the pencil line. For large circles, you can measure from a central point, as described for the Trompe l'Oeil table cover (page 102), putting pins at 3–5cm/1–2in intervals, then tacking and cutting next to the tacking line. Alternatively, attach a piece of string or cotton to a drawing pin in the centre of the cloth, and move it round in a circle, placing the pins that way (**fig. h**).

Avoiding confusion Projects such as the Birds in the Trees quilt (page 130), with dozens of tiny pieces, can get into a terrible muddle – keep all the pieces for each bird in separate envelopes, similarly all the leaves, pink dots, and so on. This way you will be certain to have all the bits to hand, and will not risk losing any.

If you have chosen different colours from those ones shown and listed for a particular project, make your own colour key, identifying the colours you are using as 'A', 'B', and so on. Keep this list handy when cutting out and when positioning pieces on the background fabric.

After cutting out your appliqué shapes, snip all the inward curves, points and corners (**fig. i**). Your snips should be *just* less than 3mm/¹⁄₈in.

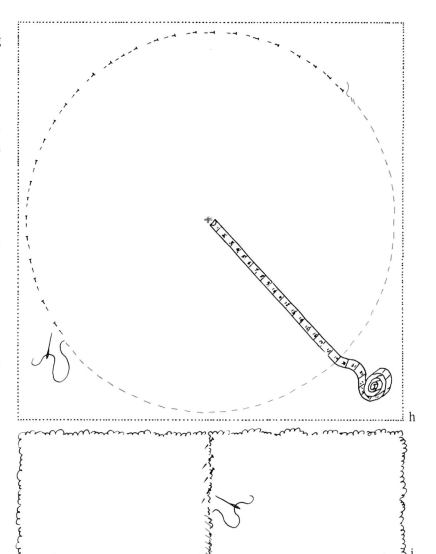

h

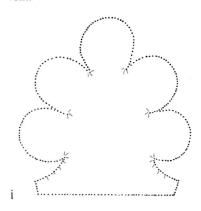

i

JOINING WADDING

You may need to join pieces of wadding to make up the width for a large quilt. Lay the two pieces, cut to the length of the quilt plus about 5cm/2in, side by side, and pin them together at intervals. Join them with cross-over stitches (**fig. j**), pulling the stitches tight enough to prevent gaps but not so tight that they strain the wadding. Do not overlap the two pieces you are joining, as this will cause a ridge in the finished quilt.

TRANSFERRING DETAILS FOR EMBROIDERY

There are several methods of transferring designs for embroidery.

j

If the material is lightweight, you can simply tape the full-size pattern to a window, tape the fabric on top, and trace the lines directly with a fabric marking pencil.

Alternatively, you can use dressmaker's carbon, which is a special non-smudge transfer paper. Place the fabric on a flat, firm surface, lay the paper, coloured side down, on top, and then position the design on top of both. Go over the lines firmly with a ball-point pen. The paper comes in several colours, to contrast with different shades of fabric; use one that will provide just enough contrast for the purpose. Always test the paper first on a spare piece of fabric.

The following method is one I use frequently. With tracing paper, trace the embroidery design from the pattern. Take a stout pin and stab along the lines you have drawn to make a series of little holes in the fabric. These will not last, but will remain visible long enough for you to lightly draw along them, joining the dots, with a fabric pencil, wipe-off pen or dressmaker's chalk.

STITCHING

Tacking This is a fairly large running stitch, sometimes called basting. It is used to hold the appliqué pieces in position while they are sewn on. As a rule, the stitches should be sewn a scant 1cm/⅜in from the raw edge.

Slipstitching This is a small and (preferably) invisible stitch to hold the turned-in edges of the appliqué

pieces down and prevent any fraying. Pull the thread firmly, keeping the stitches tight, but not so tight that the fabric puckers.

I normally work slipstitching with the piece being applied lying towards me (**fig. k**). I find that this method helps me to turn under the edges smoothly, and the work goes quite fast. However, many people prefer to work slipstitch with the appliqué pieces lying away from them, and if you find this more comfortable, you should work this way. The aim is to achieve a smoothly turned and firmly stitched edge.

When slipstitching pieces that overlap each other (for example, the carrots on the Carrot Patch quilt, page 114), only sew those parts that will show when the work is complete. This makes less work, obviously, but also ensures a flatter finish with no ridges.

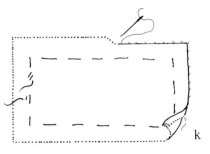

k

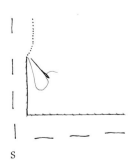

KEY
The illustrations in this book use the following symbols:

················	raw edge
——————	turned-under edge/seam
⌒⊤⊤⊤⌒	snips in fabric edge
←——————→	place on straight grain
– – – ∿	tacking
————————	slipstitch
– – – – –	topstitching/running stitch

l   m   n   o

Points These are best approached methodically. Work up to one stitch length from the tip of the point on one side (**fig. l**). Turn the point in, and make a stitch right on the end (**fig. m**). Turn in the second side and stitch along (**fig. n**). **Fig. o** shows the underside of the work.

Corners Much the same technique applies as for points – that is, do not attempt to turn under both sides of a corner or point before you sew. On an outer corner sew up to the angle of the corner, stopping a little short of it. Turn under the adjacent side, and make a small stitch right on the corner at a 45° angle (**fig. p**). Then

turn in the second side and sew that (**fig. q**). This way you can achieve really sharp corners and points without bulky lumps or fraying. It is much the same as folding 'hospital corners' on a sheet.

On an inner corner (**fig. r**), stitch into the corner, before continuing along the next side (**fig. s**).

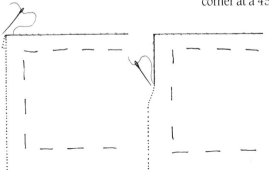

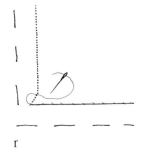

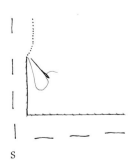

p   q   r   s

Circles and curves When sewing circles or any rounded shape, it is only too easy to get little corners appearing, which spoil the smooth curve. The best thing to do is to coax the fabric into a curved shape as you go round, and not to attempt to get it perfectly turned in before you start sewing. Use your needle to push in or pull out a little fabric at a time.

Straight lines, especially long ones, will be straighter and easier to sew if you turn in the edges and press them before sewing. For example, the Falling Oak Leaves and Beautiful Balloons curtains, the Coral Reef quilt and the Stars and Hearts quilt all have some straight pieces which will be quicker to apply – and look neater – if you turn them in and press them in advance.

Backstitch This is used to make a solid line (**fig. t**) when embroidering details, such as the cat's features in the tea cosy project (page 24).

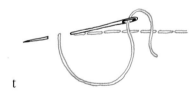

t

French knots These little dots are used for decorative purposes (**fig. u**). They can be worked in a contrasting colour, as on the four-sided bag (page 50).

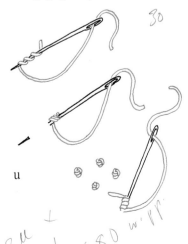

u

Topstitching (running stitch)
This is a straight in-and-out running stitch (**fig. v**), usually worked round the edges of the appliqué shapes after slipstitching and pressing. It holds the pieces flat and strengthens the work, as well as being decorative and adding texture. It can also be used purely decoratively to add detail to a piece – as, for example, on the mother cat in the tea cosy project (page 22). Make the stitches as even as possible, and choose the stitch size to suit the design; small-scale designs such as the coffee pot cosy (page 84) require smaller stitching, as do details such as the features on the reclining mermaid at the bottom of the Coral Reef quilt (page 46).

Tacking is removed, as a general rule, after the topstitching is completed and before giving your work a final press. It is best to keep it in place while working the topstitching, as it holds the piece flat and prevents any possibility of it becoming distorted or buckling as you sew the running stitch round it.

Satin stitch This is used to fill an area when embroidering details such as the cat's eyes (page 24). Work the outline first in small backstitch or running stitch, then fill it with parallel lines (**fig. w**). Satin stitch is basically simple, but keeping the stitches parallel can be tricky. Establish the slant by starting near the middle of the shape – not at the end or corner – then work outwards.

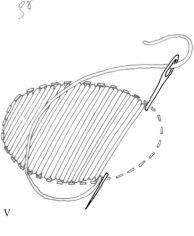

v

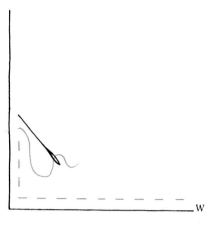

W

PRESSING

Normally I press the work at almost every stage – before cutting out, after slipstitching, after topstitching (having removed tacking). It is much easier to press as you go along, and in fact sometimes quite difficult to do it after a project is finished, as with many layers one sometimes gets bumps. Use the iron no hotter than you need to, and iron *very* gently where there are several overlapping layers. Use a pressing cloth to avoid making a sheen on fabrics that are prone to this. On tiny pieces use just the tip of the iron to smooth them. A small travelling iron is useful for fiddly places.

FINISHING

Several of the projects in this book are finished with a binding round the edge. This is an easy way of finishing off a piece, and it offers the possibility of adding an extra line of colour to frame the design. Generally speaking, edging strips are machine-sewn onto the right side of the piece, turned over to the back and hemmed onto the lining. The corners can be either mitred or sewn straight. Mitring can be decorative as well as neat. However, the straight type of corner can also be a decorative feature, as in the 'Home Sweet Home' hanging (page 64), where the black selvedge of the edging fabric is part of the design.

To make a straight corner, trim the underlying edging piece level with the edge of the quilt (or other object), and turn in the end of the other edging strip to the same length; press. Overlap the two ends neatly and sew as invisibly as possible along the joins.

Mitred corners are easiest to make with a single edging strip that continues all round the piece, rather than with separate strips on each side. Fold the surplus fabric at the corners as shown in **fig x**.

Joining bias strips Bias-cut strips should be joined on the straight grain of the fabric – that is, along the diagonal ends of the strips (**fig. y**).

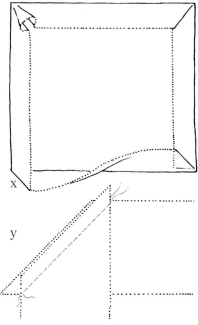

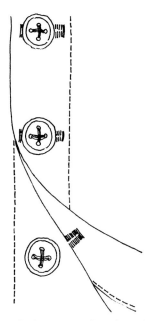

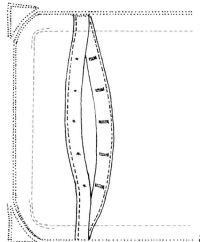

MEASUREMENTS
You will sometimes find variations in the metric/imperial equivalents given in this book. For example, you may find 1cm/$\frac{3}{8}$in in one place and 1cm/$\frac{1}{2}$in in another. These variations are intentional; in each case, an appropriate measurement in the context of *that system* has been chosen. Always use either metric or imperial – never try to mix the two.

CUSHIONS
There are several different ways of making up a cushion. When I make a cushion or a quilt – or, indeed, anything else – I like the fastenings, lining and other functional parts to be not only serviceable but an embellishment of the whole.

For this reason I prefer to use buttons or ribbon ties on cushions rather than zips or hooks. All the cushion projects in this book were made with button fastenings. The cutting instructions include an allowance for overlapping and for turning under the edges.

1 Turn under 5mm/$\frac{1}{4}$in on the two opening edges; press. Fold under these edges again by the required amount – usually about 3–4cm/ 1$\frac{1}{4}$–1$\frac{1}{2}$in has been allowed; pin and tack them in place. Before tacking, check the overlap by placing the two sections side by side with the opening edges lapped and so that their outer edges will match those of the top cover.

If the overlap is not adequate for buttoning, you will need to reduce the turning on one or both edges.

Machine stitch the turnings in place.

2 Work buttonholes in the overlap edge by hand or by machine – most modern machines will work buttonholes. However, you should first work one or more test buttonholes in a spare piece of the fabric (double thickness) to make sure it will produce satisfactory results and that the buttonhole is the right size. As a general rule, make the length equal to the diameter of the button plus its thickness.

If your machine has trouble producing a neat buttonhole, it is safer to work the buttonholes by hand.

3 Sew the buttons to the other edge, opposite the buttonholes (**fig. z**).

4 To join the top and back covers (without piping): place the back sections – unbuttoned – on the top cover with right sides facing and edges matching. Pin, tack and machine stitch round the edges. Press the seam flat. Cut diagonally across the corners to reduce the bulk. You may wish to work a little extra stitching at these points for reinforcement (**fig. aa**). Now press the seam open. Turn the cover right side out through the opening.

To pipe an edge

1 First prepare the piping as follows. Cut and join (if necessary) a bias strip long enough to cover the piping cord, which should be a few centimetres/inches longer than the distance around the finished edge of the cover (measured at the seamline). The bias strip should be as wide as the circumference of the cord plus at least 2.5cm/1in for seam allowances.

Wrap the strip round the cord, right side outside. With the zipper foot on the machine, stitch close to the side of the cord (**fig. bb**).

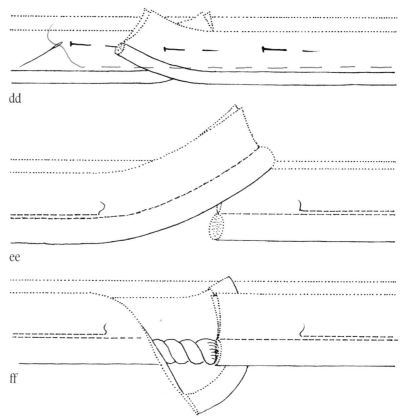

dd

ee

ff

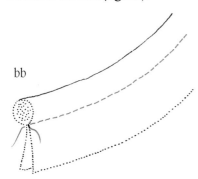

bb

2 Place the piping on the right side of the top cover, with the cord towards the centre and the seam allowance towards the edge. The stitching should lie on the seamline, or slightly outside it.

Pin and tack the piping in place. Clip the seam allowances at the corners so that they will lie flat (**fig. cc**). Using the zipper foot, stitch the piping in place.

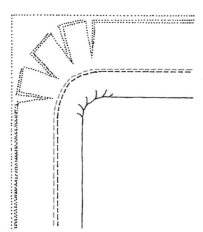

cc

To join piping ends, you can use one of the following methods. The first is suitable only for quite narrow piping.
Method 1: At the point of joining, overlap the ends smoothly; tack them in place, then stitch (**fig. dd**).
Method 2: Stitch the piping in place up to within 5cm/2in of the join. Trim one end of the piping straight; cut the other end to overlap the first by 2.5cm/1in (**fig. ee**). Pull this second cord out of the bias covering and trim off 2.5cm/1in. Smooth the bias fabric back over the cord, then unpick the stitching back to the end of the cord. Turn under about 1cm/ ³⁄₈in of the fabric end. Butt the cord ends together, then wrap the fabric end over the other piping (**fig. ff**).

Tack the joined piping in place and complete the stitching.

3 When the piping has been attached, join the top and back covers as described above.

Boxed cushion

A boxed cushion has a flat section, or gusset, joining the top and back covers. This form of construction is essential on a round cushion (apart from very flat ones) in order to preserve the round shape.

1 Join the short ends of the gusset to make a ring of the required size. Press the seam open. Pin and tack one edge of the gusset to the top cover, first having applied piping if you are using it. Clip the seam allowance to make it lie flat. Machine stitch (**fig. gg**).

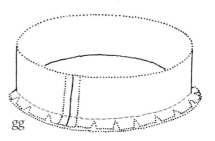

gg

2 Pin and tack the other edge of the gusset to the back cover in the same way. In order to prevent the two sections from flopping about, fasten one button at each end, and tack the two sections together for a short distance. Machine stitch (**fig. hh**). Turn the cover right side out.

Grading seams In order to reduce bulk where several layers of fabric are joined – as on the piped seams of a cushion cover – it is often necessary to grade the seam allowances, by trimming them to different widths (**fig. ii**).

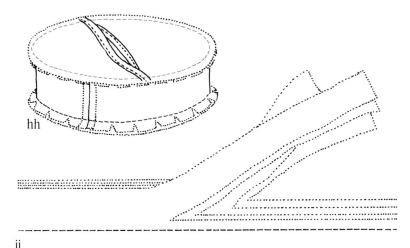

hh

ii

CURTAINS

There are many different ways of making curtains. If you are making your own, you should first consult a book on soft furnishings for detailed instructions on measuring windows and planning the amount of fabric to buy. You will almost certainly need to adjust the proportions of the curtains shown in this book in order to suit your own windows.

If you are using a heading tape, you should buy more than twice the width of your windows (ask the salesperson for guidance), then pleat up the tape itself to see where the

pleats will fall, so that you can position them correctly. (This is less essential if you are using a pencil-pleated heading, as on the Beautiful Balloons curtains, page 90, than it is for French pleats, which have spaces between them.) Mark the finished ends of the tape (that is, where they will be turned under for neatening). Then smooth the tape out flat and measure it. This will be the finished width of the curtain panel.

I strongly recommend interlining most curtains, as it makes them hang better, gives additional

protection to the main curtain fabric – not to mention your beautifully worked appliqué – and conserves heat. However, this is best done by a professional. The instructions that follow are for basic lined curtains and for those in which you are making your own pleats, rather than using a heading tape.

Basic method, lined curtains

1 Trim one side edge of the lining panel so that it measures 3cm/1in less in width than the curtain panel. Trim the lining at one end so that it is 9cm/3½in shorter than the curtain panel.

2 Pin, tack and machine stitch the lining and curtain together, right sides facing, along their side edges, placing the lining 3cm/1in down from the top edge of the curtain and taking 1.5cm/⅝in seam allowance. Leave the last 6cm/2½in of the lining unstitched (**fig. jj**). Press the seam allowances towards the lining.

3 Turn the curtain right side out. Centre the lining as shown, so that a small amount of curtain fabric is visible at each edge (**fig. kk**). Fold the top edge down 1.5cm/½in and then another 1.5cm/½in, enclosing the lining. Pin and tack it in place. Hem it to the lining by hand (**fig. ll**).

jj

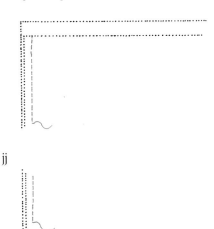

kk

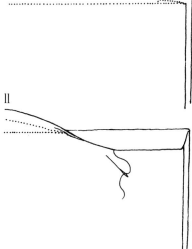

ll

4 Cut the heading tape to the finished width of the curtain plus about 3cm/1¼in for turning under. If you are using tape with cords, add about 10cm/4in to this measurement, then pull out the cords at one end for 10cm/4in and cut away the excess tape; in this way, you will have some cord to get hold of when pleating the curtains. If you are using tape with pleats spaced at intervals (e.g. French pleats), make sure you position the tape correctly in relation to the edges of the curtains.

Turn under the ends of the tape and pin and tack it to the top edge of the curtains, about 5mm/¼in from the top. Machine stitch it to the curtain round all edges (**fig. mm**).

5 To hem the lining, first turn the curtain wrong side out. On the lining, turn under 1cm/½in; press. Turn this edge under another 5cm/2in; press. Tack and machine stitch the folded edge in place (**fig. nn**).

6 It is a good idea to hang up the curtains at this point, first turning up a single temporary hem and tacking it in place. Leave the curtains to hang for a few days. Adjust the hem allowance, if necessary, and mark the finished length with a line of tacking. Trim the hem allowance to measure 10cm/4in.

Turn up 5cm/2in on the lower edge; press. Turn under another 5cm/2in; press and tack this in place. Hem the curtain by hand.

Fold the side edges in, turning up

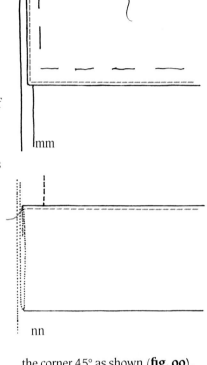

mm

nn

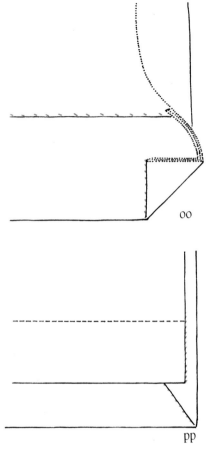

oo

pp

the corner 45° as shown (**fig. oo**). Slipstitch it in place.

Tack the lining over the curtain edge as shown, and slipstitch it in place from the end of the machine-stitched seam to the lower edge (**fig. pp**).

Heading for hand-made pleats

1 Cut the lining 6cm/2½in shorter than the curtain, and trim one side so that the lining is 3cm/1in narrower than the curtain.

2 Turn under and press 8cm/3in on the upper edge of the curtain. Trim

the folded buckram strip to measure 4cm/1½in less than the width of the curtain. Slip it under the top hem fold, leaving 2cm/¾in at each side; tack it in place (**fig. qq**).

3 Turn under and press 8cm/3in on the upper edge of the lining; press.

Stitch the curtain and lining together along the sides, as described in Step 2 of the Basic Method, but placing the lining about 3mm/⅛in down from the curtain edge (**fig. rr**).

4 Turn the curtain right side out. Centre the lining and press the side edges. Slipstitch the lining to the curtain along the upper edge.

5 Complete the curtain as described in Steps 5 and 6 of the Basic Method, and make pleats of the desired size, style and number.

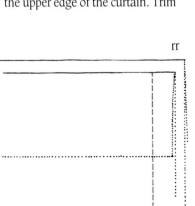

rr

qq

The
Projects

The versatility and beauty of appliqué, and the wonderful opportunities it offers for self-expression, are revealed in the pages that follow. Twenty specially-created projects show a wealth of appliqué designs, both figurative and abstract, that can be used to adorn objects as diverse as curtains and cushion covers, wall hangings and waistcoats. Some projects are clearly more complex than others and absolute beginners would probably be better advised to start with something simple, such as Cat Family.

Cat Family

Children will love this friendly family of cats. They are easy and fun to make, and do a highly efficient job of keeping tea and boiled eggs warm. The tea cosy is made up here with a cream-coloured calico cat sitting on a check tablecloth; she is surrounded by her eight kittens – four white and four black, one on each side of the four egg cosies. You could, if you wish, make more or fewer egg cosies, or put a cat on just one or both sides of the tea cosy.

All of the fabrics are washable cottons, and the wadding is medium-weight polyester. The tea cosy measures approximately 28cm/ 11in tall by 37cm/14½in wide.

Materials

Medium-weight cotton fabrics, 90cm/36in wide. I have used the colours indicated in the list below. You can, of course, use quite different colour combinations if you wish.

A Light blue – for background: 40cm/½yd

B White – for cats and kittens: 60cm/¾yd (or 1m/1yd if cut double, see the Note on page 144)

C Checked fabric (the one I used is seersucker) – for tablecloth: 10cm/ ⅛yd (or piece approx. 20 × 40cm/ 8 × 16in)

D Black – for kittens: 10cm/⅛yd (or piece approx. 20cm/8in square)

E Yellow – for binding: 40cm/½yd (or enough to cut a total of 4m/ 4⅜yd of bias strips averaging 3.5cm/1½in in width)

F Plain coloured or printed fabric of your choice – for lining: 40cm/½yd Medium-weight polyester wadding: 40cm/½yd

Ribbon 1.2cm/½in wide: 70cm/ ¾yd

Grey and white quilting or sewing thread

Stranded embroidery cotton in turquoise and apple green.

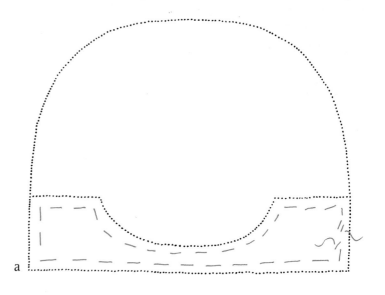

a

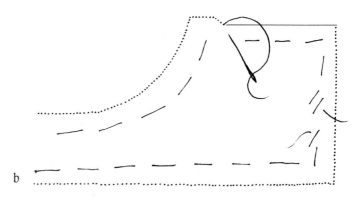

b

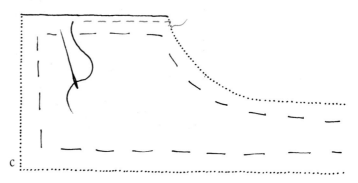

c

1 Cut out the fabric pieces as instructed on page 144. (See also the general instructions on pages 12–16.)

2 To make the tea cosy appliqué, first position the tablecloth piece on the background fabric, with the lower edges even. Pin and tack it in place (fig. a). Turn under the straight upper edges of the tablecloth 5mm/ ¼in, then tack and slipstitch them (see page 15) to the background (fig. b). But do not stitch the curved edge. Topstitch 3mm/⅛in from the slipstitched edges (fig. c) in an appropriate colour (see page 16).

3 Position the cat on the background, overlapping the raw 'scooped out' edge of the tablecloth. Pin, tack (fig. d) and slipstitch it in place, taking special care at the corners where you have snipped the fabric. Press.

Topstitch 3mm/⅛in from the edge all round the cat. Work a double line of stitching for the tail and back leg. If you are confident enough, use a fabric pencil to draw the lines first, then rub them out carefully afterwards. Otherwise trace these details, and the facial features, from the pattern, using one of the methods described on page 14. Remove all tacking.

d

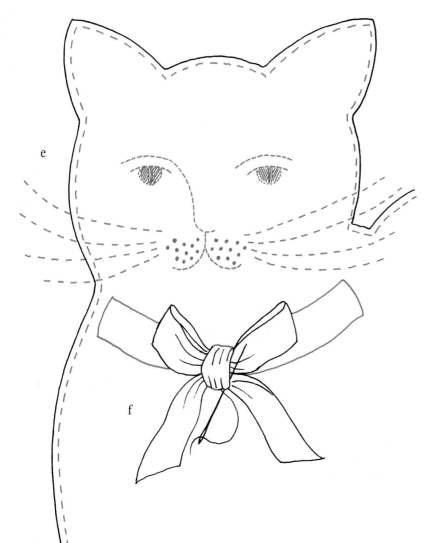

e

f

4 Embroider the cat's features in backstitch, using a single strand of the grey thread. Outline the eye shape in backstitch; then fill in with satin stitch, worked horizontally or diagonally, using two strands of turquoise. Make a few lines of vertical satin stitch in green to suggest the pupils. Work French knots (see page 16) in grey, then embroider the whiskers in running stitch (fig. e).

5 To make the bows, first cut the ribbon in half, then in half again, leaving four equal lengths. Turn under 5mm/¼in at one end of each piece and press. Set two pieces aside for the other cat. Pin and tack the turned-under ends to the neck of the cat, positioning them as shown in the photograph. Tie the ribbon in a neat bow and slipstitch the ends in place. Slipstitch the centre of the bow (fig. f) then trim the ends.

If you want two cats, repeat steps 2–4 on the other side (fig. g).

g

6 Now the cosy can be made up.
Assemble the three layers of each side with the lining wrong side up on the bottom, then the wadding, then the appliquéd piece, right side up on top. Make sure that the edges match, then pin and tack them together.

Cut a length of the wider binding long enough to go easily round the curved edge with about 3cm/1¼in extra, plus two lengths the same measurement as the lower edge. Pin one of these shorter lengths along the lower edge of the appliquéd side of the cosy, right sides facing and raw edges matching. Tack (fig. h),

then machine stitch through all layers, 1cm/⅜in from the edge. Fold the binding to the lining side, turn under the raw edge 6mm/¼in, and pin, tack (fig. i) and slipstitch it to the lining, covering the machine stitching. Bind the lower edge of the other side in the same way.

h

i

j

k

7 To join the two sides of the cosy, pin them together, with the linings on the inside, matching the edges exactly. Tack through all the layers about 2.5cm/1in from the curved edge. Pin the remaining strip of binding round one side, leaving at least 1cm/⅜in extending at each end to tuck in for a neat finish. Tack the binding on (fig. j), taking your needle through all layers, then machine stitch, a scant 1cm/⅜in from the edge. Grade the wadding and lining seam allowances (as explained on page 19) to reduce bulk. Then fold the binding to the

other side, turn in the raw edge 5mm/¼in, and tack and slipstitch the binding in place (fig. k), covering the line of machine stitching.

8 To make the egg cosies, follow the same basic procedures as for the tea cosy. Work the appliqué on each side before making up the cosies. Note that the topstitching and embroidery use smaller stitches than those on the tea cosy. Arrange the four different kittens as you please: an alternative colourway is shown on the right.

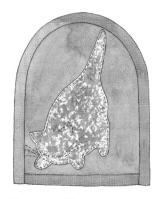

One kitten could be a ginger tom!

Brilliant Blooms

This large, colourful cushion would look marvellous by itself on a wicker armchair or as the centrepiece on a big sofa, with smaller cushions made up in the same colour. It could also work well as a floor cushion in a child's bedroom. It is about 55cm/22in square.

I have made it up here in ten colours, choosing a fairly dark lavender blue linen for the background, both for its colour and for its weight. For the appliqué I have used three different pinks – a coral, a fuchsia and a rose pink, three quite similar yellows – pale, medium and dark, a dark turquoise and a bright green. The touches of black have the effect of making the bright colours even more vivid.

Materials

Linen and assorted cotton fabrics 90cm/36in wide. I have used the colours indicated in the list below. You can, of course, use more, fewer or quite different colours for your version of the cushion. The quantities suggested are the most appropriate purchasable amounts or, in some cases, the appropriate size scrap from your collection.

A Deep lavender blue – for background: 1.3m/1 1/2yd (or 70cm/3/4yd of 122cm/48in fabric)
B Deep turquoise – for inner border: 30cm/3/8yd (or piece approx. 25 × 50cm/10 × 20in)
C Coral pink – for border edging, petals, etc: 30cm/3/8yd
D Rose pink – for petals, etc: 20cm/1/4yd (or piece approx. 20 × 30cm/8 × 12in)
E Fuchsia pink – for petals, etc.: 10cm/1/8yd (or piece approx. 10 × 35cm/4 × 14in)
F Golden yellow – for leaves, stems: 20cm/1/4yd (or piece approx. 20 × 40cm/8 × 16in)
G Mid yellow – for leaves, stems: 20cm/1/4yd (or piece approx. 15 × 30cm/6 × 12in)

a

H Pale yellow – for leaves, stems: 20cm/1/4yd (or piece approx. 15 × 30cm/6 × 12in)
I Bright green – for diagonal border strips: 20cm/1/4yd (or piece approx. 20 × 35cm/8 × 14in)
J Black – for border strips and random pieces: 10cm/1/8yd (or piece approx. 20 × 25cm/8 × 10in)
Black cotton sewing or quilting thread
7 Buttons
Cushion pad 55cm/22in square

1 Cut out the fabric pieces as instructed on page 146. (See also the general instructions on pages 12–16.)

2 Position the four inner border pieces (Fabric B) with their outer edges 8cm/3 1/4in from the edges of the main piece. Pin and tack them in place down the centre, lapping one corner over the next all round the square.

3 Arrange the flower stems in the central square, tucking their ends under the tacked strips, with their heads pointing towards the centre. Hold them in place with a few pins, while you put the leaves and petals in place, adjusting the petals as necessary so that the flowers fill the square more or less evenly without touching each other. Pin and tack all these pieces in place (fig. a). Keep the tacking stitches well in from the edge of each piece because you will be turning under the edges by 3mm/1/8in and you will need to lift some petals up in order to stitch those underneath.

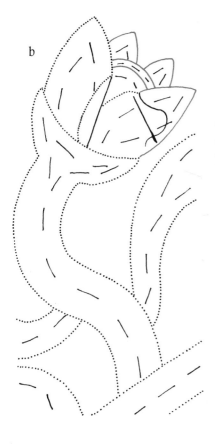

b

4 Now sew on the flowers, slipstitching the petals, leaves and stems (see page 15). Start with the underlying petals and work up to those on the top. For example, when stitching Flower II, begin with the two small petals (Fabric D), stitching both sides down to the point where they will be covered; then stitch the Fabric F centre, then the Fabric E centre, then the outer petals (fig. b).

Next, slipstitch the leaves and stems (fig. c), again working from the lower pieces to the upper ones. For example, in Flower I, stitch the stem itself, then the calyx.

When you have finished all the stitching, press the work under a pressing cloth. Do not remove the tacking stitches (fig. d).

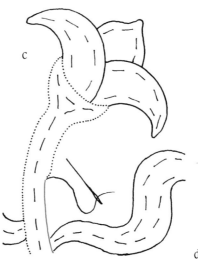

c

d

5 Now arrange the geometric border pieces as shown in fig. e. Basically the elements are the same on all four sides. Sides 2 and 4 are identical but have different distributions of colours; 1 and 3 are similar, with slight variations. Pin and tack the pieces in place, making sure you allow enough overlap for the overlying pieces to be turned in 3mm/$\frac{1}{8}$in without any raw edges appearing.

Fold the three Fabric J strips (Side 3) in half lengthways; press. Tuck a strip under each wide strip so that when the latter's raw edges are slipstitched about 3mm/$\frac{1}{8}$in of the folded strip will be visible.

Side 4

Side 3

Side 1

e   Side 2

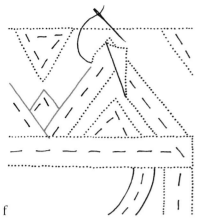

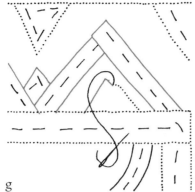

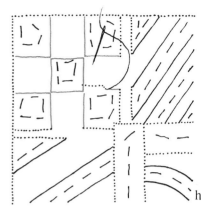

f

g

h

6 Slipstitch the pieces on each side, working from lower pieces to upper ones. On Side 4, for example, first stitch the black diamonds, then the green strips (fig. f), then the turquoise strips, and then the pink triangles (fig. g).

Next, tack and slipstitch the squares in each of the corner sections (fig. h), then the black strips alongside them.

Finally, slipstitch the main border strips along both long edges. Press the work carefully through a cloth.

7 The small black shapes can be sewn on the background in a random fashion. Pin and tack them in place, then slipstitch the edges.

Now topstitch (see page 16) all the appliqué pieces, apart from these random shapes, using black thread. Remove all the tacking, and press the work, through a cloth, on both sides.

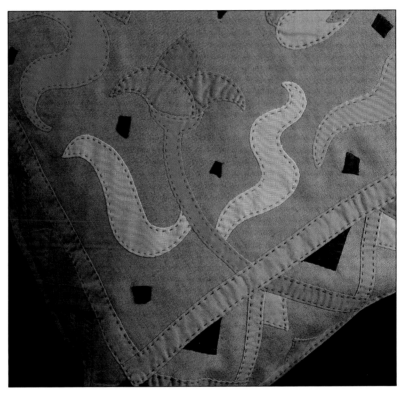

i

8 To make the flat edging strip for the cushion, join the edging strips (Fabric C) to make a single strip, 240cm/95in long. Press the seams open. Fold the strip in half lengthways, then press it flat. Work running stitch along the folded edge.

Tack the strip to the right side of the main piece, placing the raw edges together and forming a tiny pleat at each corner (fig. i). Join the ends neatly.

9 Make up the cushion cover as described on page 17.

A soft pastel scheme would look equally pretty.

Swags and Diamonds

This quilt, although large, is one of the simplest projects in the book. None of the motifs overlaps the others, the shapes are uncomplicated and the design is symmetrical – a simple repeating pattern of diamonds and small circles, with a border composed of curved swags and larger circles. All of these are traditional elements which appear quite frequently in North American appliqué quilts.

I have chosen a very dark blue furnishing cotton for the base fabric and colours ranging from bright emerald green to brilliant turquoise for the appliqué. Most of these are Indian silks, and some of them are 'shot', so that the silk changes colour depending on the direction of the light. For the topstitching I have used a bright lime green perlé cotton.

In the instructions I have not specified which fabrics to use for the circles at the corners of the diamonds. Since your colours will differ slightly or considerably from mine, you will want to choose those that contrast most effectively.

The finished quilt measures approximately 233cm/92in square.

Materials

Silk and cotton fabrics (90cm/36in wide unless otherwise stated). I have made the quilt in the colours indicated in the list below. You may, of course, decide to make it in quite different colours.

A Dark blue, at least 122cm/48in wide – for the quilt top: 4.7m/5$\frac{1}{8}$yd
B Apple green – for side swags and binding: 1.2m/1$\frac{3}{8}$yd
C Turquoise cotton – for top and bottom swags: 60cm/$\frac{3}{4}$yd
D Kingfisher blue – for corner motifs: 20cm/$\frac{1}{4}$yd
E Emerald green – for leaf shapes, diamonds: 20cm/$\frac{1}{4}$yd
F Deep sea green – for large border circles, diamonds: 30cm/$\frac{3}{8}$yd
G Plain or printed cotton – for lining, at least 122cm/48in wide: 4.7m/5$\frac{1}{8}$yd
Medium-weight polyester wadding: 2.4m/2$\frac{5}{8}$yd, if at least 233cm/92in wide; or 4.7m/5$\frac{1}{8}$yd if narrower.
No. 5 perlé cotton (lime green): two skeins

1 Cut out the fabric pieces as instructed on page 148. (See also the general instructions on pages 12–16.)

2 The cut-out pieces are arranged on the centre panel as shown in fig. a. You will find it easier to get them in the right positions if you either fold the fabric in half crossways and lengthways, pressing lightly after each fold, or measure and mark the vertical and horizontal centres with dressmaker's chalk.

Begin by positioning three Fabric C swags at each end. Place their lower edges about 11cm/4$\frac{1}{2}$in from the edge and leave 5.5cm/2$\frac{1}{4}$in between them. When you are sure that they are in a straight line, pin, then tack them in place a scant 1cm/$\frac{3}{8}$in from their edges. Then pin and tack four large circles and four three-lobed leaf shapes between the swags (Fabric B at one end, Fabric E at the other). These pieces should be positioned so that, when their edges are turned under, there will be about 5mm/$\frac{1}{4}$in space between them at their closest points (figs a, b and c). If your fabric is narrower than 138cm/54in, the outer leaves and circles must be applied later (see Step 6).

Now position the diamonds, starting with the two rows at the

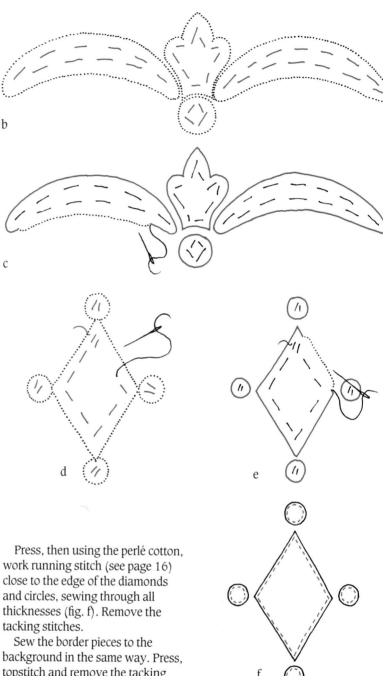

centre. These should be about 11cm/
4½in from the horizontal centre
mark (that is, 22cm/9in apart). The
horizontal distance between them
should be 28cm/11in. I have
positioned the shot fabrics so that
the weave of the silk runs alternately
one way then the other. Make sure
that the diamonds are vertical and
tack them in place.

Pin and tack a small circle at the
corners of each diamond, with the
raw edges overlapping slightly so
that a very small space will be left
between the shapes after stitching.

3 Slipstitch the shapes to the
background, turning under 3mm/
⅛in as you go (see page 15). Begin
with the diamonds, keeping their
sides straight and their points sharp
(figs d and e). Press them carefully.

Now slipstitch the four small
circles at the points of the diamonds,
keeping them as round as you can.
(Hints on how to keep angles and
corners sharp and circles rounded
are to be found on pages 15-16.)

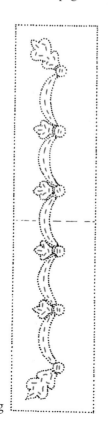

Press, then using the perlé cotton,
work running stitch (see page 16)
close to the edge of the diamonds
and circles, sewing through all
thicknesses (fig. f). Remove the
tacking stitches.

Sew the border pieces to the
background in the same way. Press,
topstitch and remove the tacking.

4 To apply the border pieces to
the side panels, first fold each panel
in half crossways and press or mark
this point. Now pin and tack five
swags to each panel, starting with
the one in the centre and placing
them about 11cm/4½in from the
outer edge. Leave 5.5cm/2¼in
between them.

Pin and tack the circles, leaf
shapes and large corner motifs to the
fabric, taking care to align the large
motifs at a 45° angle to the corners
(fig. g).

Slipstitch all the motifs to the
fabric. Press, then topstitch as
before. Remove the tacking.

5 Join the centre and side panels, taking 2cm/³⁄₄in seam allowance on the centre piece and as much as necessary on the side panels in order to make the quilt measure 233cm/92in across. Trim away the excess fabric from the side panels, and press the seams open.

6 Apply the remaining swags to the top and bottom borders, crossing the seams as shown (fig. h). If your fabric is narrower than mine, you may also need to apply the remaining leaf shapes and circles omitted from Step 2.

Give the quilt top a final press.

7 Join the side and centre lining panels. Trim the excess at the sides to make a square measuring 233cm/92in. Join the wadding, if necessary (see page 14), to make a square of the same size.

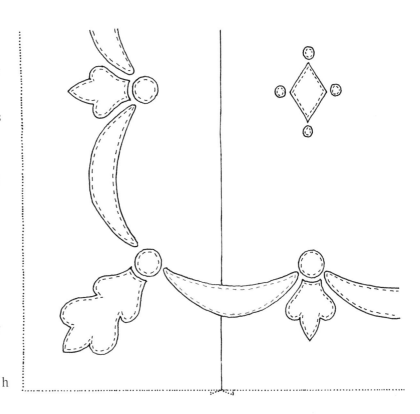

h

8 To join the three layers of the quilt, place the wadding in the centre and the fabrics (right side outside) on top and bottom. Pin, then tack the layers together down the centre, then at two or three points to the right and left of this line. Also tack round the four sides, 5cm/2in or so from the raw edges (fig. i).

i

9 Secure the quilt layers. If you like, you can work quilting round the shapes, or you can simply tie the layers together at intervals, as I have done. With a long double strand of sewing thread to match the quilt fabric, work through the layers about 20 times, making a loop about 5cm/2in long (fig. j). Cut the loop (fig. k), and tie the strands in a firm knot (fig. l). Trim the ends evenly (fig. m).

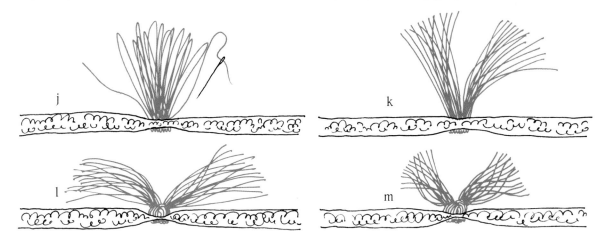

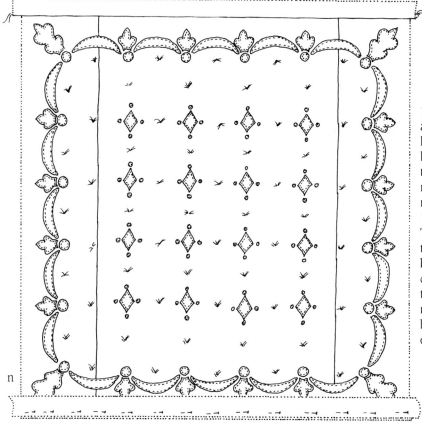

10 The binding strips can now be applied. Join the strips to make four lengths, each about 240cm/94in long, then pin and tack two of them to opposite edges of the quilt top, right sides facing and raw edges matching. Machine stitch about 1cm/^{3}/$_8$in from the raw edge (fig. n). Trim any ragged edges of wadding that may be sticking out. Turn the binding to the wrong side of the quilt. Fold under the raw edge and tack it in place, covering the line of machine stitching. Slipstitch the binding to the fabric (fig. o). Trim the ends level with the quilt.

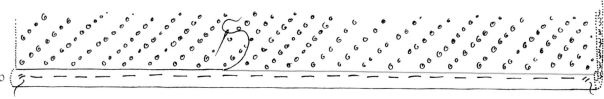

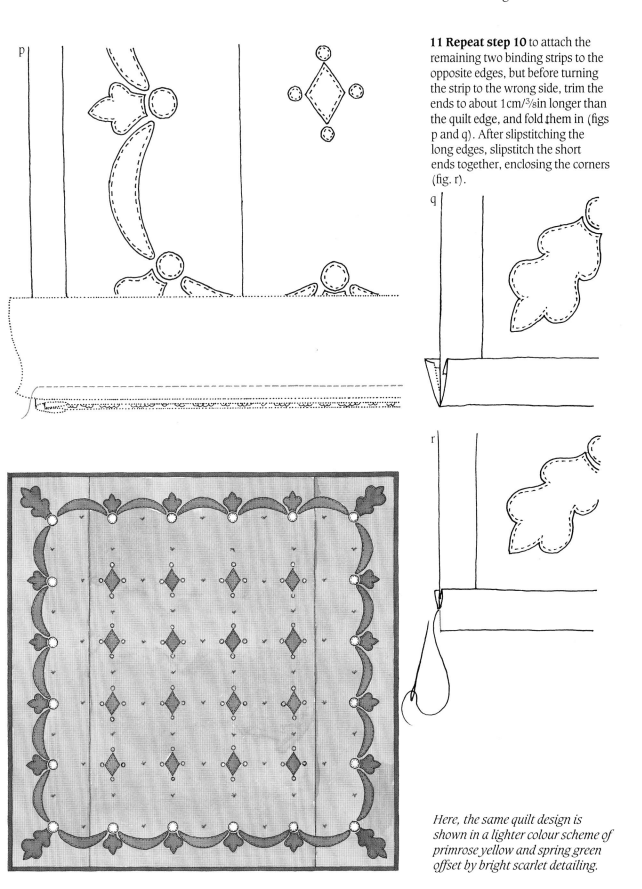

11 Repeat step 10 to attach the remaining two binding strips to the opposite edges, but before turning the strip to the wrong side, trim the ends to about 1cm/³⁄₈in longer than the quilt edge, and fold them in (figs p and q). After slipstitching the long edges, slipstitch the short ends together, enclosing the corners (fig. r).

Here, the same quilt design is shown in a lighter colour scheme of primrose yellow and spring green offset by bright scarlet detailing.

Falling Oak Leaves

These curtains have a simple repeat design of stylized oak leaves, with a dotted border. They are easy to make, and the stitching itself is very simple, but it is vital to get the borders perfectly straight and the oak leaves placed correctly. This means taking great care in the preliminary stages.

I have made the curtains in an elegant, pale yellow chintz, slightly glazed, with two shades of blue chintz for the appliqué and a deep shade of the same blue for the lining. I have interlined them, as this makes a much more luxurious, draught-proof and hard-wearing pair of curtains. An extra layer of padding also makes them hang better, and will protect your hard work.

Each curtain measures 220cm/86½in long by 115cm/45in wide; however, the design could easily be adapted to other widths or lengths. The oak leaves are fairly large, and might not suit a small window; but they would look marvellous on a huge pair of curtains for, say, French windows, or even on hangings for a four-poster bed.

Materials

Furnishing cotton or chintz, 122cm/48in wide. I have used the colours listed below; you may wish to make the curtains up in a quite different colour scheme.
A Lemon yellow – for background: 4.9m/5½yd
B Dark blue – for lining: 4.7m/5¼yd
C Medium blue – for the borders: 1.5m/1¾yd
D Pale blue – for the leaves and dots: 1.5m/1¾yd
Curtain interlining fabric, such as domette, at least 122cm/48in wide (optional): 4.4m/4⅞yd
Buckram, at least 90cm/36in wide: 30cm/⅜yd
Pale blue and medium blue cotton sewing or quilting thread for topstitching

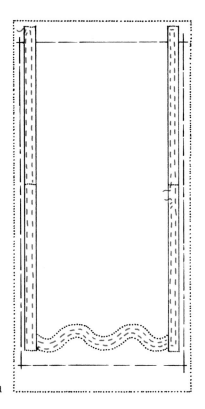

a

Set square (optional) and dressmaker's chalk
16 curtain hooks
4 brass curtain rings (2.5cm/1in)

1 Cut out the fabric pieces as instructed on page 162. (See also the general instructions on pages 12–16.) The two panels are identical; repeat the instructions that follow to make the second appliqué panel.

2 Mark the finished size of the curtain on one length of the background fabric using dressmaker's chalk. Allow 7cm/2¾in at the top and 9cm/3¼in at the bottom for hems and 2cm/¾in at both sides for seams. Use a metre/yard rule and set square (or other right-angled object) to make sure the lines are straight and corners square. This gives a line to measure from and will help you place the pieces accurately and straight.

3 Position the wavy border along the lower edge of the curtain. The lowest part of the curves should be 5cm/2in from the chalk line, and the ends should be equidistant from the two sides. Pin and tack the border in place, working at least 1cm/⅜in from the edges.

4 Prepare the vertical border strips by folding in and pressing 5mm/¼in along both edges. Use the weave of the fabric to help get them straight. Place them down both sides of the panel, about 4cm/1½in from the chalk line. They should overlap the corners of the wavy border by about 1cm/⅜in. The upper strip should overlap the lower one by the same amount and should extend past the marked upper finished edge by about 5cm/2in, as the border goes over the top edge of the finished curtain. Tack down both edges of the strips to prevent them shifting (fig. a).

5 Slipstitch the borders, starting with the wavy one, turning under the raw edges as you go (see page 15). Lift up the straight border pieces to reach the corners, but do not stitch the ends of the wavy border; leave them flat, and trim back the outer corners (fig. b), so that they will not show when the vertical border is sewn down. Press the work.

Now slipstitch the vertical borders in place, working down one side and up the other. Trim the ends where they overlap the wavy border, and fold them carefully to make a neat join. Treat the join half way up the sides in a similar way, turning under the upper strip and sewing it over the lower one. Press.

6 Topstitch (see page 16) all the way round the border pieces with matching thread, 3mm/$\frac{1}{8}$in from the edge. Work the lines of running stitch across the joins at the corners as well. Remove the tacking.

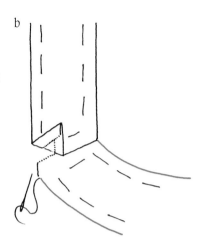

b

7 To position the oak leaves, you will find it easiest to lay the curtain out flat, either on the floor or on a large table. Arrange them as shown in fig. c, positioning the centre line of leaves first. Mark the centre of the curtain with a line of tacking, or fold the curtain in half vertically and lightly press a crease in it. Place the bottom centre leaf 39cm/15$\frac{1}{2}$in from the marked finished edge and pin it in place. Position the top centre leaf 11cm/4$\frac{1}{2}$in down from the marked upper edge. The remaining centre leaf goes half way between these two. The outer leaves in the horizontal groups of three should be placed with their outermost curves 13cm/5in from the vertical borders.

Position the rows of two leaves half way between the rows of three, both vertically and horizontally. Tack all round the leaves, including the edges of the centre slash, at least 1cm/$\frac{3}{8}$in from the edges (fig. c).

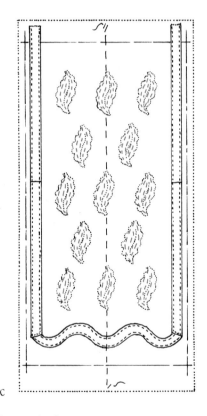

c

8 Slipstitch the leaves in place, taking particular care at the points and stems and keeping the curves smooth. Slipstitch the edges of the slash also (fig. d), clipping into the corners to make a neat curve.

When all the leaves have been sewn down, press them carefully and topstitch them, following the curves and points (including the slash), and keeping the line of sewing parallel to the stitched edge. Remove the tacking.

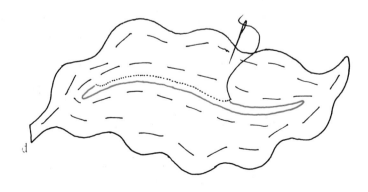

d

9 Now position the dots. There are five on the wavy border and ten on each vertical border. Place the uppermost dots 15.5cm/6in from the marked upper edge of the curtain (not from the end of the border) and the remaining dots the same distance apart down the sides. The dots on the wavy border should be 14.5cm/5 ½in apart.

Tack, and then slipstitch them in place, taking special care to keep the edge smoothly rounded (fig. e). You may find it helpful to mark the finished edge on each dot first, using a paper template 4.5cm/1¾in in diameter, or a compass set to this measurement. You can use this line as a guide when turning in the edge.

When all the dots are slipstitched, press them and topstitch them in the same way as for the oak leaves. Remove the tacking.

To make the tiebacks
1 Position the appliqué shape in the centre of the right side of one of the yellow tieback pieces. Pin, tack and slipstitch it in place. Press it, then topstitch round the edges of the appliqué in the usual way. Remove the tacking.

Place the buckram on the wrong side of the tieback piece, centring it so the seam allowance is even. Turn this over the edge of the buckram, and pin and tack it in place (fig. g).

2 Join the bias strips (Fabric D) to make two strips, each 135cm/53in long, one for each tieback (see page 13). Press them in half lengthways. Tack each strip just under the edge of the tieback, so that it extends 5mm/¼in outside it. Join the ends neatly by turning under one end and placing this folded end over the other one. Working from the right side, slipstitch the edge of the tieback piece to the binding strip. Press. Work topstitching round the edge in the usual way, through all layers. Remove the tacking.

10 When all these stages are completed make up the curtains (fig. f), following the instructions on page 19. The curtains shown here have a hand-pleated heading, but you can use a slotted or drawstring headed tape if you prefer.

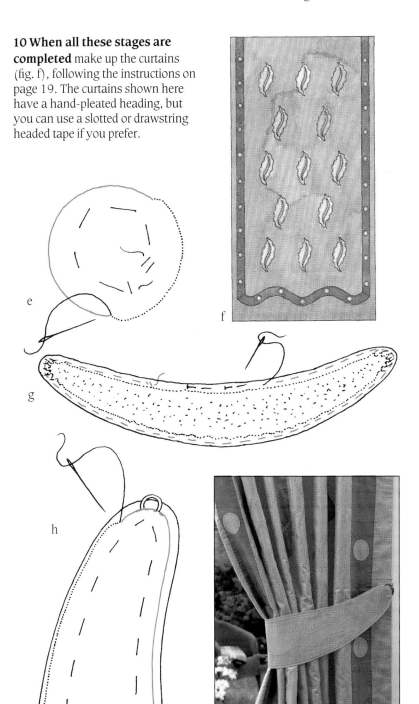

e

g

h

f

3 Now place the lining piece on the wrong side of the tieback, and pin and tack it in place. Slipstitch it to the tieback, turning under 5mm/¼in as you go; the edge should conceal the slipstitching in the binding. When you reach the end, slip a brass curtain ring between the tieback and the lining, then continue the

slipstitching, working a few oversewing stitches to either side of the ring for extra strength (fig. h). Take care not to let the stitches show on the front of the work. Press, and remove tacking stitches.

Make the second tieback in exactly the same way.

Animal Parade

Animals from all over the world march around this brightly coloured frieze nursery. It is made of felt – a great material to use for appliqué for the obvious reason that you don't have to turn under the edges! You can include a lot of detail, with sharp points and corners that would be difficult to achieve if you were turning the edges in.

However, felt is not very strong when cut into thin pieces, so work carefully to prevent the shapes from becoming distorted or losing some of their fine details.

All the animals on this frieze are moving from right to left; but you could make them face alternate ways, if you prefer. You could also adjust the length, by subtracting or adding sections. The frieze measures just under 4.5m/4⅞yd in length, but you could extend it to make an animal parade all the way round a small bedroom.

Materials

Felt (90cm/36in wide). I have used the following colours and quantities. You could, of course, use quite different colours and adjust your quantities if you decided to make a shorter or longer frieze.
A Dark blue – for background: 80cm/⅞yd

B Medium blue – for background: 80cm/⅞yd
C Red – for borders, cow, bears: 1m/1yd
D White – for polar bears, sheep: 30cm/⅜yd
E Buff – for moose, seal: 30cm/⅜yd, or piece approx. 30 × 25cm/12 × 10in
F Bright green – for crocodile, snake, grass: 30cm/⅜yd, or piece approx. 30 × 25cm/12 × 10in
G Dark pink – for camel, baby bear: 20cm/¼yd, or piece approx. 20 × 25cm/8 × 10in
H Light pink – for pig, camel: 20cm/¼yd, or piece approx. 20 × 25cm/8 × 10in
I Mint green – for leaves: 10cm/⅛yd, or piece approx. 20cm/8in square
J Deep turquoise – for leaves: 10cm/

⅛yd, or piece approx. 20cm/8in square
K Black – for zebra stripes: 10cm/⅛yd, or piece approx. 20cm/8in square
L Yellow – for geese legs: small scrap
Heavyweight calico, 90cm/36in wide: 1.6m/1⅞yd
Sewing or quilting thread to match the two shades of blue felt

1 Cut out the fabric pieces as instructed on page 149. (See also the general instructions on pages 12–16).

2 The edging strips are positioned before you work the appliqué. Pin, then tack a wavy strip to the bottom and a straight strip to the top edge of the right side of each panel. The strips should overlap the panel edges by 5mm/¼in (fig. a).

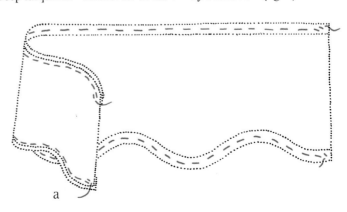

a

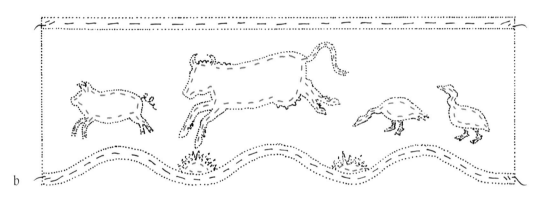

b

3 Apply the farm animals to the first (far left, dark blue) panel, pinning them to the background and spacing them evenly. The pig's snout should be 4cm/1 ½in from the left-hand edge and the second goose's tail 3cm/1 ¼in from the right-hand edge. Slip the legs of the geese just under the lower edge of the body. Position the cow with a sprightly kick in her back legs, as if she has just jumped over the moon. Tuck the clumps of grass under the edge of the lower wavy strip by about 3mm/⅛in. Then tack all the pieces in place (fig. b).

Now stitch the animals and grass in place, using the dark blue thread and running stitch (see page 16), worked about 3mm/⅛in from the edge. Take care in delicate places, such as the pig's feet and the blades of grass, not to pull or rub the felt.

4 Work the appliqué on the remaining panels in the same way, matching the colour of your thread to that of the panel. Space the animals evenly and do not place any part of them closer than 2.5cm/1in from the side edges. Special notes for individual panels are as follows:

Panel 2 I have placed one of the penguins so that he seems to be sliding down the slope of the wavy edge (fig. c). And one of the seal's tails overlaps the edge slightly.

c

d

e

Panel 3 The mother and father bear are plodding straight ahead after the tortoise, while baby bear is turning his head to see how the hares are doing. The tufts of grass are tucked under the wavy edge, as for Panel 1, but here the stitching also runs along the lower edge (fig. d).

Panel 4 The zebra's black stripes are tacked on after the white body is tacked; then the running stitch is worked in one operation. The mane is tucked very slightly under the neck and is held in place with a single line of running stitch close to the neck edge.

Panel 5 The moose's two antlers are positioned after the body has been stitched in place, and are stitched separately, one overlapping the other (fig. e). The horns and ears of the goat and sheep are sewn on together with the bodies.

Panel 6, with its camels and cats, pyramids and palms, is very straightforward with none of the pieces overlapping any others.

f

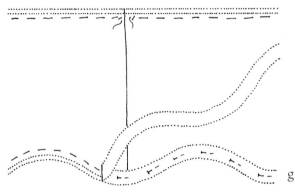

g

5 To make up the frieze, first remove the tacking, and press each panel very carefully from the wrong side.

Tack and machine stitch the calico backing pieces together to make one long strip, taking 1cm/³⁄₈in seams. Press the seams open.

Place the six panels on the calico strip, wrong sides facing, with the felt edges butted together over each seam. Pin them in place. Position one of the short wavy strips over each join, hiding the edges of the panels. Pin (fig. f) and tack the strips in place.

Turn the frieze wrong side up. Position the six long red wavy strips along the bottom edge, aligning them with the ones on the front and so enclosing the raw edge of the calico (fig. g). Do the same with the straight edging strips and the two short wavy strips at each end. Pin then tack all these pieces in place. Turn the frieze right side up.

6 Prepare the hanging hoops by joining pairs of loops with small running stitches along both edges (fig. h). Position them along the top edge of the frieze, tucking them between the two red felt straight strips at 21cm/8¼in intervals, three loops to a panel. Pin them in place.

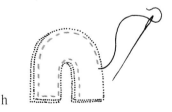

h

7 To complete the frieze, work running stitch along both edges of all the wavy and straight strips, using the dark blue thread and taking the needle through all thicknesses. Make sure you catch in the hanging loops securely as you go (fig. i).

Press the frieze from the wrong side, and remove all tacking stitches.

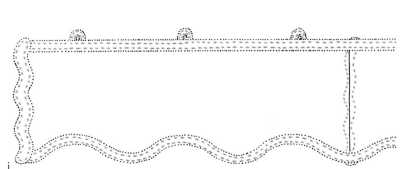

i

Buds in Spring

This bedspread has a fresh and simple design of flower buds and leaves scattered on a plain background, with a pretty scalloped edge. It is made for a single bed and measures 223cm/88in long by 152cm/60in wide; but the design could easily be adapted for a double bedspread.

I have made it in a medium-weight white linen, with the appliqué in light blue and turquoise cotton, topstitched in a medium blue thread, slightly darker than the turquoise. The lining is white cotton. There is a fair amount of work in it, but it is all very straightforward.

Materials

Linen and lightweight cottons 90cm/36in wide, unless otherwise stated. I have made the bedspread in the colours indicated in the list below. You can, of course, make it in any other colours of your choice.
A White linen – for background: 4.5m/5yd
B White cotton – for lining: 4.5m/5yd (alternatively, use 228cm/90in wide sheeting, and buy half the amount)
C Light blue plain-woven cotton – for bias edging strips and flowers: 70cm/³⁄4yd
D Turquoise plain-woven cotton – for stems and leaves: 40cm/¹⁄2yd
Medium blue and white cotton sewing or quilting thread for topstitching
Piece of cardboard 15cm/6in square to make circular template
Dressmaker's chalk or water-soluble pen

1 Cut out the fabric pieces as instructed on page 154. (See also the general instructions on pages 12–16.)

2 Position the flowers and leaves on the centre panel. First measure off 33cm/13in from one end, and mark this distance with a line of tacking;

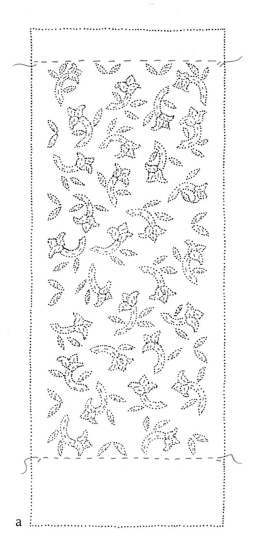

a

this area will be left plain and will hang over the end of the bed. At the other end mark off 15cm/6in. Arrange the flowers randomly within the remaining area (fig. a), making sure that they are evenly spaced and that none are closer than 5cm/2in to the side edges. Each flower has a stem, one centre petal, two outer petals, and two or three leaves. Vary the positions of the leaves slightly, using any that are

left over to fill obvious gaps. I have put a couple of leaves together pointing outwards at intervals around the edge.

Pin all the pieces down, making sure that when the edges are turned under and stitched there will be no gaps. Have a final check that your flowers are evenly spaced, and then tack them all in place, at least 1cm/³⁄8in from the edge.

3 Slipstitch each flower starting at the top end of the stem. Lift the edges of the petals and slipstitch (see page 15) down the side of the stem to the bottom, along the slanting end and up the other side. Leave the top flat and unstitched (fig. b).

Next, stitch the centre petal and then the two outer ones – in some flowers lapping the right petal over the left, in others vice versa. Finish with the top one – the only one that needs to be stitched all the way round (fig. c). On the other two, you need hem only the part that will be exposed, before simply moving your needle across to start on the petal that overlaps it.

When all the sprigs and leaves have been stitched in place, press them carefully.

Topstitch round the edges of each sprig, 3mm/⅛in from the edge (see page 16), going round the petals and stem in one operation. Then topstitch the leaves. When this is complete, remove the tacking.

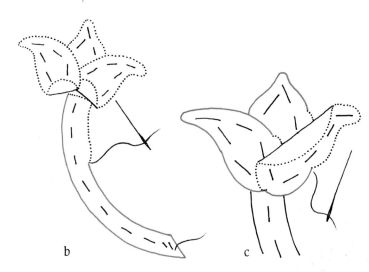

b

c

4 Join the side panels to each side of the centre panel. Pin and tack the lengths together, taking a 1.2cm/½in seam allowance, then stitch by machine (fig. d). Press the seams open. Clip the selvedges, if you have left them on, at about 10cm/4in intervals; this makes the fabric more flexible.

Join the two lengths of lining down the centre, and then press the seam open.

5 Attach the lining at this stage. Lay it on the top fabric, which you have spread out, right side down, on a flat, clean surface. (This is easier than placing the linen on top, since the lining is lighter and more manoeuvrable.) Begin by pinning the lining to the bedspread all the way down the centre, smoothing the fabric outwards to get rid of wrinkles. Tack along this line. Work two or three more lines of tacking from one side to the other (fig. e).

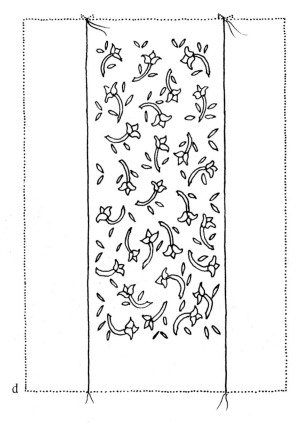

d

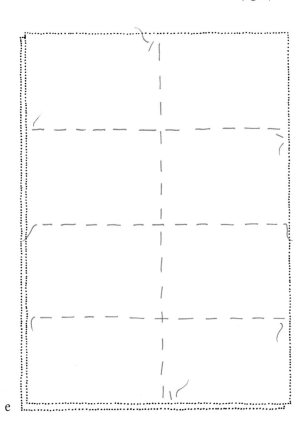

e

6 To make the outer scalloped edges along each side of the spread, first draw a line all the way down each side, marking the final outer edge. It should be 33cm/13in from the side seam. Use a water-soluble pen or dressmaker's chalk and a metre/yard rule, and check the distance at several points to make sure the line is straight. Do *not* trim away the excess fabric.

Now mark a series of semi-circles for the scallops on the side and bottom edges. Begin by placing your circular template at the upper right-hand corner of the bedspread, in the right angle made by the top edge of the fabric and the marked line. Draw round it to a point 7.5cm/3in from the marked line and mark these points on both sides of the template.

Using the chalk or marking pen, draw a series of semi-circles all the way down the side (fig. f), drawing up to the mark on each side of the template and ending with the last scallop about 13cm/5in from the bottom edge. The opposite side is then marked in the same way.

To mark the bottom edge, place the template to one side of the centre line. (Double check by measuring carefully from each side, in case your line of tacking is slightly off-centre.) Mark round it, then mark three more scallops out towards the corner. Then repeat the procedure on the other side of the centre line.

The corner points are marked by drawing a straight line from the outer corner of each scallop to the marked corner of the spread (fig. g).

7 Now tack all round the edge of the bedspread, 2.5cm/1in in from the marked line and the straight top edge, working through both layers (fig. h).

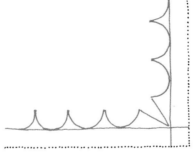

g

f

Work on the central panel is now complete and the scalloped edges are ready to be finished and trimmed (fig. i).

h

i

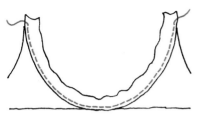

8 Sew on the bias-cut binding strips by machine. Round each semi-circle sew a 24cm/9½in strip, right sides together, putting the raw edge of the strip exactly along the marked line and leaving 5mm/¼in free at each inner corner. Tack, then machine stitch, 5mm/¼in from the edge (fig. j).

Attach the long strip of binding (pieced as required – see page 17) to the straight top edge and round the top scallops on each side (fig. k). Similarly, attach the two 28cm/11in strips to the corner points, again leaving 5mm/¼in free at the ends.

Cut along your scalloped pencil line all the way round the bedspread and trim the top, if necessary, to the edge of the binding (fig. l).

9 Turn the binding over to the wrong side. Turn in the raw edge and the unstitched ends of the strips and pin them down onto the lining. Check that the binding is turned in evenly all the way round the bedspread, then tack.

Slipstitch the binding to the lining, including the short turned ends (fig. m). At the corner points, fold the excess binding neatly on both sides, and slipstitch it in place with tiny stitches.

j

k

l

m

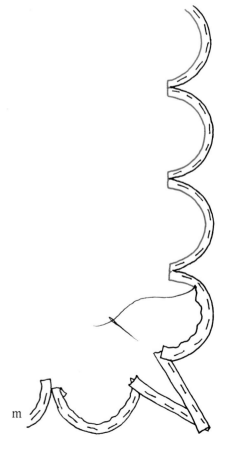

10 Now place a small circle between each scallop, over the join, and tack it in place. Make sure that it will cover the ends of the binding when the edges are turned under (fig. n).

Slipstitch round each circle, taking care to preserve the shape. Topstitch, press and remove the tacking stitches (fig. o).

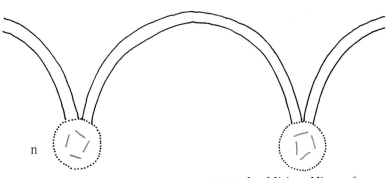

n

11 Work additional lines of running stitch in white to keep the two layers together. I have put them just inside the side seams, just below the central area of appliqué and 2.5cm/1in in from the bound edge. I have also put 12 small circles of running stitch at 28cm/11in intervals in two lines on the centre panel (fig. p). This is really quilting rather than topstitching, as its function is to hold the two layers together and only incidentally to add decoration and texture.

o

p

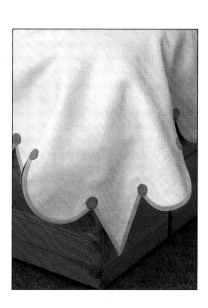

Provençal Garden

This capacious drawstring bag is just the thing for carrying your current knitting, embroidery or sewing project – if, like me, you tend to take it everywhere and work on it at odd moments. It would also make an attractive general purpose bag.

I created the original version of this bag some years ago in silk and scraps of antique chintz. This one is made of a thick hand-woven Indian cotton with a fairly rough texture. It has a Provençal print cotton lining, and cotton and wool appliqué. There is cotton wadding between the layers.

There are four sides. Two have a design of urns and foliage cut from two different plain green cottons. On one of them I have embroidered lots of little French knots in red for added texture and colour. The other two sides have baskets woven from ribbon, containing a mixture of plain green leaves and some cut-out printed chintz leaves. For one of the baskets I have used bought bias binding, woven and plaited, and for the other I used a piece of rather faded blue wool ribbon, weaving it for the basket and sewing it round two short pieces of piping cord for the base and the rim of the basket.

Materials

Assorted cotton and wool fabrics, 90cm/36in wide. My bag is made up in the colours indicated in the list below. You may wish to choose other colours.
A Deep blue – for background: 90cm/1yd
B Blue and red print – for lining: 90cm/1yd
C Red – for binding and covering cord: 1m/1yd
D Bright turquoise – for arches and column bases: 30cm/¼yd
E Cream background print – for columns: 20cm/⅛yd
F Bright yellow – for keystones, capitals and urns: 10cm/⅛yd
G Dull gold – for cut-out urn pieces: 20cm/¼yd
H Dark green – for embroidered leaves: 20cm/¼yd
I Emerald green – for wavy leaves: 20cm/¼yd
J Beige – for basket: 10cm/⅛yd
K Leaf-printed chintz: leaves should be up to 22cm/9in tall. If plain colour is used, cut leaves on the bias, from 30cm/¼yd of fabric.
L Faded turquoise leaf-printed fabric: 20cm/¼yd
Packet of bright green bias binding
Packet of beige bias binding
Faded turquoise ribbon, 2cm/¾in wide: 1m/1yd
Red stranded embroidery cotton: 1 skein
Cotton sewing or quilting thread in the colours to match arches, keystones, cut-out urn pieces and plain-coloured leaves
Medium cotton or polyester wadding: 90cm/1yd
Piping cord, No. 5 (approx. 8mm/⅜in diameter): 1.5m/1⅝yd
16 2.5cm/1in curtain rings (optional)

1 Cut out the fabric pieces as instructed on page 155. (See also the general instructions on pages 12–16.)

2 Place the columns, column bases and arch on one rectangle of the background fabric. Pin and tack them in place, leaving 5mm/¼in space between them and an equal space on both sides. On my bag I have tucked in a thin strip of bias binding under the inner edge of the arch. Extra bits of this sort are optional, but if you feel like taking the trouble, they add further richness and colour to the design. You can do it by cutting a 30cm/12in length of bias binding in half lengthways, and tucking it under the edge at the pinning stage. Tack it in place, and make sure you catch it in when stitching the arch in position later (fig. a). Check that the columns are aligned with the straight grain of the background fabric, then pin and tack all the pieces in place.

Repeat the process on the remaining three panels.

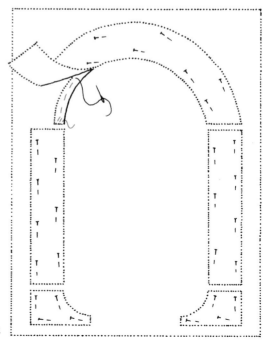

a

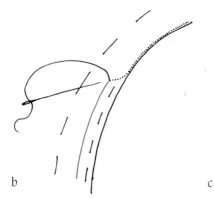

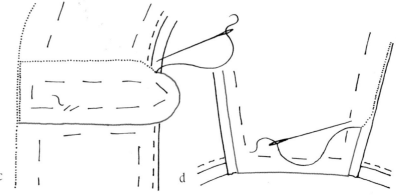

b

c

d

3 Complete the sewing of these pieces by first slipstitching round the inside edges (see page 15), turning under 3mm/⅛in as you go (fig. b). You can stitch all five pieces in one operation, starting at the bottom of one base and finishing at the bottom edge of the other one. Do not hem along the bottoms of the bases or along the outside edge of the columns and arch.

Then topstitch the pieces (see page 16) 3mm/⅛in from the edge, making sure you take the needle through all the fabric layers. Repeat the process on the remaining panels. In the bag shown here I have left out the topstitching on the columns because the printed wool did not seem to require it, but if I had made the columns in a plain fabric I would have carried the topstitching on all the way round.

4 Position the capitals, the lower rims of the columns and the keystone as shown, then pin and tack them in place. (You may wish to insert two thin strips of bias binding on either side of the keystone, as for the arch.)

Slipstitch (figs c and d) and topstitch these pieces along the inner edges only.

Repeat Step 4 on the remaining panels. Press, but do not remove the tacking stitches, as they hold the outer edge of all the pieces in place (fig. e).

f

e

Side ɪ: Urn with red-spotted leaves
1 Place the cut-out urn over the solid urn piece (right sides up), then tack the two pieces together round their edges. Centre the urn between the columns, leaving 3.5cm/1⅜in between its lower edge and the lower edge of the base fabric. Check that it is straight, then pin and tack it in place (fig. f).

2 To apply the leaves, place them on the background in the order shown (fig. f), tucking 1cm/³⁄₈in under the top edge of the urn. Pin and tack them in place. Remember that as you slipstitch each leaf you will need to lift the edge of any that overlap it, so keep your tacking well in from the edge (fig. g).

Slipstitch round the leaves in the order shown, turning under the edge 3mm/¹⁄₈in as usual. You can slipstitch and topstitch in one operation if you are using the same colour, as I have here. Work up one side and down the other, then go back the way you came, using running stitch, 3mm/¹⁄₈in from the edge. When all nine leaves are slipstitched and topstitched, press them and remove the tacking.

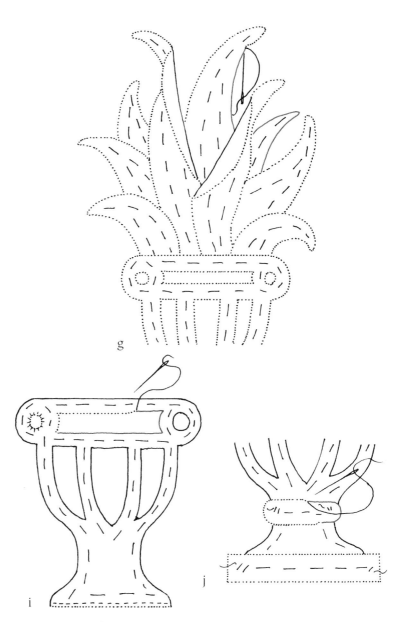

g

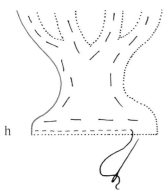

h

i

j

3 Now slipstitch the urn to the background fabric, beginning with the top edge. Make sure that the lower raw edges of the leaves are still covered when turning under the edge. When you reach the lower edge of the urn, do not turn it in, but cross over to the other side with small running stitches, as close to the edge as you can (fig. h). Carry on stitching up the other side and round the curve until you are back where you started.

4 Complete the urn by turning under the edges of the six cut holes,

and slipstitching round them (fig. i). Pay special attention to keeping the straight lines really straight, and take care at the corners not to let any threads escape (see page 15). Press the urn, then topstitch along all the hemmed edges. Remove the tacking.

Put on the two base pieces of the urn last. Pin, tack, slipstitch (fig. j) and topstitch them. Press and remove the tacking stitches.

5 Embroider the leaves with French knots, using three strands of embroidery cotton (see page 16). Do not fasten off between knots.

k

Side II: Urn with wavy leaves

1 To apply the urn, first position the three upright urn pieces over the main piece as shown, and tack them in place.

Then position the two urn pieces on the background fabric, centring them between the columns and leaving 5mm/¼in between them and 3.5cm/1⅜in between the lowest point and the edge of the background fabric. Pin and tack these pieces in place, then slipstitch and topstitch the three upright pieces to the main urn piece and background along their vertical edges only.

Slipstitch and topstitch the edges of the bottom piece of the urn, leaving its top edge raw.

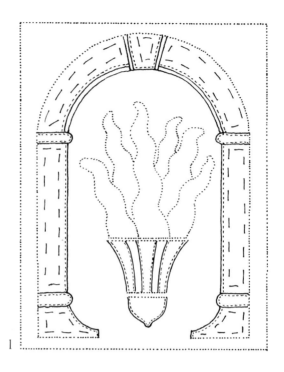

l

2 Place the leaves on the background fabric in the order shown, leaving a gap of 3mm/⅛in between their lower edges and the top edge of the urn (fig. l). Pin and tack them, leaving yourself room to lift the edges of the overlapping ones, as you did on Side I. Slipstitch them in the same order, leaving the bottom edges raw; topstitch, press, and remove the tacking.

Pin and tack the remaining five small pieces of the urn in place (see fig. m). When you have slipstitched (fig. n) and topstitched them, remove their tacking stitches and give the work a final press.

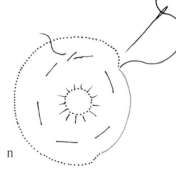

n

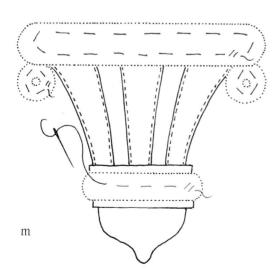

m

Side III: Diagonal-weave basket

N.B. I have put some large fern leaves, cut from a remnant of chintz, in the woven basket. You could use something similar, or flowers cut from any suitable remnant. Failing that, you could make up some leaves, as on Side I, perhaps in a different green.

1 To make the basket, first place the basket piece on the background fabric, centring it between the columns and leaving 3.5cm/1³⁄₈in between its lower edge and the edge of the background fabric. Pin and tack it in place, using matching thread and working no closer than 1.5cm/⁵⁄₈in from the edge (fig. o).

If you are using 1.2cm/½in bias binding or a similar sized ribbon you will need four pieces 12cm/4³⁄₄in long, four of 9cm/3½in and six more about 7cm/2³⁄₄in. Weave them together to cover the basket piece, using the longer pieces in the middle (fig. p). The shape will be ragged, but do not worry. Keep the strips parallel and at a 45° angle to the edge of the background fabric.

Pin the woven strips to the basket shape at about 1cm/½in intervals, then trim round the edges, leaving at least 5mm/¼in hanging over (figs. q and r). Turn the ends under the sides of the basket and tack them in

o

place. Also tack along each strip to hold the weaving in place, and remove the pins. Leave the top and bottom edges ragged; they will be covered by the two plaited pieces.

2 Position whatever foliage you are going to use with the bottom edge of the pieces about 3mm/¹⁄₈in from the top edge of the basket. Pin,

tack and slipstitch the pieces to the background in the usual way. Topstitch if appropriate. I have not topstitched my cut-out chintz leaves because I did not want to interfere with the printed pattern. The running stitch would, however, hold all the leaves nicely flat. Try topstitching a leaf and see whether it works with your particular print.

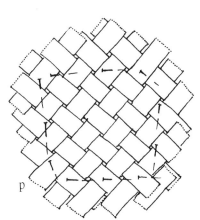

p

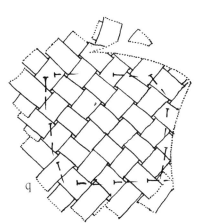

q

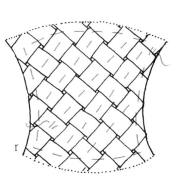

r

3 To make the plaits, cut three 20cm/8in and three 18cm/7in lengths of bias binding, then fold all the pieces double lengthways. Join each group of three with a pin at one end (fig. s), make two neat plaits and pin them at the other end.

Put the two plaited strips in position over the raw edges of the basket, trimming away any ends of the weaving that poke out. The plaits should cover all the ends at the top and bottom of the basket. Trim and tuck in the ends of the plaits neatly; pin and tack (fig. t). Slipstitch round the entire basket, sewing down the sides and along both sides of both plaits (fig. u). Bring the needle up in several places to anchor the weaving with a few invisible stitches (fig. v). Press and remove the tacking (fig. w).

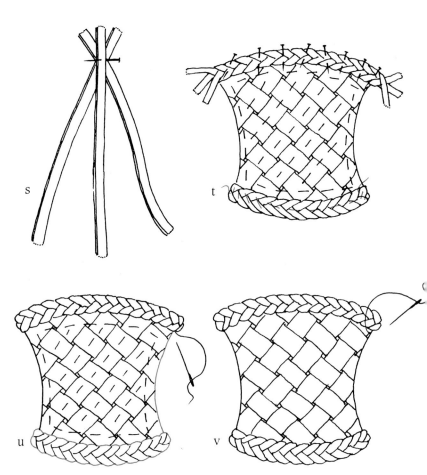

Side IV: Vertical-weave basket
N.B. On this side I have filled the basket with a mixture of printed cut-out leaves and plain green leaves similar to those on Side I.
1 To make the basket, position the basket piece on the background fabric, and pin and tack it in place, 1.5cm/⅝in in from the edge.

Cut seven pieces of ribbon, each 11cm/4½in long, position them over the basket piece, and weave them as for the basket on Side III, but straight up and down (fig. x). Trim the edges and secure them as described in Step 1, Side III.

2 Position the foliage pieces and sew them down as described in Step 2, Side III.

3 To make the top and bottom of the basket, cut two pieces of piping cord, one 13cm/5in long and one 8cm/3¼in long, and corresponding lengths of ribbon, a little longer than

the cord. Wrap the ribbon round the cord, first turning in the ends, and sew it over the cord, enclosing the ends with stitching (fig. y).

Sew the pieces of cord over the top and bottom edges of the basket, making sure you cover all the raw edges (fig. z).

When you have completed Side IV

(fig. aa), press all four panels and remove all the tacking stitches except those round the outside edge of the arch and columns.

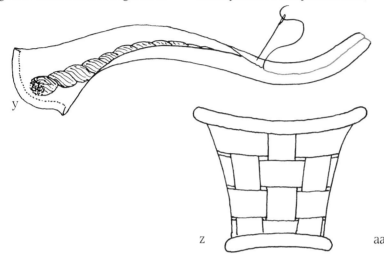

y

z   aa

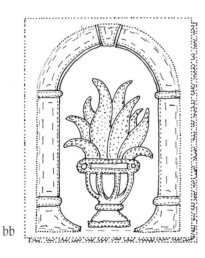

bb

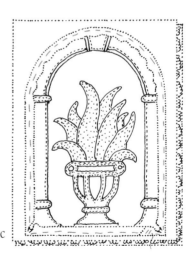

cc

Making up the bag
1 To assemble the layers, place a rectangle of lining fabric wrong side up, then place a piece of wadding and a finished panel, right side up, on top. Pin through all the layers then tack them together round the edges of the design, keeping your stitches inside the arch (fig. bb).

2 For the edging, cut four lengths of the bias-cut Fabric C, each 130cm/51in long, and one piece 120cm/47in long. (I have used a red satin weave curtain lining material, similar to the blue green I used on the arches, cut in bias strips and joined by machine to get the length. A ready-made bias strip, though, will not be as strong.)

Pin a long bias strip round the

edge of one panel, putting right sides together and matching the raw edges exactly; position the ends along the bottom edge. Where the ends meet, sew them together by hand, using small running stitches. Trim the seam and press it open. Tack the binding in place, working through all the layers (fig. cc), then machine stitch all the way round, 5mm/¼in from the edge.

dd

3 Trim the panel edges to the edge of the bias strip, cutting through all the layers (fig. dd). Turn the strip over to the back and, tucking under the raw edge, pin it to the lining fabric (fig. ee). Tack and slipstitch it down (fig. ff).   For a bit of extra colour, you could add a thin strip of bias binding between the edging and the lining, using the method described in Step 2 on page 50.

Apply the binding to the remaining three panels in exactly the same way.

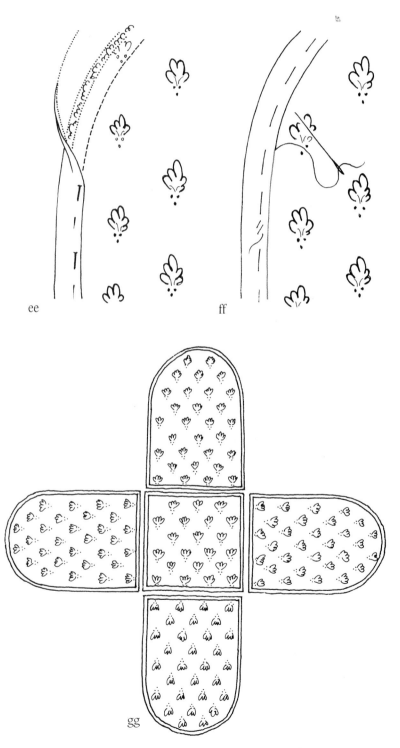

ee   ff

gg

4 For the base, make a 'sandwich' of the three square pieces: lining, wadding and main fabric. Tack them together round the edges, then bind the edges with the shorter strip as just described in Steps 2 and 3.

Decide on the order you want the four panels to be in. Then lay them out, face down, with the square base panel in the centre (fig. gg). Pin all four sides of the base to the adjacent panel edges, then tack all the way round, working back and forth over the join.

5 Join the base to the side panels with slipstitch, using double thread for strength. Then sew the sides together in the same way, working from bottom to top. When you have sewn up the first side, turn the bag wrong side out to sew the other three seams. Make sure as you go up each side that the feet of the columns and the columns themselves are level with one another. When you reach the top of the columns, oversew a few stitches on the spot, for strength.

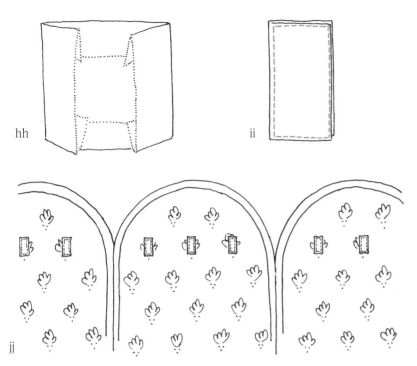

hh

ii

jj

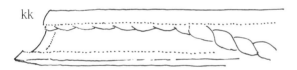

kk

ll

6 Sew rings or fabric loops to the inside of the bag for the drawstring. If you are using small brass curtain rings, sew four of these across the inside of each panel at the height of the top of the columns.

To make fabric loops, cut 12 pieces of lining fabric, each 5cm/2in square. Turn in 5mm/¼in on all four sides of each piece and press (fig. hh). Fold each one in half, so that you have 12 folded rectangles. Press again. Machine stitch all the way round each folded piece very close to the edge (fig. ii). Sew the loops firmly to the inside of the bag, three to a side, positioning them as shown (fig. jj) and using double thread. When sewing each loop, take the needle through to the right side and back again a few times, invisibly, to join all the layers.

7 Make the drawstring by covering a 120cm/47in length of piping cord with a bias strip of fabric. I have used a piece of the same red material that I used for the binding on the panels.

Cut a strip of fabric on the straight grain, 3cm/1in wider than the circumference of the cord, and slightly longer. Turn under and press 5mm/¼in on one long edge. Place the cord on the opposite edge, on the wrong side of the fabric, then roll it towards the pressed edge (fig. kk). Pin this edge to the cord (fig. ll), then slipstitch it in place. Tuck in the ends and work a few stitches to secure them firmly.

Thread the cord through the loops, then sew the ends together.

Stars and Hearts

Traditional motifs of stars and hearts are used in a bold and simple way on this cosy cot quilt. The twelve frilly rosettes at the corners of each square add extra colour and a third dimension, which I always love on quilts. Babies will love them too, so it is important to ensure that they are sewn on very firmly!

I have made the quilt in fine wool and cotton, in warm tones of cream, red and gold. The lining is a cream and red checked Liberty wool.

The quilt measures approximately 93cm/36½in long by 65cm/25½in wide.

Materials

Assorted cotton and wool fabrics, 90cm/36in wide (unless otherwise stated). I have used the colours indicated below. You may wish, of course, to make the quilt in quite different colours.

A Cream viyella – for base fabric: 1m/1¼yd

B Red checked wool – for lining: 1m/1¼yd

C Gold cotton – for lattice: 1m/12¼yd

D Coral red cotton – for outer edging and rosettes, 122cm/48in wide: 50cm/⅝yd

E Dark red cotton – for hearts and stars: 20cm/¼yd

F Pink cotton – for inner edging, 122cm/48in wide: 20cm/¼yd

G Cream-yellow cotton – for rosette centres: 10cm/⅛yd

Lightweight polyester wadding: 1m/1¼yd

Medium-weight non-woven iron-on interfacing: 10cm/⅛yd

Cream-coloured sewing or quilting thread for topstitching

1 Cut out the fabric pieces as instructed on page 161. (See also the general instructions on pages 12–16.)

2 Start with the lattice strips. Turn under and press 5mm/¼in on the long edges, except for one edge

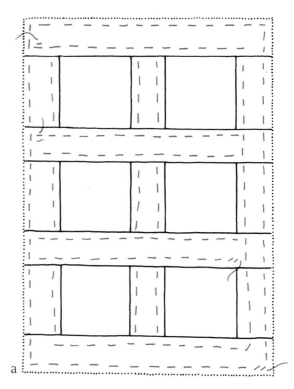

a

on both of the long strips and two of the shorter ones; these will be covered by the outer binding.

Place them on the base fabric, aligning their outer edges. Here the horizontal strips overlap the vertical ones, but you could place the vertical ones on top, or interweave them.

The six squares of base fabric left exposed should measure 18.5cm/7¼in; the exact size does not matter, so long as they are all the same.

Pin the lattice strips in place, then

tack them at least 1cm/⅜in from the folded edges (fig. a).

3 Fold the inner edging strips in half lengthways and press. Tuck them under the edges of the lattice, so that 3mm/⅛in of their folded edges are visible (fig. b). Pin, then tack through all the layers.

Slipstitch (see page 15) the edges of the lattice strips in place round each square and where they overlap; work through all the fabric layers. Then topstitch (see page 16).

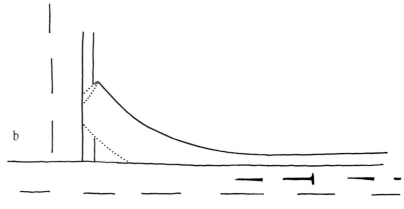

b

4 Position the hearts and stars in the squares, making sure that they are centred and straight; then pin and tack them in place (fig. c). Slipstitch them to the base fabric, turning under the edges as you go. Then work a double line of running stitch round the edge of each motif. Remove all the tacking stitches.

5 Now make the rosettes. Machine stitch the short ends of each of the 12 short fabric strips, with right sides together, to make a loop (fig. d). Press the seam open. Fold the loop in half lengthways, wrong sides together, and press. Work gathering stitches 5mm/¼in from the raw edges (fig. e). Pull on the thread to gather the fabric into the rosette shape (fig. f). Fasten off securely and trim the thread ends. Pin the rosettes to the crossing points, then tack them in place about 2.5cm/1in from the centre.

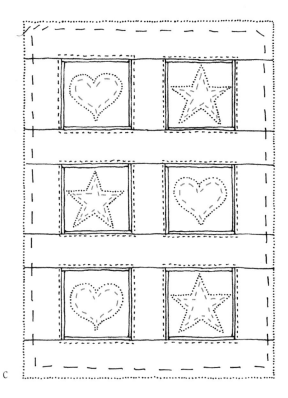

c

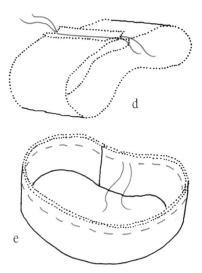

d

e

f

g

6 Attach the rosette centres. First stiffen them by fusing the smaller interfacing circles to the wrong side of the fabric circles, making sure the interfacing is centred. Then pin a circle over each rosette, covering the raw gathered edges.

Slipstitch the circles in place, tucking under the edges as you go (fig. g). Make small stitches, taking your needle vertically through all the layers to hold the rosettes firmly in place.

Topstitch round each circle, 3mm/⅛in from the edge, again using a vertical stabbing movement to fix them securely. Remove the tacking stitches. The appliqué is now finished (fig. h).

h

7 To assemble the quilt, place the lining (wrong side up) on the bottom, then lay the wadding and the quilt top over it. Make sure the edges match, then pin and tack them together, 2.5cm/1in from the edge. Also tack straight down and across the middle of the quilt and round each square, about 5mm/¼in from the edge (fig. i).

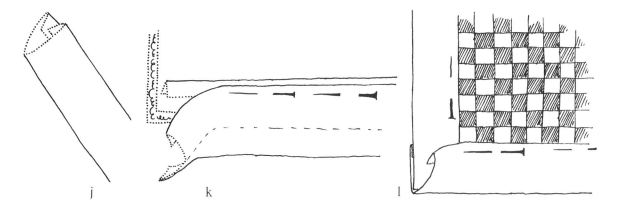

Quilt round each square, working small running stitches just inside the edging, as shown above. Make sure that the needle goes through all thicknesses. Ideally, this should be done on a quilting frame, but if you have tacked carefully, a table will do.

8 To attach the outer edging strips of the quilt, first turn under and press 5mm/¼in on both long edges. Fold the strips in half lengthways and press (fig. j).

Place them over the edge of the quilt on the right side only, with the centre fold slightly outside the quilt edges. Pin them in place, leaving the ends free.

Tuck the narrow inner edging strips under the outer strips, leaving 3mm/⅛in exposed (fig. k). Pin and tack through all layers all the way round.

Slipstitch the outer edging in place on the right side of the quilt, taking the needle through all the layers. At the corners, lap the shorter strips over the longer ones, and slipstitch them together.

Topstitch round the outer edging strip 3mm/⅛in from the hemmed edge, again taking the needle through all layers so as to hold the wadding securely between the two fabric layers.

9 Now fold the edging to the underside of the quilt, covering the two lines of stitching. Pin (fig. l) and tack it in place, folding the corners in neatly (see page 17). Slipstitch the edging to the lining and to itself at the corners, making a neat right angle. Remove all the tacking stitches, and press round the edges.

j   k   l

'Home Sweet Home'

Over the years, I have made a number of appliqué and embroidery portraits of houses. Some have been made into cushions; others are in the form of small pictures, set into specially made box frames. The one I have made here is designed to hang from a rod, which is slotted through loops on the back of the hanging.

The idea of making an embroidered portrait of your house is not a new one: in seventeenth-century England large embroideries sometimes included a representation of the house they were designed to hang in – occasionally surrounded by its garden. These were grand and beautiful homes, of course, but almost any kind of dwelling can be treated in this way.

The American colonial house in this hanging is based on one in New England. Like many houses of the period, it is clad in clapboard, which I have represented with strips of rather old and yellowed bias binding – ideal for suggesting faded white paint. (You can achieve a similar effect by immersing new binding in weak tea.)

If the walls of the house are of brick or stone, the house should be cut in one piece from a suitable plain-coloured fabric. The holes for the windows can be cut and bound with tape as described below. With plain walls you can go to town with details, including window boxes or balconies, or smother the house with climbing roses if you like. Feel free to put in plants to suit the picture, even if they do not actually exist – you can plant them later!

The finished hanging measures 42cm/16½in square.

Materials
Assorted fabrics, 90cm/36in wide. I have used the colours indicated below; you will probably choose different colours for your house.

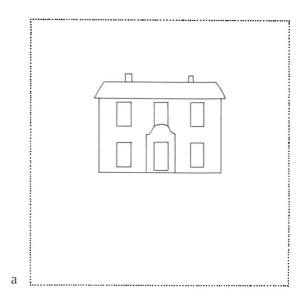

a

A Small beige and red print – for background: 50cm/½yd
B Large-scale floral print – for motifs: minimum of 10cm/⅛yd, depending on fabric design
C Light blue – for sky: 10cm/⅛yd, or piece approx. 10 × 33cm/4 × 13in
D Beige – for foreground: 10cm/⅛yd, or piece approx. 10 × 33cm/4 × 13in
E Cream floral print – for side pieces: 10cm/⅛yd, or piece approx. 12cm/5in square
F Rust – for roof: 10cm/⅛yd, or piece approx. 23 × 5cm/9 × 2in
G Dark grey – for windows: 10cm/⅛yd, or piece approx. 10cm/4in square
H Blue – for door: scrap approx. 5 × 6cm/2 × 2½in
I Cream – for porch: scrap approx. 9 × 6cm/3½ × 2½in
J Blue stripe – for border strips: 10cm/⅛yd (or 50cm/½yd, if using a lengthways-striped fabric)
K Lining: 50cm/½yd
Calico – for base fabric: 50cm/½yd
Cream bias binding, 1.2cm/½in wide: 4.5m/5yd
Drab green bias binding for window

frames: 70cm/¾yd
Tiny scraps of cream fabric for chimneys; lace and/or printed fabric for curtains
Narrow piping (optional) to harmonize with outer binding: 1.6m/1¾yd
Four decorations (optional) for corners
Sewing or quilting thread in cream, black, beige, brown (toning with the roof fabric) and drab green
Medium-weight polyester wadding: 50cm/½yd
Tracing paper, including piece 40cm/16in square

1 Cut out the fabric pieces as instructed on page 158. (See also the general instructions on pages 12–16.)

2 Draw the main outlines of the house on the piece of calico (fig. a), with the lower edge of the house 17cm/6½in away from the lower edge of the fabric. To do this, prick holes in the tracing at all the corners with a pin. Mark through the holes with a pencil, then join the marks using a ruler to get straight lines.

3 Position the background pieces
– the sky, the two side pieces (Fabric E) and the foreground (Fabric D) – so that they overlap the outer drawn lines of the house by about 5mm/¼in. Trim the sky piece as shown to allow for the roof (check this against roof pattern). Pin and tack them in place (fig. b), working far enough from the edges so that you will be able to lift them later to check the position of the pencil lines.

Position the five pieces for the window backgrounds so that they overlap the pencilled lines by 3mm/⅛in. (I have used a charcoal grey silk with a slight sheen that looks like glass.) Hold them in place with tacking.

4 To apply the cladding, open out and press flat one of the folded edges of the bias binding. Cut the binding into short strips of the following lengths (the number of strips of each length is given in brackets): 3cm/1¼in (32); 4.5cm/1¾in (16); 8.5cm/3⅜in (20); 3.5cm/1⅜in (16); 20cm/8in (1). These numbers and lengths will, of course, need to be adjusted if your house differs from mine.

Arrange the strips of binding on the house shape, working from the bottom upwards and overlapping them with their folded edges downwards (fig. c). Pin, then tack the strips in place, keeping them as

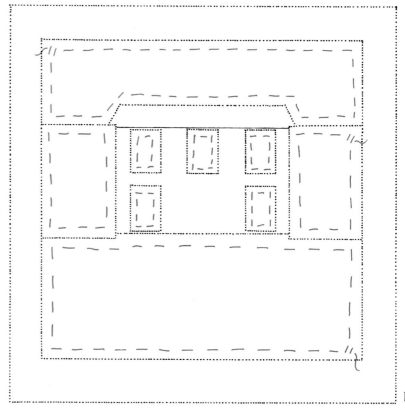

b

parallel as possible and spacing them evenly. They should just meet your pencilled lines, but if any overlap, trim them as required.

Using matching thread and a small, even running stitch, sew the strips in place close to the folded edges, taking the needle through all thicknesses. Remove the tacking.

Cut two more lengths of binding,

each 12.5cm/5in long, fold them in half lengthways and press. Pin, tack (fig. d) and slipstitch them to the side edges (see page 15), covering the raw edges of the horizontal strips. Turn in the bottom ends neatly, but leave the upper ends raw. Work running stitch along both sides of these two corner boards and across the bottom. Remove the tacking.

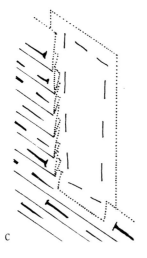

c

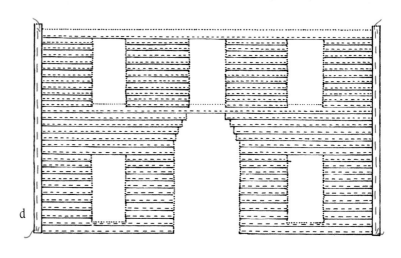

d

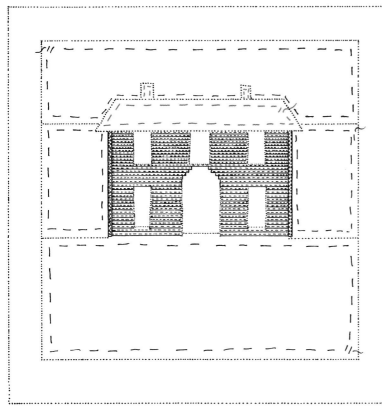

e

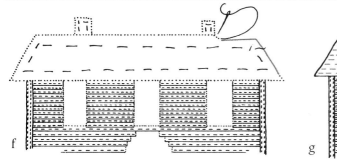

f

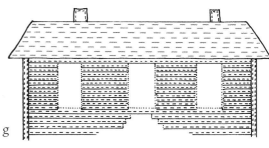

g

5 The roof and chimneys can now be applied. Pin and tack the chimneys onto the roof, about 4cm/1½in from the ends, with the bottom edges overlapping the roof line.

Pin and tack the roof piece over the roof outline (fig. e), then slipstitch it in place, turning under 3mm/⅛in as you go and turning under and slipstitching round the chimneys as you come to them (fig. f). Press.

Work parallel lines of running stitch across the roof, in a toning colour, keeping the lines about 3mm/⅛in apart and staggering the stitches like bricks or tiles, as shown. Work small running stitches round the chimneys, using matching thread. Remove the tacking (fig. g).

6 Now apply the windows. Cut five 12cm/4¾in lengths of bias binding in your chosen colour for the outer window frames. Trim each strip lengthways, cutting off one folded edge as shown, so that you are left with a strip about 8mm/³⁄₁₆in wide, with one folded edge.

Sew one of these strips round each window, using small slipstitches and placing the folded edge of the binding over the ends of the cladding strips by a scant 3mm/⅛in (fig. h). To make neat 90° corners, work a tiny stitch right on the corners of the windows (see page 15).

When you have sewn round all

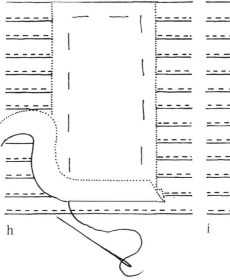

h

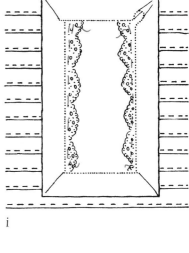

i

four sides, you will have a spare 3mm/⅛in or so to turn under for a neat finish (fig. i).

If you are putting in curtains or blinds, do this before stitching down the inner edge. I have slipped in tiny pieces of lace and delicate printed fabric for curtains on the upper windows. Fold a tiny scrap of the fabric to the width you want, finger press the fold and slip the scrap under the window frame. Pin or tack it in place. Fold under the inner raw

edge of the binding, and slipstitch it in place, securing the curtains as you go and making neat mitred corners as you come to them (fig. j).

Work small running stitches round the inner and outer edges of the binding, using matching thread. Embroider the inner window frames and glazing bars using backstitch. For the inner frames and across the centre, work round twice, using double thread; use a single strand for the thin glazing bars.

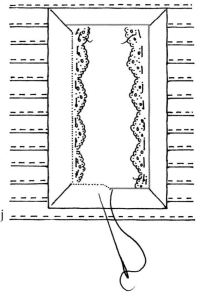

j

k

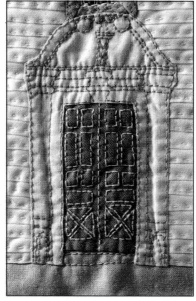

7 The door and porch can now be pinned and tacked in place. Slipstitch the lower edge of the door, then all round the porch, turning under 3mm/⅛in. Press.

Transfer the details of panelling and carving to the fabric using dressmaker's carbon (see page 14). Embroider them using backstitch and one strand of thread (fig. k). The motif on the tiny column in the centre is worked in detached chain or daisy stitch. Snip and remove tacking as you go along if it gets in your way.

8 Decorative foliage on the outside of the house can now be added, using either embroidery or appliqué (fig. l). The creeper shown here is worked in backstitch and French knots (see page 16). You could make a border of embroidered lavender or rosemary in front of the house, or add some Virginia creeper or wisteria trailing around the front door. I have sometimes used cut-out bits of foliage from a small-scale printed fabric – making, for example, twin bushes or box hedges or bay trees in tubs to place either side of the door.

l

9 Now arrange the flowers and foliage around the house. I have framed mine with trees, flowers and leaves which I salvaged from an antique chintz curtain in very poor condition. I cut and joined the pieces of tree trunk to form a continuous snaking bough, and arranged the groups of leaves at intervals along it. The flowers were cut out individually and arranged in profusion below the house, along with more leaves and a basket of fruit cut from another old chintz, which also supplied the pieces that fill the spaces between the sides of the house and the trees.

Cut floral motifs, branches, and leaves from your chosen printed Fabric B, leaving a scant 5mm/¼in around the edges. Arrange these prettily around the house, leaving some sky and foreground showing. Use some leaves to cover the raw edges where the side pieces meet the sky and the foreground. Pin, then tack these motifs in place, a scant 1cm/⅜in from the edges (fig. m).

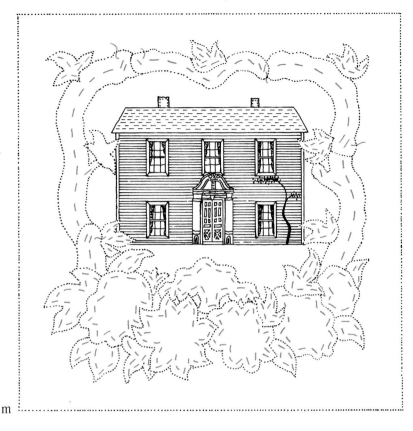

m

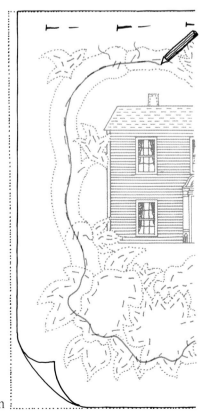

n

10 Place the large square of tracing paper over the work, and lightly trace round the floral surround, about 1cm/⅜in inside the outer cut edges (fig. n). This will serve as the trimming line for the Fabric A background. Cut the tracing along the marked line. Pin it over the background and trim away the excess fabric.

Place the fabric on the picture, centring it carefully. Pin, then tack it in place, about 1.5cm/⅝in from the edges, slipping the inner edges under the motifs. You may need to undo or loosen a few tacking stitches to do this. Replace them after you have tacked Fabric A.

Turn under and slipstitch the edges of the floral motifs, starting with those underneath and working upwards, snipping curves and corners where necessary (fig. o). Press the work carefully through a cloth, smoothing each leaf or flower with the tip of the iron. Remove the tacking from the flowers and leaves.

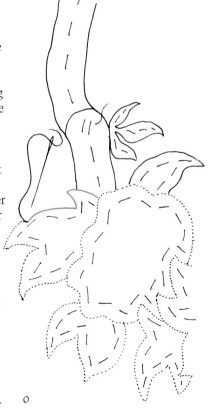

o

11 Make up the picture. Turn under and press 5mm/¼in on one (inner) edge of the four border strips. I have made decorative use of the black selvedge on my blue and grey striped silk border. It provides an extra line in the border and emphasizes the overlapping arrangement of the strips. I have tucked in some piping in blue and white stripes to make another line of colour. Pin the border strips, right side up, round the edges of the picture, overlapping them in a clockwise direction (fig. p).

Cut lengths of piping, if you are using it, to fit the inner edges of the border, plus a little extra. Tuck these under the border strips. Tack the strips to the background, taking in the piping edges (fig. q).

Assemble the three layers – lining, wadding and appliqué panel – right sides outside. Pin, then tack through all layers (fig. r).

Work a line of running stitch 5mm/¼in inside the inner edges of the border, taking the needle through all layers with a stabbing movement. I have used black thread for this, so that it shows as part of the whole design. Work another line along the inner edge of the border strips, again through all layers, thus attaching the border and piping to all the underlying fabrics.

p

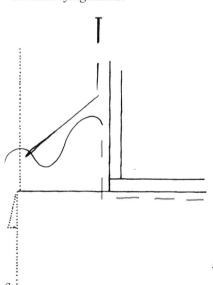

q

r

12 Turn in the outer edges of the border strips and the lining, enclosing the wadding (trim this back, if necessary). Join these with a third line of running stitch 3mm/⅛in from the edge (fig. s).

Turn under and press 5mm/¼in on the longer edges of the four fabric loops. Fold the strips in half lengthways, matching the turned-in edges. Press. Machine stitch close to the open edges (fig. t). Turn under and press 5mm/¼in on each short end. Pin and tack the loops to the upper edge of the lining, placing them about 2cm/¾in down from the top. The outer ones go about 3cm/1¼in from the side edges, with the inner ones evenly spaced between them. Sew them firmly to the lining fabric (fig. u).

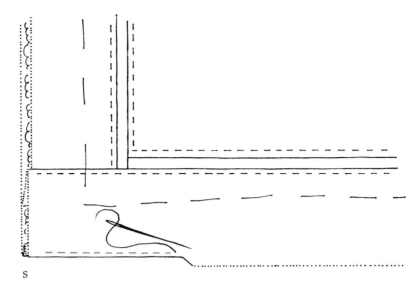

s

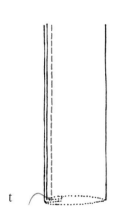

t

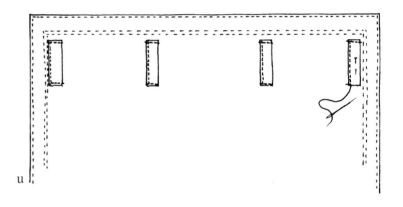

u

Sew the braid decorations to the four corners. Those I have used here are tiny crocheted fruits and leaves cut from lampshade trimming (fig. v).

A word of encouragement
However carefully you measure, and however accurately you cut the pieces of fabric for your house, it is likely to end up slightly askew in places. Do not worry about this; fabric is a flexible material and will not behave like paper, or wood, or bricks and mortar. The aim is not to make an architectural drawing, but an attractive picture. So pin, tack and stitch as neatly as you can, but do not despair if dead-straight lines elude you – it's nicer that way!

v

Fleur-de-Lys Variations

Beautiful floor tiles in yellow and terracotta are to be found in hundreds of different designs in many medieval English churches. They also form part of the decoration in the Gothic Revival churches of the Victorian period.

For this set of six cushions I have chosen six variations of the fleur-de-lys motif from a church in Cambridge. The fleur-de-lys figured prominently in medieval art and appears on many of these tiles. I have made the cushions up in the traditional colours of the tiles themselves, and have added blue to complement the earthy yellow and brown. I found a scrap of printed fabric that contained just the right shades of corn yellow, terracotta and blue, and have used this to join the yellow and brown appliqué centre of the cushions to the blue border. It is a tough cotton furnishing fabric that does not fray easily; I have taken advantage of this and cut the strips with pinking shears to give a decorative serrated edge, then simply secured them with running stitch. I have carried the terracotta over onto the blue by using it for the four leaf shapes in the corners of each cushion, and have finished the cushions off with a mottled blue piping.

Each cushion measures approximately 40cm/16in square.

Materials

Medium-weight cotton fabrics (90cm/36in wide unless otherwise stated). I have used the colours indicated in the list below. You may, of course, choose different colours.
A Blue – for border and back covers: 3.2m/3½yd
B Yellow – for centre square: 50cm/½yd
C Terracotta – for motifs: 50cm/½yd
D Print – for pinked edging strips, 122cm/48in wide: 20cm/¼yd
E Print – for piping: 1m/1yd

Cream sewing or quilting thread for topstitching
Medium-sized, pre-shrunk piping cord: 10m/11yd
6 cushion pads, 40cm/16in square
4 small buttons
Set square
Dressmaker's chalk

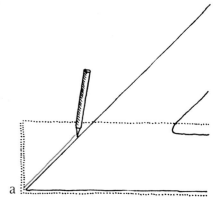

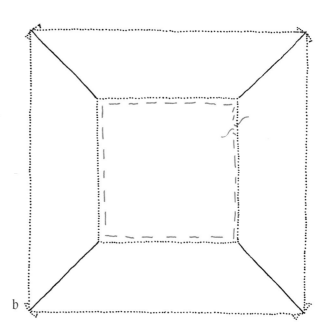

1 Cut out the fabric pieces as instructed on page 164. (See also the general instructions on pages 12–16.) Note. The following instructions relate primarily to Cushion I. However the procedure is essentially the same for all six cushions.

2 To join the top cover pieces, first place two of the rectangular border pieces together with right sides facing and edges matching. Then, using the set square and chalk, mark a 45° angle from the lower left-hand corner on the top piece up to the top edge (fig. a). Tack the two pieces together inside the line, then machine stitch 1cm/⅜in from the line. Cut away the corners of the two pieces along the marked line. Repeat to join all four of the border pieces with 45° angles. Press the seams open.

Place one of the centre squares over the border, right sides up. Pin, then tack round the edges (fig. b).

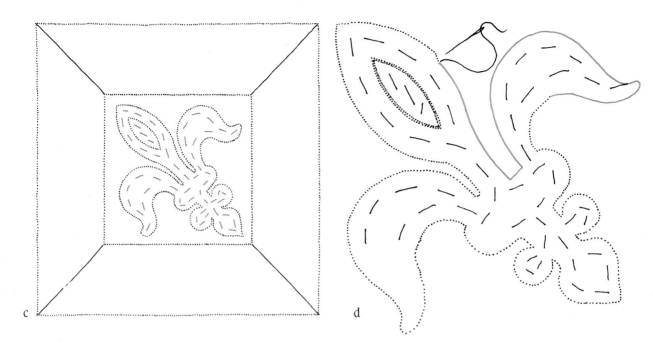

c   d

3 Apply the central motif. First place the main pieces of the fleur-de-lys and its inner leaf shape on the centre square, making sure that the points are directed exactly into the corners. At this stage the leaf shape fits exactly into the main motif. Pin and tack the shapes in place, a scant 1cm/³⁄₈in from the edges (fig c).

Slipstitch (see page 15) round the large shape first, turning in 3mm/ ¹⁄₈in as you go along and trying to keep the curves as smooth as possible (fig. d). Turn sharp points at the corners. Next, turn under and slipstitch the inner, cut-out edge. Finally, slipstitch the inner leaf shape. Remove the tacking stitches and press.

Now work running stitches (see page 16) 3mm/¹⁄₈in from the edge round the entire motif. Press (fig. e).

e

f

4 To complete the appliqué, position four leaf shapes on the four corner seams, 4.5cm/1³⁄₄in from the outer corners. Pin and tack them in position.

Then place the four pinked strips over the join of the centre square and border, with each strip overlapping the end of the next one (fig. f); pin and tack them in place. Trim any bits of the centre square that are visible around the edges. (If you want to use a fabric for the joining strip that is not suitable to be pinked and left raw, cut strips of fabric wide enough to be turned in and hemmed instead.)

Turn under and slipstitch the edges of the leaf shapes, making the points as neat and sharp as possible. Press. Work running stitch 3mm/¹⁄₈in from the edge of each leaf.

Also work running stitch round the pinked strips, 3mm/¹⁄₈in from the inner points of the pinking (fig. g). If you have not pinked the edges, turn them under and slipstitch them before working the running stitch. Remove the tacking and give the top cover a final press.

5 Make up the cushion as instructed on page 17.

Cushion II is worked in similar fashion to the first. It is a slightly more complicated version of the fleur-de-lys motif, but cut in only one piece.

Cushion III is a smaller and simpler fleur-de-lys surrounded by geometric shapes. These are easy to apply, but make sure you keep right angles really square, and points sharp.

Cushion IV has an even smaller fleur-de-lys with groups of leaf and petal shapes enclosed in curved strips at each corner.

Cushion V has a fleur-de-lys with a central circle in two pieces. Tack the main piece on carefully, making sure that the points of the four fleur-de-lys shapes point directly at the corners.

Cushion VI has six appliqué pieces. They should all be pinned and tacked in place before the stitching is worked. Make sure that the circle overlaps the ends of the four fleur-de-lys by 6mm/¹⁄₄in. Slipstitch the fleur-de-lys pieces first, then the circle, with its four oak leaf shapes, and lastly the eight-petalled flower shape in the middle.

Far right *A jewel-like colour scheme, combines wine red with light and dark jade green.*

g

II

III

IV

V

VI

Coral Reef with Mermaid

A lively procession of sea horses and water serpents, shoals of fish and a mermaid swim around the coral reef border of this quilt. The central panel has a simple repeat pattern of small fish and dots. The quilt measures about 228 × 154cm/91 × 61in, and will cover a single bed generously.

Some of my quilts rely for their effect on a restrained use of colour, but this is quite the opposite. I have used a rich scheme of 23 reds, purples, blues and greens, bound at the edge with a striped ikat cotton containing many of the same colours. For the lining I have used an ikat sari, which I bought in Orissa, India, where this kind of weaving is a speciality. It has a bright fuchsia pink ground with stripes in many colours, including some of those in the quilt top. It adds hugely to the richness of an object – whether quilt, curtain or cosy – to have it beautiful all the way round. Then there is not so much a right side and a wrong side as two complementary sides,
making something really satisfying and complete.

Materials

Soft, closely woven cotton fabrics, 90cm/36in wide. In the list below, the number of colours has been reduced, to give a broad indication of how they were used. You may, of course, decide to use fewer, more, or quite different colours for your own version of the quilt.

A Sky blue – for border and dots: 3.2m/3½yd
B Pale blue – for centre panel: 1.6m/1¾yd
C Sage green – for triangles (central panel border): 40cm/½yd
D Ice blue – for mermaid's body: 40cm/½yd
E Cadet blue – for sea horse, fish head, etc: 40cm/½yd
F Deep turquoise blue – for fish scales, sea horse: 40cm/½yd
G Grey-violet – for large fish stripe: 20cm/¼yd
H Deep mauve – for serpent, mermaid's hair: 40cm/½yd
I Bright red – for small fish, serpent circles: 20cm/¼yd
J Dark blue – for coral, large fish tail: 30cm/⅜yd
K Bright green – for narrow edging strips: 20 cm/¼yd
L Mauve – for serpent: 40cm/½yd
M Bright pink – for medium fish, serpent triangles: 10cm/⅛yd
N Purple – for small fish: 10cm/⅛yd
O Pale mauve – for serpent triangles: 10cm/⅛yd
P Charcoal grey – for rock: piece 15cm/6in square
Q Terracotta rose – for small fish: 10cm/⅛yd
R Yellow – for fish in coral: tiny scrap
S Striped cotton – for binding: 90cm/1yd, if cut on the bias; 50cm/½yd, if cut crossways
T Lining: 4.8m/5¼yd
Lightweight wadding: 2.4m/2¾yd, at least 157cm/62in wide (if widths
must be joined, double the quantity)
Pale blue cotton sewing or quilting thread for topstitching and quilting
Dark mauve and dark grey-blue sewing thread for embroidery
Flexible curve (optional) and dressmaker's chalk

1 Cut out the fabric pieces as instructed on page 166. (See also the general instructions on pages 12–16.)

2 Start with the appliqué on the central panel. I have made the panel out of three separate pieces, so there are two seams running across it. I have turned these to advantage by working lines of quilting alongside them – a useful expedient if you need to piece part of a quilt. Snip the small fish at the corners, and arrange them evenly over the fabric, leaving 16cm/6¼in between their tails and noses and 11cm/4¼in between the rows. When you are satisfied that the fish are placed evenly, and that they are all straight – that is, horizontal – pin, then tack (see page 15) them in place (fig. a).

Place the dots between the fish, again measuring the distances with a ruler or tape measure to get them absolutely evenly spaced. Pin and tack.

Slipstitch round all the pieces (see page 15), turning in 3mm/⅛in as you go. Press them carefully, then topstitch round each piece 3mm/⅛in from the edge. Press, and remove the tacking.

a

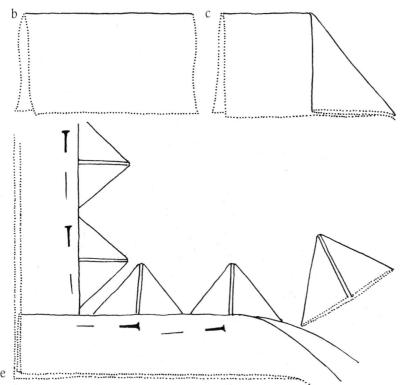

3 Make the border for the central panel, starting with the zigzag edging. Fold each 5cm/2in square in half to form a rectangle (fig. b), then fold the corners down to make a triangle (figs c and d). Press.

Now fold each of the narrow Fabric A strips in half lengthways and press. Place the strips, folded edge inwards, along the four sides of the centre panel, matching the raw edges, and pin them on. Take one of the folded triangles, and tuck it under the folded edge of a strip, quite close to a corner, so that the point is towards the centre and at least 5mm/¼in of the triangle is covered by the folded strip. Secure it with a pin. Tuck in another triangle next to the first, and pin. Continue in this way all the way round the edge, spacing the triangles evenly and

pinning through all thicknesses (fig. e). When you have made sure that they are all straight, evenly spaced and tucked in by an even amount, tack along the folded strip, through all the triangles and the centre panel (fig. f).

4 Apply the serpents to the long border strips. First centre one serpent on a side border piece, making sure that it lies parallel to the edges, and pin it to the fabric in a few places. Note that the two serpents are facing in opposite directions, one pointing to the head and one to the foot of the quilt.

Place the triangles along the serpent's back, and pin all pieces to the border at short intervals. Tack along both sides of the serpent, working round each triangle as you

come to it (fig. g). Cut the slit for the serpent's mouth, and snip the curve at the corner. Slip the tongue piece in under the mouth, making sure it is far enough in so that when the mouth edges are turned under and stitched, the edge of the tongue will still be concealed. Pin and tack.

Fold the squares for the teeth (eight are used for each serpent) in the same way as those for the zigzag edging. Set these on one side.

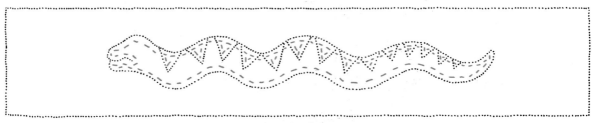

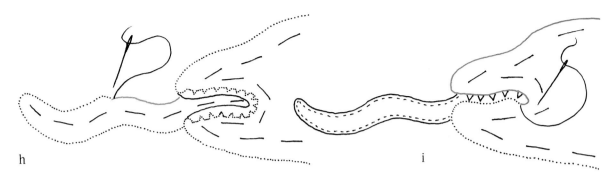

h   i

5 Slipstitch the tongue to the border fabric (fig. h). Press, then work topstitching all round it.

Slipstitch the serpent to the border, making sure the curves are quite smooth. As you reach each triangle, slipstitch its inner two sides to the serpent; then continue along the outer edge, treating the raw edges of triangle and serpent as one. When you reach the mouth, insert the teeth (with the triangle fold underneath) as you stitch, starting at the inner corner of the mouth and tucking them in as you go; leave only a small, sharp point showing (fig. i).

Pin and tack the circles at intervals along the serpent's back. Then pin and tack the almond-shaped eye piece in place. Slipstitch, press and topstitch all these pieces. Finally sew on the small round iris in the eye. Press carefully.

Sew the second serpent onto the other long border piece in the same way as the first one.

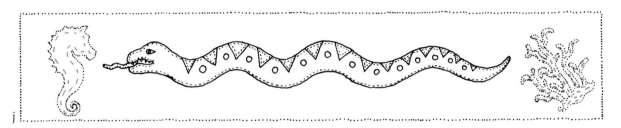

j

6 The clumps of coral are placed with their base 'rock' lying across the bottom corners of the quilt (fig. j). They are very curvy, so snip them carefully, and position the branches to make an attractive bush-like arrangement. To make sure that they are balanced across the corner, pin the rock diagonally about 13cm/ 5¼in in from the corner at an angle of 45° and with the ends equidistant from the border edges. Use this as a guide when arranging the branches of coral. I have put a few small fish among the branches, some behind and some in front. I felt that two or three were enough, but you could have fun putting in whole shoals if you like. Pin, tack, slipstitch, topstitch and press the coral and fish; then apply the rock in the same way, covering the lower edges of the coral branches.

7 The sea horses can now be positioned in the remaining corners of the long border pieces. They look towards the foot of the quilt, so that one of them is following a serpent, while the other appears to be having a confrontation with one (fig. j).

Snipping is all-important on a curly shape such as the sea horses' tails, so make sure you have made enough tiny snips before you start sewing. The same applies to the curved shape that lies on top of the basic sea horse piece.

Make sure that they are perfectly upright when you pin them on, then sew them on in exactly the same way as for the serpents (fig. k).

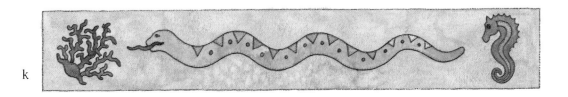

k

8 To work the appliqué on the top border piece, first fold the border in half crossways to find the centre; mark this with tacking. Position the head of the large fish 25cm/10in to the left of the line of tacking, with its upper lip about 17cm/6¾in from the upper raw edge, then pin it in place.

Position the tail with its inner points 10cm/4in to the right of the centre line of tacking, making sure that it is at right angles to the border edges (fig. l). Pin it in place.

Using the flexible curve (or, if you are confident enough, your eye) and dressmaker's chalk, draw a smooth curve from head to tail to indicate the upper and lower body lines of the

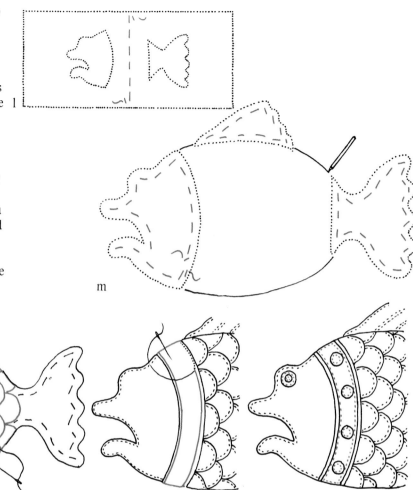

fish. Adjust the head or tail if necessary. Pin the top fin along the curve, about 2.5cm/1in from the head. Tack (fig. m) and slipstitch these pieces in place; press.

9 Pin and tack the scales, starting at the tail end and working towards the head. Using the drawn line as a guide, place them carefully, so that when the edges are turned no gaps will appear. Trim the scales as required to fit the body shape, then slipstitch them in place, taking care to keep a smooth curve at the edges (fig. n). Topstitch all of the applied fish pieces.

The wide, curved 'collar' stripe is put on next. First fold the narrow bias strips (Fabric K) in half lengthways and press. Set two aside

for the mermaid scales, and press the other two again, curving them slightly – one with the fold outside, one with it inside. Position the collar between the head and the scales, and pin it in place. Tack, then slipstitch, tucking in the bias strips – leave about 3mm/⅛in showing. Trim and turn in the ends (fig. o).

Next, sew on the four dots (Fabric J), the tailfin pieces and the larger eye dot, topstitching in the usual way, Sew on the smaller eye dot, topstitch and remove tacking (fig. p).

10 The smaller fish at the top end of the quilt are now positioned and sewn on in the same way. Before tacking them in place, lay the border alongside the short end of the central panel and check that the fish do not extend more than 3cm/1¼in beyond the inner edge of the narrow border; otherwise they will be caught in the seam. Apply the curved stripes to the medium-sized fish at the same time as the main shapes, just as you incorporated the triangles on the serpents (fig. q).

q

11 To position the mermaid
first mark the centre of the bottom border piece with tacking. Then measure 39cm/15¼in to the left of this line to give the position of her right elbow. Mark this point about 5cm/2in up from the raw edge. Using this as a starting point, place the main body/head piece and the six tail pieces on the border, overlapping the left edges on the right ones and forming a graceful curve (fig. r). She should measure about 79cm/31in in length. When you are satisfied with her shape, and sure that all the pieces overlap enough so that there will not be any gaps when the stitching is finished, pin, then tack them on.

12 Prepare the edging for the tail pieces by cutting six pieces, each 6cm/2½in long, from the remaining folded bias strips. Press each piece in a sharp curve, folded edge outwards.

Starting at the tailfin, slipstitch each tail piece in place. On the third and fifth tail pieces, tuck the curved bias strips under the scales. Press.

Add lines of running stitch all the way round each piece (fig. s), making the stitches smaller and closer to the edge than usual on the body so that you can get finer detail on her face.

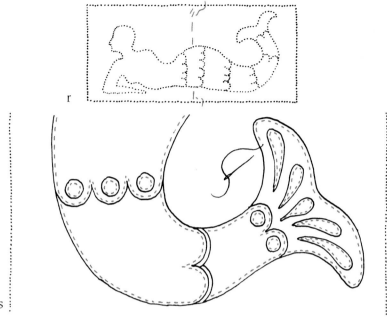

Decorate the second, fourth and sixth tail pieces with dots (Fabric K), placed inside the curve of the scales. Pin and tack these in place, then add the tailfin pieces and the two tiny dots for her nipples. Slipstitch, press and topstitch all these pieces. Remove the tacking.

Now position the mermaid's left arm (fig. t), and arrange her flowing tresses. Pin and tack all these in place. Slipstitch the arm first, then press and topstitch it. Also work a double curved line of running

stitches to define the left breast.

Slipstitch the locks of hair, starting at the top, overlapping them and making sure you keep an attractive curve at the hairline round her forehead (fig. u). Topstitch, press and remove the tacking.

Embroider the mermaid's mouth and eyelid fold in backstitch, using blue-grey thread. Work twice round the eye and eyebrow. For the iris, use mauve, working round the edge in backstitch, then filling the shape with satin stitch.

13 Now join all the border pieces
to the central panel. Begin by joining
the short multicoloured border strips
to make two strips 162cm/64in long
and two 87cm/34in long. Press the
seams open. Turn in 5mm/¼in on
both edges of all the strips and press.

Position the four appliquéd border
pieces around the four sides of the
centre panel, overlapping it by
1.5cm/½in (fig. v). Put in a few pins
to prevent it all from shifting, and
pin the narrow pressed strips over
the join (fig. w). Also pin the wide
border pieces where they join,
lapping the long pieces over the
short ones and making sure you
keep the whole thing flat. Tack along
both sides of the narrow strips, and
turn in their ends to make neat
corners (fig. x). Tack the joins of the
wide border pieces. Slipstitch along
the edges of the narrow strips, round
their folded ends, and along the joins
of the border pieces. Topstitch along
the seams, joining the wide border
pieces. Press.

v

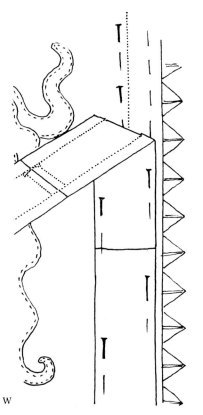

w

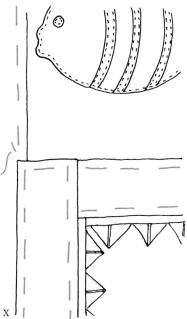

x

14 The quilt top is now ready to
be joined to its backing and to the
wadding. Join the two lining pieces
along one long edge by machine and
press the seam open. Trim the lining
to measure about 3cm/1¼in larger
than the quilt top on all sides. Trim
the wadding to about the same size
(first joining the widths if
necessary). It is always a good idea
to cut the wadding and the lining
slightly larger than the quilt top. Pin
the lining, wadding and quilt top
together, making sure all three are
flat and that there are no wrinkles.

y

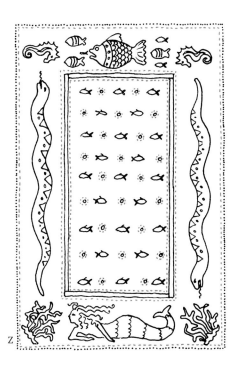

z

15 Tack through all layers
straight down the middle from top to bottom, all the way round the centre panel along the narrow strip, and all the way round the quilt about 3cm/ 1¼in from the raw edge of the quilt top. Tack round each dot on the centre panel, about 5mm/¼in from the dot (fig. y). If you plan to quilt any other parts of the work, tack near these also, to hold the layers in place.

The purpose of the quilting is to tie the layers together in a decorative manner. I have quilted round the inner and outer edges of the border, along the edges of the multicoloured strip and round the dots in the centre (fig. z); but you could have great fun quilting round the other shapes, or making wavy lines across the centre panel and round the border, for example. Work the quilting in running stitch, as for the topstitching. Ideally you should use a quilting frame, but it is quite possible to work without one if you do enough tacking. When you have finished tacking, trim the edges of the quilt.

16 To bind the edges of the quilt, first join the binding strips to make a piece about 7.8m/8⅝yd long. Press the seams open. Pin the strip to the edge of the quilt top, right sides together and edges matching. Tack, then machine stitch through all thicknesses, about 5mm/¼in from the edge (fig. aa). Turn the binding strip over to the back of the quilt, turn in the raw edge and pin (fig. bb). Tack all round the quilt on the back, tucking the edging strip in evenly and covering the line of machine stitching (fig. cc). Slipstitch. Press lightly, then remove all tacking.

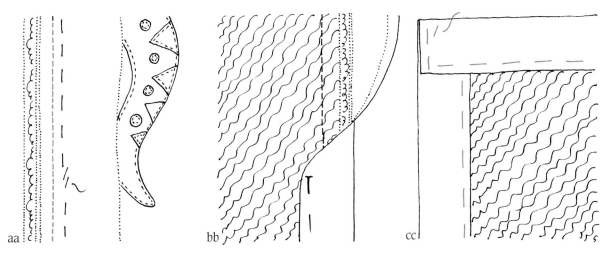

aa

bb

cc

Venetian Gothic

This three-sided cosy is tall enough to fit over all but the very largest coffee or chocolate pot – and will keep drinks piping hot while you warm the croissants, answer the telephone . . . and so on.

On each side there is a Venetian window with striped marble columns. For the background fabric I have used a piece of old black silk satin left over from an evening jacket my mother had many years ago. The fabric has a bright red and yellow striped selvedge, and I have cut the three pieces so that this selvedge forms the bottom edge of the main pieces.

For the appliqué I have used Indian dupion silk in four colours, changing their distribution on each side so that the three sides are quite different from one another, yet matching. I have used some striped Egyptian cottons for the columns, for the edge piping and for the thickly padded bottom edge. These cottons have a slippery shiny finish and are woven in glorious rich colours that go well with the Indian silks. But – a word of caution – the Indian silks fray very easily, especially if you are working with small pieces such as those used in this design. So, unless you are confident about using them, I would suggest trying the cosy out in cottons first.

Materials

Silk and/or cotton fabrics, at least 90cm/36in wide. I have made the cosy in the colours indicated in the list below. You may, of course, wish to make it in fewer, more or quite different colours. I have shown one alternative on page 89.
A Black satin – for background: 40cm/½yd
B Lining: 40cm/½yd
C Red and gold stripe – for wide binding: 30cm/⅓yd
D Black and gold stripe – for narrow

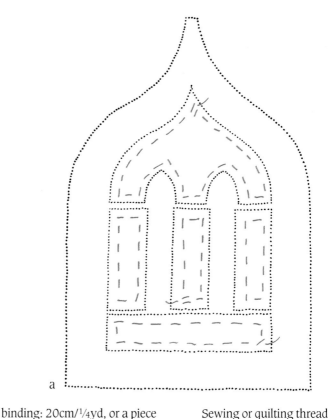

a

binding: 20cm/¼yd, or a piece approx. 20 × 50cm/8 × 20in
E Bright gold – for arches, Side 1: 20cm/¼yd
F Woven stripe – for columns, Side 1: 10cm/⅛yd, or a piece approx. 15cm/6in square
G Silver grey – for arches, Side 2: 20cm/¼yd
H Woven stripe – for columns, Side 2: 10cm/⅛yd, or a piece approx. 10 × 40cm/4 × 16in
I Copper-brown – for arches, Side 3: 20cm/¼yd
J Red – for binding, Side 3: 20cm/¼yd, or piece approx. 20 × 30cm/8 × 12in
K Woven stripe – for columns, Side 3: 10cm/4in, or piece approx. 15cm/6in square
Medium-weight (4oz) polyester wadding: 40cm/½yd
Cotton yarn for pompoms: 50g/2oz ball
Piece of thin cardboard, approx. 20cm/8in square

Sewing or quilting thread to match plain-coloured fabrics

1 Cut out the fabric pieces as instructed on page 172. (See also the general instructions on pages 12–16.)

Turn under and press about 8mm/generous ¼in on both side edges of the centre columns and one side edge of the other.
Note: each side includes the same pieces and is assembled in the same way as the others. Keep all the pieces for each side together.

2 Position the arches, columns and base piece on one of the background pieces. The outer columns should be equidistant from the side edges, and the lower edge of the base 4cm/1½in from the bottom edge. Leave 3mm/⅛in between the columns and the arched piece and 3mm/⅛in between the columns and the base. Pin and tack these pieces in place (fig. a).

3 To apply the bias strips, first join the individual cut strips to make a single strip 95cm/37in long. Turn under and press 6mm/¼in on the long edges. Cut one piece 16.5cm/6½in long from the end. Place this shorter piece over the top edge of the base, also covering the lower ends of the columns; pin and tack it in place. Pin and tack the longer strip over the outer edges of all the pieces, starting and ending at the top point (fig. b). At the two bottom corners, fold the strip neatly in two stages as shown (figs c and d).

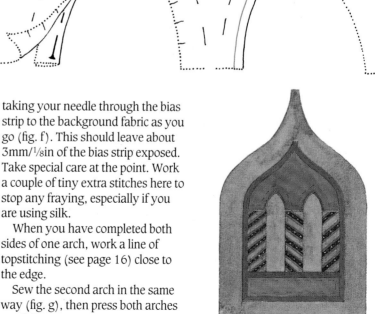

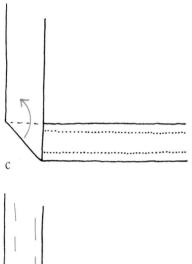

4 The inner arches can now be stitched. First slipstitch the four folded and pressed inner edges of the columns to the background fabric (see page 15). Cut inner edging strips, each 4.5cm/1¾in long; fold them in half lengthways and press. Slip each one under the curved edge of an arch, so that its folded edge runs directly under the cut edge of the arch. Pin and tack each strip in place, lifting up the arch slightly to do so (fig. e).

Turn under 3mm/⅛in along the cut edge and slipstitch it down, taking your needle through the bias strip to the background fabric as you go (fig. f). This should leave about 3mm/⅛in of the bias strip exposed. Take special care at the point. Work a couple of tiny extra stitches here to stop any fraying, especially if you are using silk.

When you have completed both sides of one arch, work a line of topstitching (see page 16) close to the edge.

Sew the second arch in the same way (fig. g), then press both arches carefully.

5 The short bias strip at the foot of the columns can now be slipstitched along its lower edge. Then cut three inner edging strips, each 4cm/1½in long, one for the base of each column. Turn under and press both ends of one strip to make it the same width as the centre column. Then turn under one end of the two outer strips.

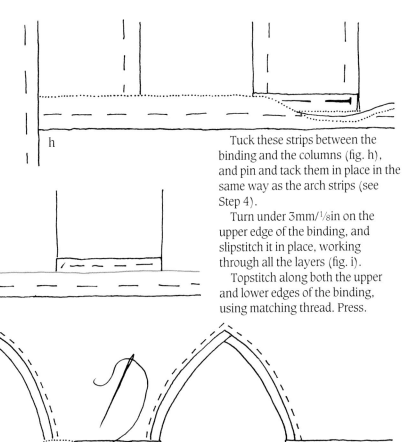

Tuck these strips between the binding and the columns (fig. h), and pin and tack them in place in the same way as the arch strips (see Step 4).

Turn under 3mm/⅛in on the upper edge of the binding, and slipstitch it in place, working through all the layers (fig. i).

Topstitch along both the upper and lower edges of the binding, using matching thread. Press.

6 Apply the three capitals to the columns, first tacking them in place (fig. j). Make sure that they are straight and at an even height. Prepare six edging strips, each 4cm/ 1½in long, as for the base of the columns (see Step 5), and insert them one above and one below each capital, folded edge outwards, leaving 3mm/⅛in exposed after turning under and slipstitching the capitals. Slipstitch the capitals in place, incorporating the edging strips (fig. k).

Topstitch round the capitals close to the edge (fig. l).

7 The long bias appliqué strip can now be slipstitched, starting with the outside edge and covering the raw edges of the pieces you have already applied. Take care to keep the shape of the curve smooth and the sides dead straight. Keep the stitching line absolutely straight right up to the bottom corner. Make a tiny stitch on the corner itself then work in a straight line from that point along the bottom edge. This way you can make crisp 90° corners.

Slipstitch round the inner edge. Then topstitch along both edges, working through all the layers (fig. m). Press.

8 Now add the ornaments. Place the five circles on the base – one directly below each column and the other two equidistant between them. Position the larger circle centrally above the middle column.

Place the finial at the point of the arch, making sure that its lower edge is straight and that, when it is slipstitched, it will not overlap the inner point of the arch. Pin and tack all these pieces in place (fig. n).

Slipstitch them in any order, taking great care to keep the circles evenly round. Topstitch close to the edges using matching thread. Press.

Finally, position the smaller circle centrally on top of the larger one; pin, tack and slipstitch, then topstitch, as usual. Press this last piece and remove all the tacking stitches.

Work the appliqué on the other two sides, following Steps 2–8.

9 Assemble the three layers of each side. Place the lining on the bottom, then place the wadding and the appliquéd piece on top. Make sure all the corners and points match, then pin and tack them together about 2.5cm/1in from their edges (fig. o).

Turn under and press 5mm/¼in along the lower edge of the top fabric; tack this hem in place. (The top fabric I used had a decorative

n

selvedge which was incorporated into the design.) Now slip one edge of the binding strip for the padded edge (Fabric C) under this folded edge or selvedge. Pin and tack the two pieces together, then work running stitch through the edges (fig. p).

10 Complete the lower binding by rolling up one of the 9cm/3½in wide strips of wadding, and placing it on

the wrong side of the wide binding piece. Bring the fabric up round it and pin it to the lining, enclosing the wadding strip. Turn in 5mm/¼in along the raw edge of the strip, and tack and slipstitch it to the lining.

Just above this rolled piece, work a line of small running stitches through all thicknesses to hold the rolled wadding in place (fig. q).

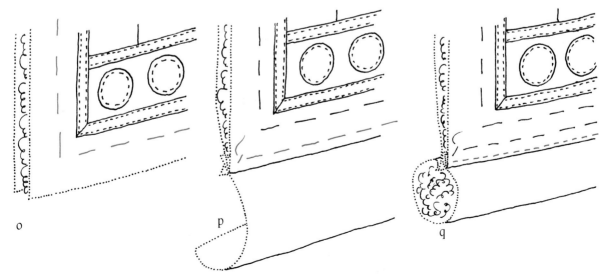

o

p

q

11 The three padded sections are now ready to be joined. Pin and tack two of the sections together with wrong sides facing, taking care to match their lower edges (fig. r). Machine stitch them together, taking a scant 1cm/⅜in seam allowance. Grade the seam (see page 19), trimming the lining and wadding close to the stitching. Repeat this process to join all three sections.

The edge binding is made by joining bias strips (Fabric D) to make a total length of 135cm/54in. Cut this into three equal lengths of 45cm/18in. Turn under and press 5mm/¼in on one edge of each strip. Pin (fig. s) and tack this edge over the stitching line on one side, and slipstitch it in place (fig. t). Then fold the binding to the other side, turn under its raw edge, and sew it in place. Trim the ends if necessary, tuck them in, and slipstitch the folded edges together.

If there are any obvious wrinkles, give the cosy a very careful press, using the tip of the iron. Do not press the iron onto the fabric.

12 Make four pompoms, about 5cm/2in in diameter, as described on page 118, using the cotton yarn. Sew a pompom to the top and to each of the corners.

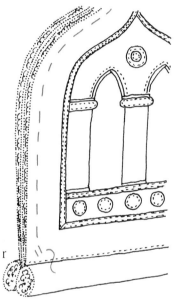

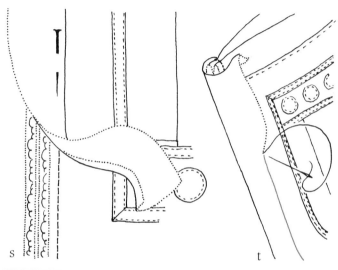

r

s

t

Above A lighter, brighter scheme, with blue, white and plum pink, for those who take their coffee in the morning.

Beautiful Balloons

As a child I was enthralled by hot air balloons. This was partly a result of having been taken to see the film *Around the World in Eighty Days*, with its exhilarating balloon flight over France, and partly because of a pair of curtains of which I was particularly fond. They had a printed design of beautiful, elaborate hot air balloons, trailing ribbons and flags.

These appliquéd curtains are quite different, but would, I hope, give as much pleasure to a child. They are made in a pale sky blue chintz, with red, white, yellow, green and blue plain cottons for the balloons and scraps of printed fabric in the same colours for the baskets. I have used quite a lot of white in the appliqué, which – along with the pale blue and the brighter colours – gives the curtains a lovely airy, summery feeling, slightly reminiscent of a seaside resort, with its Punch and Judy tents, flags and deckchairs.

The instructions given are for a pair of curtains, each measuring 169cm/66½in long by 122cm/48in wide. For larger curtains you could either spread the balloons out or add a few more; for a smaller pair you could have fewer balloons. However, the design is so large and bold that I do not think it would suit curtains much smaller than these.

Materials

Assorted cotton fabrics (90cm/36in wide unless otherwise stated).
I have made the curtains in the colours indicated below. You could, of course, make them up in more, or fewer, colours.
A Pale blue lightly glazed chintz, 125cm/49in wide for curtains: 3.6m/4yd; standard 122cm/48in wide fabric is also suitable – the curtains will be very slightly narrower
B Curtain lining: 122cm/48in wide, 3.6m/4yd
C Yellow – for border, balloons:

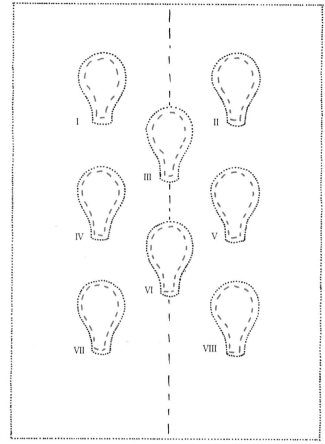

a

1.2m/1⅜yd
D White – for balloons: 90cm/1yd
E Red – for decorations: 20cm/¼yd
F Blue – for decorations: 20cm/¼yd
G Bright green – for decorations: 20cm/¼yd
H Pale green – for decorations: 10cm/⅛yd
X One or more printed fabrics – for baskets: total of 20cm/¼yd
White satin ribbon: 3mm/⅛in wide, 12.8m/14yd
White sewing or quilting thread
Curtain heading tape: 2.5m/2¾yd

1 Cut out the fabric pieces as instructed on page 159. (See also the general instructions on pages 12–16.)

2 Start by positioning the eight main balloon shapes on the background fabric. If you fold the curtain in half lengthways and press it lightly first, you can use the crease as a guide in positioning them. Place the two top balloons 18cm/7in to either side of the centre crease and 19cm/7½in down from the raw upper edge. Make sure they are vertical, then pin and tack them in place, a scant 1cm/⅜in from the edges. Position the bottom two balloons 36cm/14in from the lower edge and 18cm/7in from the crease; pin and tack them in place. Space the remaining balloons evenly between these first four (fig. a).

Slipstitch round the edge of each balloon (see page 15), turning under 3mm/⅛in as you go. Press and work running stitch (see page 16), 3mm/⅛in from the edge of each balloon. Remove the tacking.

3 Apply the decorations and baskets. You can do all the work on one balloon before moving on to the next, as described here, or you can pin and tack all these small pieces in place, then do the slipstitching and topstitching. (In a few cases, noted below, certain pieces must be completed before others are positioned.) The illustrations show the positions of the various pieces (fig. g). The designs on the balloon vary, so some of the ribbons are longer than others. Cut the four ribbons to fit each balloon as you come to it.

Balloon I Pin and tack the three vertical stripes to the balloon and then the top and bottom scalloped pieces. Place the basket 5.5cm/2¼in below the balloon, making sure that it is straight, then pin and tack (fig. b).

Cut four lengths of ribbon, long enough to extend from the lower scalloped piece to the basket, plus 1cm/³⁄₈in. Pin and tack each ribbon in place, making sure that it is straight, then work running stitches down the centre (fig. c).

Turn under and slipstitch the edge of the basket, catching in the ends of the ribbon and making neat corners.

Then turn under and slipstitch the edges of the vertical stripes, leaving their ends raw as they will be covered by the scalloped pieces. Do the same with the two scalloped pieces, aligning their outer edges with the edges of the balloon (fig. d).

Press the work. Finally, topstitch round all the edges.

Balloon II For this balloon and the remaining ones, you must complete all the stitching on the small horizontal or curved strips before stitching the ribbons in place (fig. e). When stitching on the dots, try to keep them smooth and circular.

Stitch the ribbons in place before slipstitching the basket (fig. f).

When you have completed all the stitching on the balloons, remove the tacking (fig. h). Press the work.

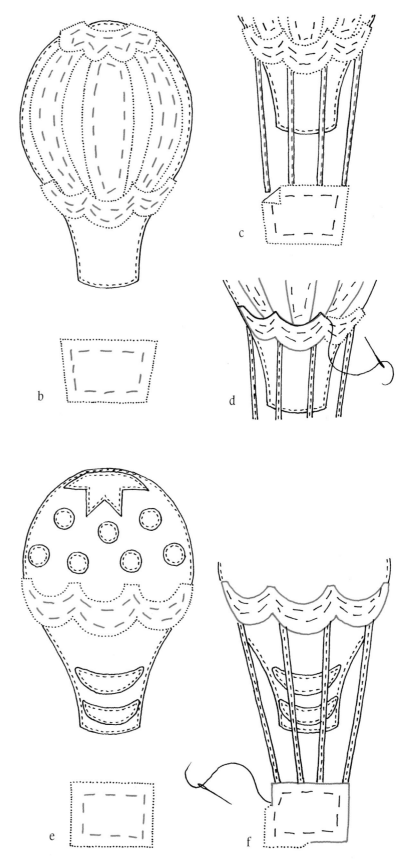

b

c

d

e

f

Making eight different balloons will give you plenty of opportunities for using up colourful scraps and inventing your own decorative motifs. These details show the colours and patterns used on my curtains.

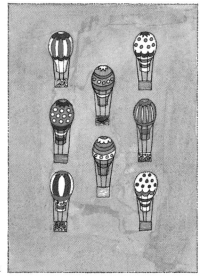

4 Now the border and flags can be added. First join the straight strips of Fabric C to make (for each curtain) two strips, each 150cm/59in long.

Press the seams open. Turn under 3mm/$\frac{1}{8}$in on both long edges and press.

Pin and tack these long strips to the curtain, with their outer edges approximately 14cm/5$\frac{1}{2}$in from the raw edges. The top of each strip should be level with the upper edge of the curtain, and the bottom of the strip level with the top of the nearest basket. Make sure that they are parallel with the edge of the curtain, then pin and tack.

Now place the two curved border pieces across the lower part of the curtain. Make sure that they are centred and that both ends are the same distance from the lower edge; pin and tack. There should be a space of about 2–2.5cm/$\frac{3}{4}$–1in between the strips at the three points where the rings will be placed. Pin and tack the flying ribbon pieces at the corners (fig. i).

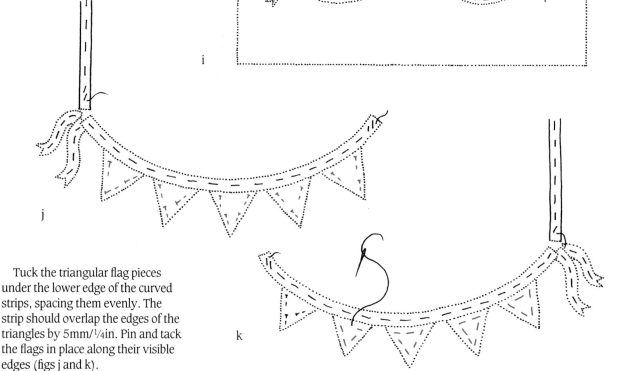

Tuck the triangular flag pieces under the lower edge of the curved strips, spacing them evenly. The strip should overlap the edges of the triangles by 5mm/$\frac{1}{4}$in. Pin and tack the flags in place along their visible edges (figs j and k).

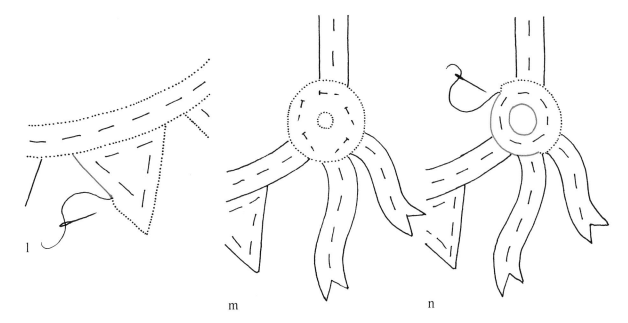

l

m   n

5 To complete the appliqué, first turn under and slipstitch the visible edges of the flags (fig. l); the other edges will be covered. Slipstitch the edges of the curved strips, turning under 3mm/⅛in as you go, then stitch the corner ribbons in the same way, taking special care to make the points sharp.

Lastly pin (fig. m) and tack the three rings in place, over the ends of the border pieces, trimming the ends as necessary so that they do not show through the holes in the centres of the rings. Slipstitch the rings in place, taking care to keep the shape circular on the inner and outer edges of each ring (fig. n).

Press the border carefully. Then work running stitch along all the edges of the border strips and flags.

Remove the tacking and give your work a final press.

6 To make up the curtains, follow the instructions on page 19. You can use a special heading tape to produce pencil pleats (as shown on these curtains) or French pleats. Or, if you prefer, you can make pleats by hand, positioning them as you like. Instructions for hand-made pleats can be found in a good general book on making soft furnishings.

Bowl of Fruit

This fruit bowl design, framed with swags and tassels, was inspired by an Early American stencilled fire screen. Stencil patterns are a rich source of ideas for appliqué, as their bold, simple shapes often translate well into cloth.

The leaves that sit among the fruit are made separately and stand out slightly from the cushion, like little ears.

The cushion (which measures approximately 41cm/16in square) is made in blues and greens, with yellow apples, but could also look lovely in soft pinks and a warm beige, in which case the fruit could be peaches or apricots. In a brighter colour scheme it might suggest a bowl of oranges.

a

Materials

Assorted medium-weight cotton fabrics, 90cm/36in wide. I have used the colours indicated below.
A Light blue – for base fabric: 60cm/⅝yd
B Gold – for apples and backing: 30cm/⅜yd
C Ice blue – for swags and tassels: 50cm/½yd
D Dark turquoise – for the bowl: 20cm/⅛yd
E Mid blue-green – for leaves: 30cm/¼yd
F Dark blue – for circles, lozenges, etc.: 20cm/¼yd
Cushion pad 40cm/16in square

Narrow piping cord, 1.8m/2yd
Dark blue sewing or quilting thread
Four buttons, 12mm/½in in diameter

1 Cut out the fabric pieces as instructed on page 174. (See also the general instructions on pages 12–16).

2 Mark the background fabric with lines of tacking in white thread (see page 15), dividing it into 5cm/2in squares (fig. a). These lines will serve as a guide for positioning the appliqué shapes.

3 To make the leaves, place two leaf shapes together with right sides facing. Stitch round them 3mm/⅛in from the edge, leaving the bottom edge open (fig. b). You can use backstitch or small running stitches to do this, or you can do it by machine.

Cut off the pointed end close to the stitching to reduce bulk (fig. c).

Turn the leaf inside out. Press it carefully, making sure you keep the shape (fig. d).

Make seven more leaves in the same way. Topstitch them (see page 16) in your chosen colour, working 3mm/⅛in from the edge (fig. e).

f

4 Now make the tassels. Fold each piece in three lengthways, with the right side outside (fig. f). Press the strip flat, so that the exposed edge lies just inside the folded edge beneath it. (This is easier if you finger-press first.)

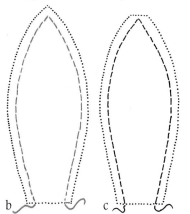

b   c

d   e

5 Position the bowl, swags, tails and tassels on the base fabric, using the tacking lines as guides. Pin and tack each piece in place (fig. g), keeping the stitches a scant 1cm/³⁄₈in from the fabric edge, so that there will be space to turn the edges under later. Make sure that the side pieces and tassels are vertical – leaning tassels look very odd. Note that the swag on the left overlaps the one on the right and that the bottom edge of each tail overlaps the top edge of the tassel below it.

Check that all the pieces you have tacked on are in the right place and that they are aligned vertically.

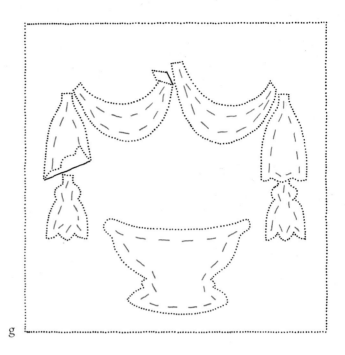

g

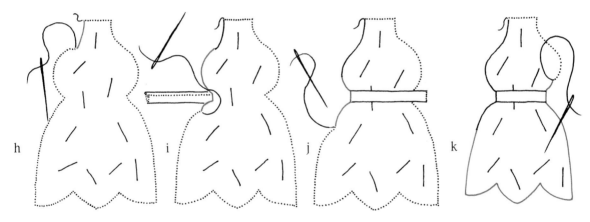

h   i   j   k

6 Stitch the tassels first. Lift up the lower edge of one tail and start at the top left-hand corner of the tassel. Slipstitch the piece to the background using tiny stitches (see page 15) and turning in 3mm/¹⁄₈in as you go (fig. h).

Stop just short of the waist of the tassel, and tuck in one end of a folded and pressed strip. Slide it in about 5mm/¹⁄₄in under the tassel, wrong side up (fig. i). Fold the strip over so that it lies flat, straight across the tassel. Carry on stitching, catching in the strip (fig. j).

Work round the three points of the tassel and up the other side, referring to the Techniques section on page 15 if you need help with the sharp points. Tuck in the other end of the strip, sewing it in as you go (fig. k). Fasten off at the top right-hand corner of the tassel. Do not stitch the top edge.

Attach the other tassel in the same way.

Continue the stitching with the two tail pieces and finally the two swags – first the right one, then the left. Stitch round the fruit bowl, leaving the whole of the top edge open; this will be stitched after the fruits are sewn on.

The main elements of the design are now in place (fig. l). Do not remove the tacking stitches, but press the work carefully through a cloth before moving to the next step.

l

7 Position the bow and the two circles on and above the swags, and place the five dots and five lozenges on the bowl. Pin and tack all of these pieces to the background (fig. m).

8 Stitch these pieces to the background in any order. They are all quick and easy to do, except for the bow, which needs extra care. It should not be too difficult, however, if you have snipped the fabric edges carefully at all the inward curves after cutting out. Press the work through a cloth when you have finished, using just the tip of the iron to go around the shape of the bow. Leave the tacking stitches in the fabric (fig. n).

m

n

9 Position the backing piece for the apples. Pin and tack it to the background fabric with the top edge of the bowl overlapping the bottom edge of the backing piece by 5mm/ ¼in (fig. o). (The raw edges will be concealed.)

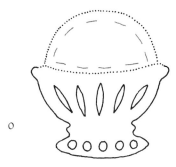

o

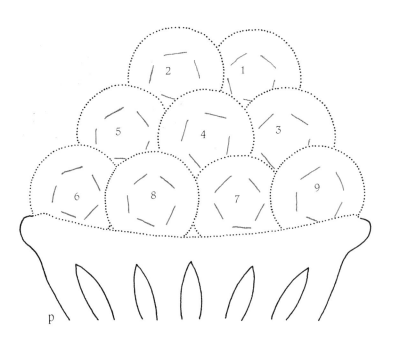

p

10 Now position the apples. Place them on the backing, arranging them as shown (fig. p), starting at the top and working down; then pin and tack them in place. Bear in mind as you tack them that when you stitch each one down you will need to lift the edge of the one that overlaps it, so keep the tacking stitches well in from the edge of each apple.

Remove the tacking stitches from the backing piece.

11 Remove the grid lines of tacking from the background fabric. Be cautious as you pull them out – you may have sewn through the lines with some of your slipstitches. If you have, snip the tacking thread carefully to release it.

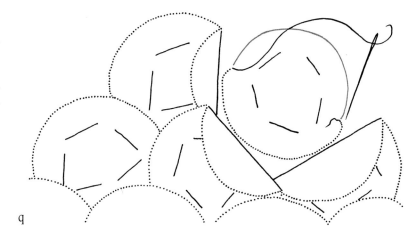

q

r

s

12 Start stitching the apples, beginning with the one at the upper right of the mound. Work round the shape, folding back the edges of adjacent apples (fig. q). Try to keep the shape smooth and round – it is all too easy to get little corners appearing, so that you end up with a polygon instead of a circle. (See page 16 for general instructions on stitching curved edges if you find this difficult.) There is no need to stitch all the way round each apple, as they overlap.

Work round the top right-hand apple to a point where you can leave the rest of it unstitched.

t

13 Apply the top left-hand apple. Tuck a leaf under the edge, holding it in place with a pin if you like, and slipstitch round the edge of the apple, turning in 3mm/^{1}/$_8$in and sewing in the leaf as you go (fig. r).

Continue in this way, sewing the apples on in the order shown (fig. p) and tucking in the leaves as described above (fig. s). Finish at the bottom right-hand corner. Press the apples, one by one, with the tip of the iron, over a pressing cloth.

Stitch the upper edge of the bowl over the apples (fig. t). Give that part a final press, before proceeding to the topstitching.

14 Work the topstitching with the tacking stitches still in.

Work running stitches 3mm/⅛in from the edge of each appliqué shape (figs u and v), making the stitches about 3mm/⅛in long. Then stitch along the other lines shown in the drawing (fig. w). If you like, you can draw guidelines, using a water-erasable pen, for the stitching that does not run parallel to the edge of a piece (the lines representing the folds on swags and tails, for example). In fiddly places, such as the bow, you can make the stitches slightly smaller, in order to follow the curves more easily; but in general try to get them as even in size and spacing as possible.

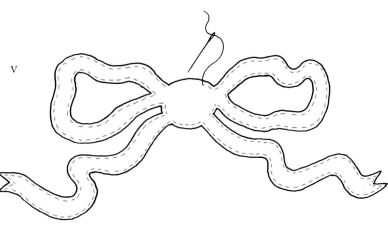

15 Remove all tacking stitches. The appliqué is now finished. Make up the cushion following the instructions on page 17.

Below: *The same design worked in a different colour scheme.*

Trompe l'Oeil

The appliqué on this table cover conveys a homely period feel – this might almost be an occasional table in a Victorian drawing room. I have made the cover in black and white, as there is so much colour elsewhere in the book and I am very fond of black and white and the positive/negative effect you can get.

While a kitten snoozes on a chair another cat slips under the table. There are various bits of needlework in progress: a knitting bag with protruding needles and balls of lacy wool and beside it a footstool bearing a pincushion in the shape of a boot. I used a black and creamy white Viyella for the bag, and tied it with striped silk ribbon.

On the white overcloth lie a pair of old-fashioned spectacles – made of grey silk and thin black ribbon – and an elegant pair of dark grey silk gloves. Near them I have placed a necklace made of different black beads – in jet, glass lustre and plastic. Some patchwork in progress hangs from the edge of the table; its needle and thread, worked in embroidery, loop past a pair of appliquéd scissors. The black and white sewing plait was an afterthought. I found it among my sewing things and thought that it would go well with the other objects on the cover.

The main part of the cover is black and white McKenzie tartan. Behind the cat is a single splash of red. The cover fits a round occasional table 61cm/24in in diameter and the same height. (Chipboard 'tables', intended simply as supports for a decorative cloth such as this, are available in kit form.)

Materials

Assorted fabrics (90cm/36in wide unless otherwise stated) in the following quantities:

A Black and white wool plaid, 140 or 152cm/54 or 60in wide: 3.7m/4yd
B White damask or similar – for overcloth: 70cm/³/₄yd
C Red Viyella or lightweight wool: 30cm/¹/₄yd
D Lining for fabric C – e.g. calico: 30cm/¹/₄yd
E Black cotton velvet – for cat: 30cm/¹/₄yd
F Small black and white checked wool – for knitting bag: 40cm/³/₈yd
G Black glazed cotton – for stool base and chair: 30cm/¹/₄yd
H Grey silk or cotton – for boot/pincushion: 10cm/¹/₈yd, or piece approx. 15cm/6in square
I Quilted black and white print – for footstool pad: 10cm/¹/₈yd; if quilted

fabric is not available, use same amounts of a cotton print and thin polyester wadding
J Soft black velvet – for pincushion pad: small scrap
K Small print – for largest jar: 30cm/³/₈yd
L Loosely woven wool check – for mat: 20cm/¹/₄yd, or piece approx. 20cm/8in square
M Charcoal grey silk, or similar – for gloves: 20cm/¹/₄yd, or piece approx. 25cm/10in square
N Pearl grey silk – for spectacles: small scrap
X A total of 13 (or fewer) printed cotton fabrics: 20cm/¹/₄yd of each
Crocheted or lace edging, approx. 6cm/2¹/₂in wide: 2.7m/3yd

Black and white striped ribbon, 4cm/
1½in wide: 1m/1¼yd
Small amounts of lace, veiling and/
or wool for 'knitting'
Black ribbon, 3mm/⅛in wide:
1.3m/1½yd
Narrow black and white braid:
30cm/⅜yd
Black bias binding, 2.5cm/1in wide:
6m/6½yd
Black bead necklace, about 40–
45cm/15–17½in long (or assorted
beads and string for making one)
Black and white sewing plait
(optional)
Black and white sewing or quilting
thread
Piece of tracing paper
Dressmaker's carbon
Fabric pencil

1 Cut out the fabric pieces as
instructed on page 175. (See also the
general instructions on pages 12–16).

2 To make the background of the
tablecloth, first join the three
sections of Fabric A by machine,
placing a narrow piece on either side
of the wide piece to form a square
measuring approximately 185cm/
72in. Take care to match the pattern,
if any, at the seams: it does not
matter if this entails making the ends
uneven, as most of these will be
trimmed away. Press the seams
open.

Fold the fabric in half in both
directions, and press the crossing of
the folds lightly to mark this point.
Then, using bright-coloured thread,
work an X at the crossing point to
mark the centre.

Measure 92cm/36in out from the
centre, and mark this distance with a
pin. Repeat at 5cm/2in intervals all
round the cloth until you have a
circle of pins (fig. a). Tack along this
pin line with small stitches.

Unfold one edge of the bias
binding, and tack it to the fabric,
right sides facing, placing the edge
just inside the line of tacking and
machine stitching along the crease
(fig. b). Overlap the ends neatly and
trim the excess fabric along the
tacking line (fig.c). Turn the bias
binding to the wrong side. Steam
press the edge, turning a little of the
fabric under at the same time and
easing the binding into shape.

Tack the free edge of the binding
to the fabric, then hem it in place by
hand. Press and remove the tacking.

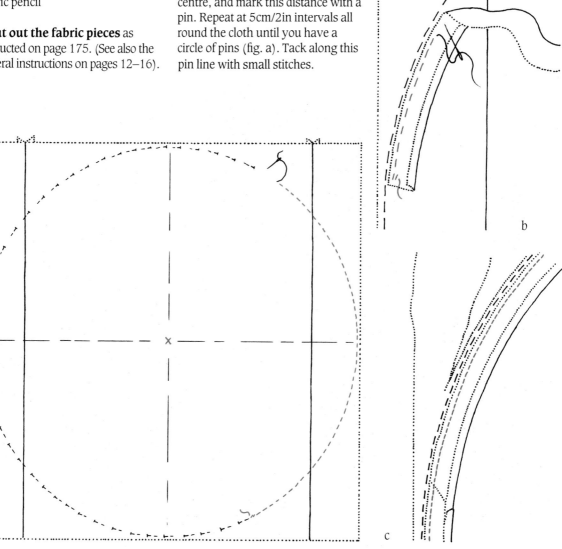

a   b

c

3 To apply the black cat, first join the background shape and its lining. Place these two sections together with right sides facing, and machine stitch them together along the lower edge. Turn the section right side out, and press the lower edge. Tack the layers together all round.

Place the background under the tablecloth, aligning the lower edges. If you are using a plaid fabric, choose a point where the stripes meet the edge at a right angle. This will make possible the best positioning of the overcloth later. Pin the background piece in place, then tack all the layers together along the edge of the background piece (fig. e).

Lift up the edge of the tablecloth to place the cat (fig. d). Trim away some of the plaid fabric to reduce bulk and prevent buckling. Hold it in place with a few pins.

Position the cat as shown (fig. f), with the front edge under the main fabric and the tail overlapping it, and tack round the shape a scant 1cm/³⁄₈in from the edge. Also tack the lifted edge of the tablecloth. Slipstitch the cat to the background, turning under 3mm/¹⁄₈in as you go (see page 15).

Slipstitch the lifted edge of the tablecloth. Then, using black thread, work small, widely spaced running stitches through the tablecloth and the upper edge of the background piece to hold them together invisibly (fig. g). Press, if necessary, very lightly, taking care not to crush the folds of the main fabric. Remove the tacking, and trim the edge of the background piece with pinking shears (or oversew it) to prevent fraying (fig. h).

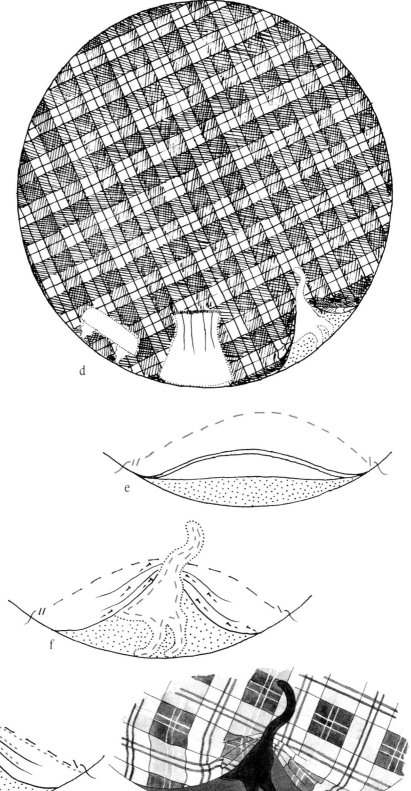

d

e

f

g

h

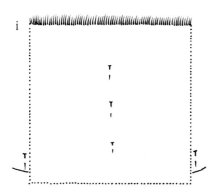

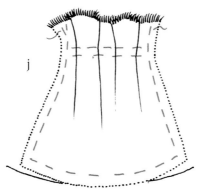

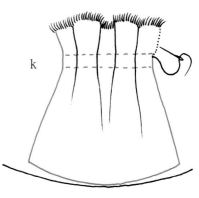

4 Now apply the knitting bag.
First measure clockwise round the circle a distance of 27cm/10½in from the left-hand corner of the background piece. Mark this point with a pin, then mark off a further 37cm/14½in. This is where the bag will go (fig. d).

If the fabric you have chosen for

the bag will fray easily, fray one of the longer sides to a depth of about 5mm/¼in; otherwise, turn under the edge and hem it.

Place the bag fabric on the cloth between the two pins and pin it down the middle (fig. i). Make a few pleats at the neck of the bag about 8–9cm/3–3½in down from the top;

pin these in place through the main fabric (this will draw the lower corners upward slightly). Tack the bag in place along the side and bottom edges and across the pleats (fig j). Slipstitch the outer edges to the cloth, and work two lines of running stitch (see page 16) across the pleats (fig. k).

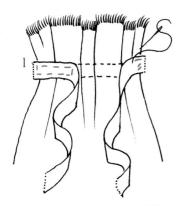

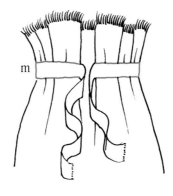

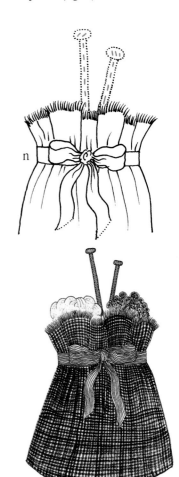

5 Cut the wide ribbon in half, and tack each piece to the neck of the bag, with the edges extending slightly (fig. l). Turn under the ends and slipstitch them in place. Sew the edges of the ribbons to the bag, using either slipstitch or running stitch, up to a point in the middle where you can still easily tie the ends into a bow, then cut the ribbon ends diagonally (fig. m).

Position the two knitting needles inside the bag. Tack them in place, with the little knobs on the ends (fig. n). Turn under and slipstitch the edges to the tablecloth. Work running stitch all round them 3mm/ ⅛in from the edge, in white thread if

they are black (fig. o). Press.

Now put the knitting in the bag. I gathered up the creamy lace net and sewed it to the inside of the bag with tiny stitches. The black veiling I loosely rolled into a ball and stitched to the main fabric (fig. p).

6 The footstool and pincushion

can now be applied. First measure off about 20cm/8in along the edge (clockwise) from the position of the knitting bag. Mark this point with a pin to indicate the position for the right leg of the footstool. Pin the two legs to the edge of the cloth, leaving about 19cm/7½in between them. Pin the pad of the footstool above them, centring it and leaving about 5mm/¼in between them (fig. d). I have used a piece of quilted cotton to give a padded effect. If you are using ordinary – unquilted – fabric, position it over the layer of wadding, with an equal amount extending on all edges, and tack through all layers (fig. q).

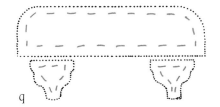

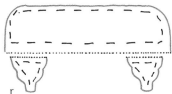

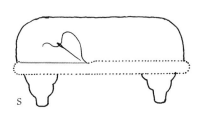

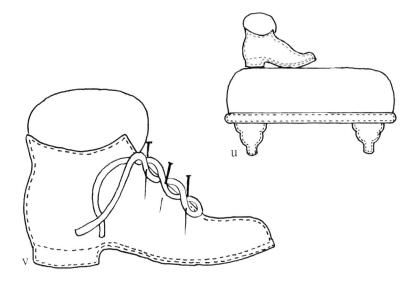

Turn under and slipstitch the edges of the legs and the footstool pad. Tuck the unpadded fabric, if you are using one, under the edges of the wadding, leaving the bottom edge of the pad and the top edges of the legs raw (fig. r).

Position the base strip over the legs and pad; pin, tack and slipstitch it in place (fig. s). Press. Work running stitch round the legs and base.

Place the boot and the pincushion pad on the footstool, with the lower edge of the boot overlapping the footstool by at least 5mm/¼in, so that when stitched it will rest firmly on the stool and not float above it. Pin and tack these pieces in place (fig. t). Turn under and slipstitch the edges of the pad, leaving the bottom edge raw. Turn under and slipstitch the edges of the boot, covering the raw edge of the pad. Press (avoiding the pad if you have used velvet for it). Work running stitch round the boot, and make an extra line along the sole (fig. u).

Pin the braid in zigzag fashion up the front of the boot (fig. v). Secure it with small running stitches, and tie the ends into a bow (fig. w).

7 Now arrange the collection of Chinese jars so that they point towards the centre of the cloth (fig. x). First measure along the edge of the tablecloth another 57cm/22in, and mark this point with a pin. This marks the position for the lower right-hand corner of the medium-sized jar. Pin and tack it in place, then pin and tack the remaining jars and vase, leaving about 4–5cm/ 1½–2in between them at their closest points. Position the lid of the largest jar 5mm/¼in under the top edge of the jar. Turn under and slipstitch the edges of all these pieces.

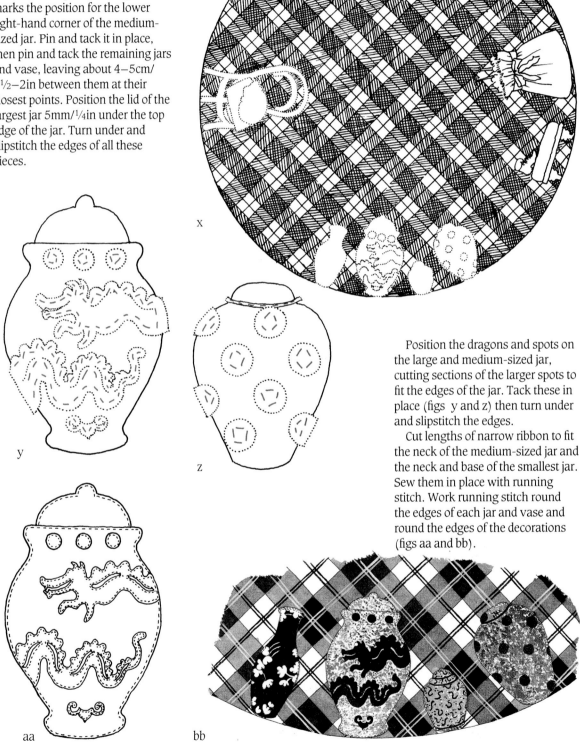

x

y

z

Position the dragons and spots on the large and medium-sized jar, cutting sections of the larger spots to fit the edges of the jar. Tack these in place (figs y and z) then turn under and slipstitch the edges.

Cut lengths of narrow ribbon to fit the neck of the medium-sized jar and the neck and base of the smallest jar. Sew them in place with running stitch. Work running stitch round the edges of each jar and vase and round the edges of the decorations (figs aa and bb).

aa

bb

8 The small bentwood chair can be applied next (fig. x). To find its position, measure another 90cm/35in along the edge of the tablecloth, and mark the spot with a pin. This is where the right leg of the chair will go. Assemble the pieces for the chair on the tablecloth, positioning the struts about 3.5cm/1½in down from the seat, and tuck them under the legs. Position the inner curve of the back so that when both pieces are turned and slipstitched, they will just meet. Tack (fig. cc) and slipstitch these pieces. Work running stitch round the edges, breaking the stitching where the legs and struts cross and where the seat meets the back. Press.

Fray the edges of the mat to a depth of about 1cm/⅜in. Place the sleeping kitten on the mat and tack it in place (fig. dd). Position the mat and kitten on the chair, and tack round all the outer edges. Turn under and slipstitch the edges of the kitten, then work running stitch round its edges. Work more running stitch inside the frayed mat edges.

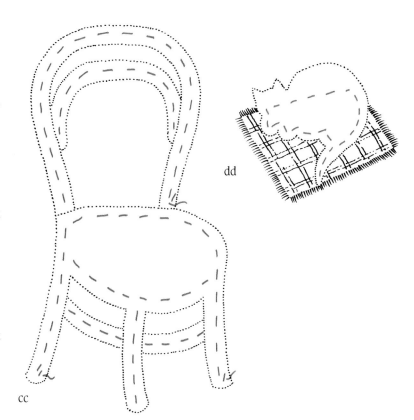

dd

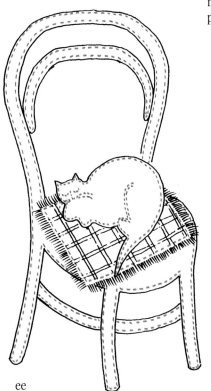

cc

Trace the kitten's features from the pattern, and transfer them to the fabric with dressmaker's carbon (see page 14). Work the outline of the back leg with a double line of running stitch, the whiskers with a single line. Work the closed eyes and nose in backstitch (figs ee and ff).

ee

ff

9 To make up the white damask overcloth, turn under and press 1cm/½in on all four edges of the cloth. Pin, then tack the edging – I have used lace – just under the edge of the cloth, right sides upwards. Join the ends of the edging diagonally at one corner; sew them together by hand, and trim away the excess. Stitch the edging to the cloth, either by hand, using two lines of running stitch, or by machine, using a fine zigzag (fig. gg).

Find the centre of the cloth, as in Step 2, and mark it with an X. Make a circle of tacking (see method in Step 2), 30cm/12in out from the centre point. This line marks the edge of the round table and will serve as a guide when positioning the objects on the white cloth. Arrange the gloves, scissors and spectacles within the circle (fig. hh). I have positioned them as described below; you may wish to alter those positions.

gg

10 Position the scissors about 23cm/9in to the left of one corner, with the underneath half 6cm/2½in from the fabric edge.

Tack this lower half to the cloth, so that it points inward at about a 45° angle. Slipstitch it in place. Position the other half over it, so that the points are slightly open. Tack and slipstitch (fig. ii). Work running stitch round the edges, adding a little circle of running stitch to indicate the screws joining them together.

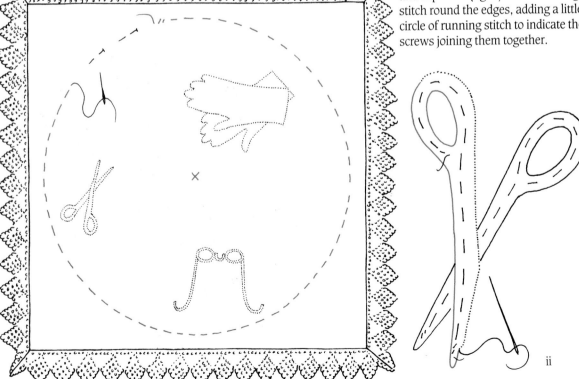

hh

ii

A little to the left of the scissors and about 8cm/3in in from the fabric edge, embroider a needle. You can work it in two or three lines of backstitch, tapering to a sharp point. To suggest thread, work running stitch in a looping line to a point about 23cm/9in in from the corner (fig. jj). This is where the patchwork will be attached.

11 To apply the gloves, place them as shown in the illustration (fig. nn), with the lower one about 8cm/3in in from the circle and pointing a little to the right of the X. Tack and slipstitch it in place, then add the upper glove. Note that both gloves have the thumbs to the left – i.e. palms together (fig. kk). Work topstitching round the edges and to delineate the fingers, then work three lines of running stitch on the upper glove (fig. ll).

12 The spectacles can now be applied. First transfer the traced outline onto the fabric using dressmaker's carbon. Position the lenses, then hold them in place with a few tacking stitches (fig. mm). The frames are made of three pieces of the narrow ribbon, one for each side and one for the bridge. Cut off enough ribbon to go round one lens and along the arm, with a little to spare. Tack it to the outline, starting at a lower 'corner' and working round the top of the lens, then along the arm (fig. nn). Attach the other pieces. Trim off the excess, then slipstitch along both edges of the ribbon, catching in the grey silk of the lenses as you go (fig. oo).

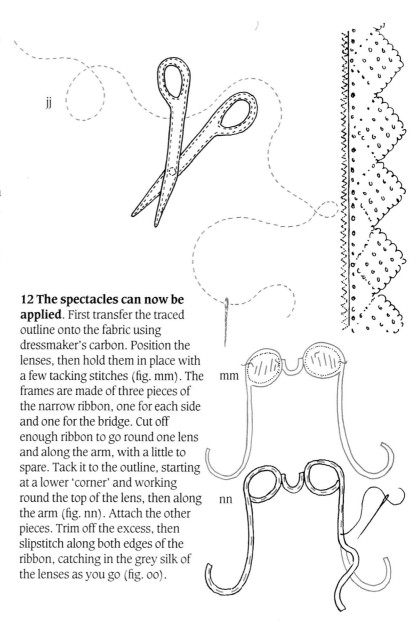

jj

mm

nn

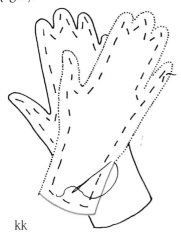

kk

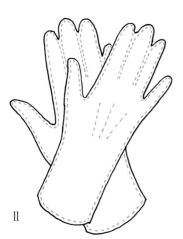

ll

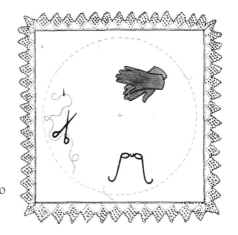

oo

13 Attach the overcloth to the main cloth. Match the two centre Xs, and align the corners of the overcloth with the straight lines of the plaid. The scissors-and-thread corner goes between the bentwood chair and the disappearing cat. Pin the cloth in place, then tack in a circle about 1cm/½in out from the original tacked circle. Using white thread, work two circles of small running stitches between these lines of tacking, joining the two cloths firmly together (fig. pp).

pp

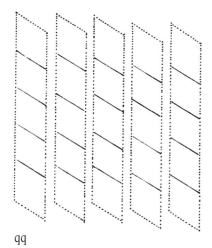

qq

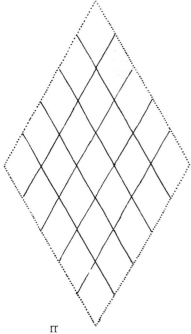

rr

14 Now make the patchwork. Machine stitch the diamonds together in strips of five (fig. qq), then join the resulting five strips together to form a piece containing five diamonds at its widest point (fig. rr). Press the seams open and cut around the edge of the patchwork with pinking shears. Gather the fabric up a little at one end, and sew it firmly to both layers of the cloth (fig. ss).

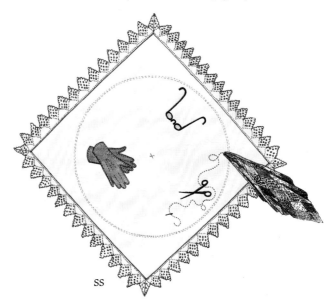

ss

15 The black bead necklace is sewn on near the gloves, again through both layers (fig. tt). Mark the shape on the cloth with a fabric pencil. Then, using double thread, work a stitch over every bead to keep it firmly sewn down (fig. uu).

tt

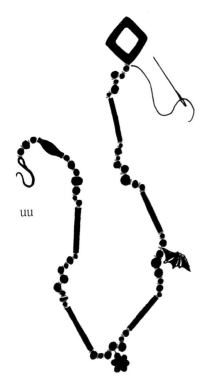

uu

16 Attach the sewing plait, if you are including one, to the remaining corner with small running stitches (fig. vv).

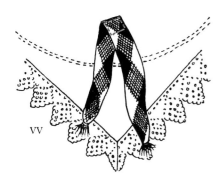

vv

Carrot Patch

This cosy and practical cot-sized quilt has a jolly design of rabbits and bunches of carrots on a patchwork background of green and white squares. I have bound the edges in a leaf-printed fabric with a background colour that matches the pale buff of the rabbits. The lining is soft cotton lawn with a small print in pastel tints of the appliqué colours.

The quilt layers can be simply tied together at several points, either invisibly or decoratively with a French knot worked in yarn or thick embroidery cotton (see page 16).

The finished quilt measures approximately 90cm/36in long by 69cm/27in wide.

Materials

Assorted lightweight cotton fabrics, 90cm/36in wide. You may, of course, use the colours of your choice. Those that I have used in the quilt illustrated here are indicated in the list that follows.

A Pale green – for patchwork: 60cm/^{3}/4yd

B White – for patchwork: 60cm/^{3}/4yd

C Bright green – for leaves: 20cm/^{1}/4yd

D Light brown – for rabbits: 20cm/^{1}/4yd

E Orange – for carrots: 10cm/^{1}/8yd

F Print – for binding: 30cm/^{3}/8yd

G Small print – for lining: 70cm/^{3}/4yd

Medium-weight (4oz) polyester wadding: 70cm/^{3}/4yd

Two balls fine white crochet cotton

Orange, pale green and cinnamon-coloured sewing or quilting thread

Black stranded embroidery cotton

Piece of thin cardboard approx. 10cm/4in square

1 Cut out the fabric pieces as

instructed on page 180. (See also the general instructions on pages 12–16.)

a

2 To make the patchwork, first join the squares and triangles as shown (fig. a) to make seven strips. Machine stitch the pieces together, right sides facing, with 1.2cm/^{1}/2in seams. Unless you are very skilled at machine stitching, it is a good idea to tack the seams first and mark the stitching line with fabric pencil. The success of the finished result depends greatly on straight, accurate stitching. Press the seams open.

To complete the patchwork, pin and machine stitch the strips together (tacking first if necessary), again taking 1.2cm/^{1}/2in seams. Make sure that the corners meet exactly. Press the seams open.

Topstitch (see page 16) along the seams of the patchwork, using orange thread and working 3mm/^{1}/8in in from the seam on both sides. Take care that the lines of running stitch do not meet each other at the corners (fig. b).

b

3 Place the four rabbits on their squares, as shown in fig. c. There are two facing each other across the middle and two with their backs to you at the top and bottom. Place them in such a way that when they are slipstitched in place they will not get in the way of the topstitching along the seams. Pin, then tack the rabbits to the fabric.

Slipstitch round the edges, turning them under as you go (see page 15) and taking special care in tight corners, such as between the ears (fig. d) and round the paws (fig. e). Work a few stitches very close together at these points to make absolutely sure that no raw edges escape.

Press the appliqué, then topstitch round the edges, using the cinnamon-coloured thread. Work the stitches slightly closer together and closer to the edge at inner corners for extra strength.

c

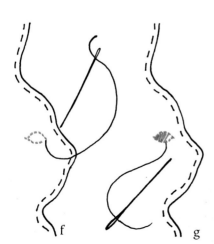

d

e

4 Embroider the eyes and whiskers. For the eyes, first define the shape with small backstitches (fig. f), using a single strand of black cotton. Then fill in the shape with satin stitch (see page 16), using two strands of the cotton (fig. g).

For the whiskers, simply work running stitches using the same thread as used for the topstitching (fig. h). These stitches, however, should be a little smaller and closer together.

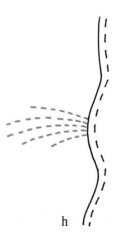

f

g

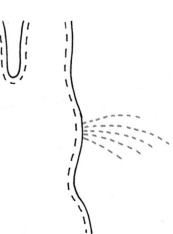

h

5 Apply the carrot tops and outer leaves, starting by placing a carrot top in the upper corner of each remaining white square (fig. c), so that, when slipstitched, its edges will clear the topstitching (fig i). Pin and tack the carrot tops in place.

Position the groups of three leaves in the white triangles at the top and bottom of the quilt, arranging them so that when the centre leaf is slipstitched in place its upper point will be 3cm/1¼in from the inner corner of the triangle. Pin and tack.

Slipstitch all the greenery in place, leaving the lower edges of the carrot tops raw as these will be covered by the carrots themselves.

Press all these pieces, then topstitch round their edges, in whatever colour you have chosen. I have used a pale green on my bright green leaves.

Work more lines of topstitching over the carrot tops to give a branch-like effect (fig. i). You could mark the lines first, using the pattern with dressmaker's carbon paper (see page 14), or simply mark them in freehand on the fabric with a fabric-marking pencil. Alternatively, stitch freehand, as I did. Start at the bottom and work a curve of running stitch up to the left, then come back the same way with a parallel curve, about 3mm/1⁄8in away from it. Continue in the same way, working four more double curved lines until you reach the top.

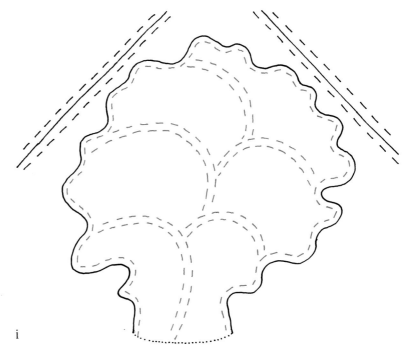

i

6 Arrange the carrots slightly differently in each square, keeping the smaller ones on the outside. I have used four carrots for each bunch, except for the one in the centre, which has three large carrots (fig. c). Make sure that when the edges are slipstitched they will fit comfortably inside the lines of topstitching round the square. Pin and tack them in place (fig. j).

Slipstitch the carrots in place, working from the bottom one upward. Stitch only the edges that will be visible, so that there are no bulky turned edges showing through the topmost pieces.

Press the bunches carefully, then topstitch round the edges using orange thread (fig. k).

Now that the appliqué is complete, remove the tacking stitches (fig. l).

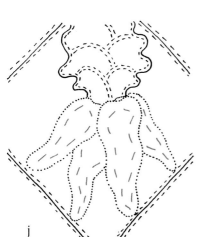

j

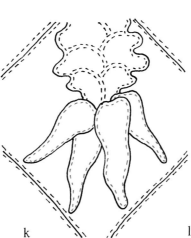

k

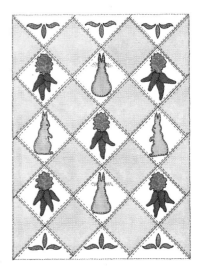

l

7 To make the pompoms for the rabbits' tails, first cut eight circles of thin cardboard, about 3cm/1¼in across. You can use any small round object, such as a large cotton reel, to draw the circles. In the centre of four of the circles, mark another circle with a diameter of about 1cm/⅜in. Cut out these smaller circles, then place the circles with cut-out centres over the solid ones to mark and cut the centre circles in the same positions.

Place each pair of circles together. Thread a long length of crochet cotton (or any thickish cotton or thin wool) into a small tapestry needle, and start wrapping it round the two circles (fig. m). Re-thread the needle as necessary, and continue wrapping until you cannot get any more thread through the hole.

Using sharp scissors, cut round the edges of the pompoms between the two layers of cardboard (fig. n). Pull the cardboard circles apart slightly, and tie a double length of thread, about 20cm/8in long, very firmly round the centre between them (fig. o). Knot it tightly. Remove the cardboard. Thread the ends into a needle, and sew each pompom securely to a rabbit as shown in the drawing (fig. p).

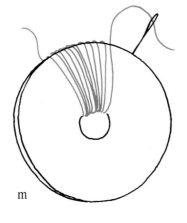

m

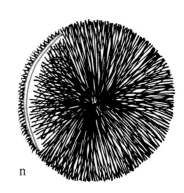

n

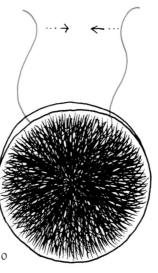

o

p

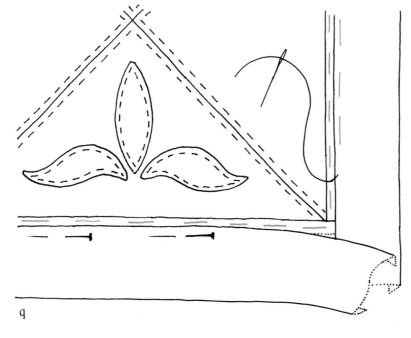

q

8 To attach the inner edging and binding strips, begin by folding each strip in half lengthways, wrong sides facing, and pressing this fold. On the wider (binding) strips, also turn under and press 5mm/¼in along the long raw edges.

Place the inner edging strips along the edge of the patchwork, folded edge towards the centre, so that they just touch the corners of the outer squares. Pin then tack them in place.

Place the binding strips over the inner strips, leaving 3mm/⅛in exposed. Pin and tack them in place, letting the strips at the top and bottom overlap the side strips.

Slipstitch the folded edge of the binding in place, working through the inner edging and the quilt top, so the three layers are firmly joined.

9 To assemble the quilt, first place the lining right side up over the wadding; pin them together, then tack about 4cm/1½in from the edges.

Lay the quilt top on the wadding, matching all the edges, then tack all the layers together, from top to bottom and across from side to side in three or four places. Also tack all the way round the edge through the binding strip (fig. r).

Using orange thread, work a line of topstitching 3mm/⅛in from the inner edges of the binding strip. Take your needle through in vertical stabbing stitches to make sure you have caught all the layers with each stitch.

10 To finish the edges, turn the quilt wrong side up, and fold the binding strips over the lining, covering the line of topstitching and overlapping the corners (fig. s). Pin and tack the strips in place, making sure that they are straight, then slipstitch them in place.

Press the strips on both sides.

11 Tie the quilt at intervals through all layers by making a few firm stitches or a French knot where four squares join (fig. t).

Warm orange predominates in this alternative scheme, making the quilt look even cosier!

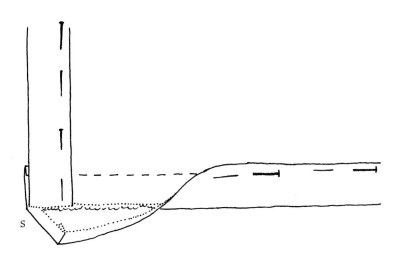

Fun with Numbers

Children will have fun learning numbers from this colourful frieze. The individual squares can be grouped as shown here, or in three rows of four squares, two rows of six or a single row of twelve. They could also be arranged to frame a door or window or sewn together to make a cover for a child's bed.

This is the kind of project for which you need to dip into your oddments bag to find just the right print or colour for a particular purpose. Many of the appliqué pieces are tiny and the use of many different colours and patterns within the basic red, white and blue overall design is what gives the frieze its charm.

You will need some flesh pink – or other flesh colour – some bright red for the ladybirds, and ideally something speckly for the birds' nest and eggs. Otherwise, an assortment of small pieces will serve.

The individual squares of the frieze measure approximately 24cm/9½in square. The squares will look and hang better if they are padded slightly. I have used a medium-weight wadding.

Materials

Cotton fabrics (90cm/36in wide unless otherwise stated). I have used the colours indicated below, but you could, of course, make the frieze in any colours of your choice.
A Calico – for background, 180cm/70in wide: 50cm/⅝yd
B Red print – for numbers: 40cm/½yd
C Blue print – for binding, loops and buttonholes: 80cm/⅞yd
D Lining: 80cm/⅞yd
Lightweight polyester wadding: 100cm/39in wide, 80cm/⅞yd
22 buttons
Square 1: piece of fabric 9 × 13cm/3½ × 5in for skirt, small scraps for legs, shirt, face and hands; felt scrap for hat and shoes; fine knitting yarn; three buttons
Square 2: scraps for houses
Square 3: scraps for kittens; fine knitting yarn and thread to match
Square 4: assorted decorations, e.g.: rickrack; narrow ribbon; embroidered braid; 'pearl' decoration
Square 5: piece of fabric 12 × 15cm/4½ × 6in for sleeve; scrap for hand; small button
Square 6: piece of red fabric about 10 × 15cm/4 × 6in for ladybirds; small

scraps of black woven fabric and black felt for their spots
Square 7: piece of brown speckled fabric approx. 11 × 14cm/4½ × 5½in for nest; piece of brown fabric approx. 25 × 12cm/10 × 5in for branches; scraps for eggs, leaves
Square 8: seam binding in several colours for pencils and matching sewing or embroidery threads
Square 9: nine plain scraps for birds
Square 10: striped fabric approx. 20cm/8in square for pyjamas; scrap for feet
Square 11: printed fabric approx. 15cm/6in square for fish
Square 12: scrap for clock face; 25cm/10in of narrow bias binding
For all squares: cream-coloured sewing or quilting thread for running stitch; sewing thread or stranded embroidery cotton in black, red, blue, and colours to match and contrast with flesh-coloured fabric

1 Cut out the fabric pieces as instructed on page 182. (See also the general instructions on pages 12–16.)

2 Apply the numbers to the squares. Because they have different shapes and some have two digits, the numbers vary slightly in their position in relation to the edges of the square, but the widest part of each digit should be between 3 and 4cm/1¼ and 1½in from the left-hand edge of the square. You may wish to check the position of some in relation to the other appliqué pieces before you tack them in place.

Make sure that all the numbers are straight, then pin and tack them in place – noting the following

special observations:

Square 3 Leave the top corner of the 3 unstitched, so that the yarn can go under it.

Square 10 These numbers are applied after the other pieces.

Square 11 Tack only down the centre of the numbers and leave the slipstitching until after the fish have been applied.

Slipstitch the numbers to the calico (see page 15), turning under 3mm/ ⅛in as you go (fig. a). Take care to keep the right angles true and the curves smooth.

Press each number carefully, then topstitch (see page 16) 3mm/⅛in from the edge.

Square 1 Pin the lady's head, shirt, hands and legs to the calico, overlapping the two shirt pieces at the centre. Tack them in place a scant 1cm/⅜in from the edge (fig. b).

Slipstitch the hands and head to the calico, turning under the edges as you go and leaving the top and bottom edges of the leggings, the neck and the wrists unstitched.

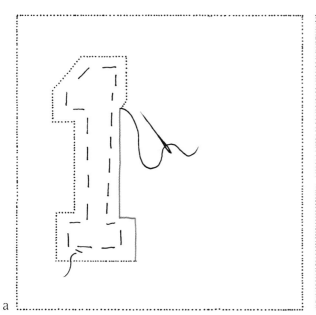

a

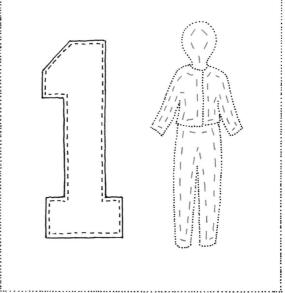

b

Pink one of the long edges of the skirt, or fray it slightly. Gather the other long edge by hand or machine (fig. c). Turn under and press 5mm/¼in on the side edges. Tuck the gathered edges under the shirt, so that when the shirt is turned and stitched the gathering stitches will not be visible. Tack the skirt in place.

Slipstitch both sides of the skirt to the calico. Then turn under and stitch the edges of the shirt.

Using the cream-coloured thread, work running stitches round all the edges except the skirt.

Remove the tacking and press.

Sew on the felt shoes, using small running stitch.

Now embroider the features, using backstitch for the lines and filling in the lips and irises with satin stitch (see page 16).

For the hair, cut short pieces of yarn, and divide them into two bunches. Sew these to either side of the face, using another strand of the yarn (fig. d). Place the hat over the top ends, and sew this on with small running stitches.

Sew the three buttons to the front of the shirt.

c

d

e

3 Work the appliqué on the remaining squares, using the same stitching techniques and stitching lower pieces before those that overlap them. Variations for individual squares are as follows:

Square 2 The windows and fanlight are embroidered in backstitch after the main pieces are slipstitched (fig. e). There is no running stitch round the windows. For doorknobs work French knots (see page 16).

Square 3 The kittens' eyelids are embroidered in backstitch; the whiskers in running stitch or backstitch, depending on the fabric and the amount of contrast required. I have used black thread for the running stitch; your choice will depend on the fabric you are using. When the shapes have been applied and embroidered, wind the yarn into a tight little ball, leaving a long end.

Sew the ball to the calico. Using matching thread, and working tiny stitches about 1 cm/½in apart, sew the remaining yarn to the surface of the fabric so that it is trailing round the square and disappearing off the edge (fig. f).

Square 4 Tuck the ends of the rickrack under the edges of the cake pieces to neaten them, and sew the

rickrack in place with a single line of running stitch using matching thread. The top and bottom edges of the main cake piece can be left raw – the lower one overlaps the cake stand – and covered with the embroidered braid. Sew this in place with spaced backstitch in matching thread. I have not topstitched the candles, but I have embroidered their flames in backstitch.

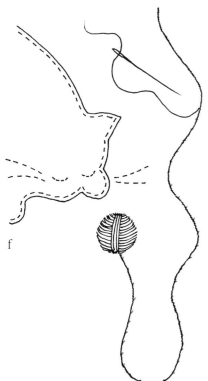

f

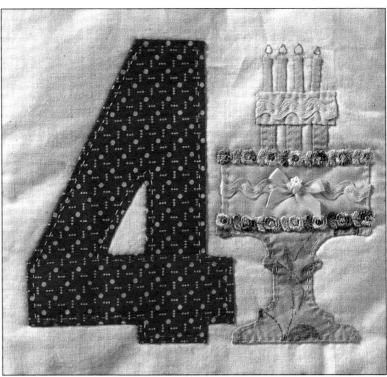

Square 5 Prepare the sleeve in the same way as the skirt in Square 1. The lower edge should be about 9.5cm/3¾in wide (trim it to fit the edge of the square). The fingernails are embroidered in backstitch, using a thread to contrast with the fabric (fig. g).

Square 6 The line dividing the ladybirds' wings is worked in backstitch. Their legs are also in backstitch. Their felt spots are secured with a single stitch in the centre (fig. h).

Square 7 I have placed the leaves slightly off the branches, and the eggs are arranged in a cluster in the middle. The lowest branch overlaps the nest (fig. i).

Square 8 To form the points of the crayons, simply turn under the top two corners. Slipstitch the edges of the binding. For the scribbles, work running stitch as you like (fig. j).

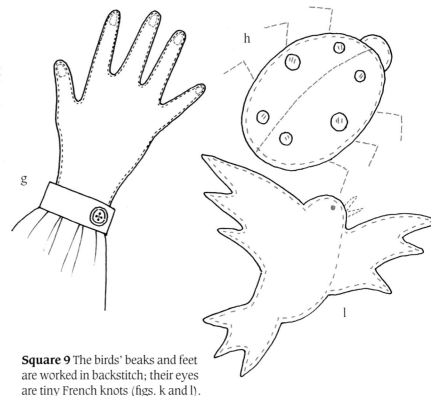

Square 9 The birds' beaks and feet are worked in backstitch; their eyes are tiny French knots (figs. k and l).

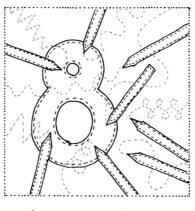

Square 10 You do not need to work the running stitch where the legs will be covered with the numbers. To mark the toes, work a few backstitches in matching thread. The toenails are also backstitched, using contrasting thread (fig. m).

Square 11 The fishes' eyes are tiny French knots.

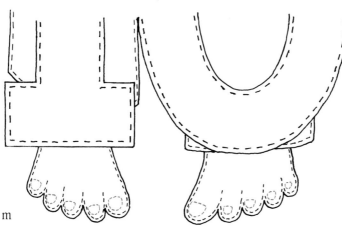

Square 12 The numerals, clock hands and stars are worked in backstitch. If you prefer, you could cut the stars and hands from felt. To edge the clock face, fold the binding to measure 5mm/¼in, trimming it if necessary, and press it in a curve, so that it will easily form a circle. Sew it in place with small, closely worked slipstitches, and finish neatly.

4 To make up the frieze, assemble the three layers of each square, with the lining on the bottom and the wadding in the middle. Pin them together, then tack them about 1.2cm/½in from the edges.

Fold each button loop strip double to make a strip 5mm/¼in wide, and then machine stitch it down the centre (fig. n). Similarly, fold the hanging loops lengthways, but use slipstitch to secure the folds in the centre of the strips (fig. o).

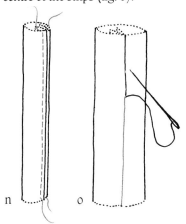

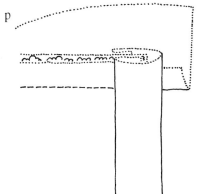

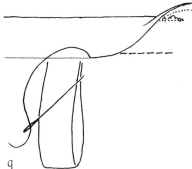

Pin two binding strips to the side edges of the appliquéd square, with right sides facing and raw edges matching. Tack, then machine stitch them, 5mm/¼in from the edge. Trim the ends so that they are even with the corners of the fabric. Press, then fold the binding to the underside of the square. Turn under the raw edge and slipstitch it to the lining fabric.

Attach the top and bottom binding strips in the same way (fig. p), but do not trim the ends. When slipstitching the top binding strip, insert one of the hanging loops in the centre (fig. q). Turn it up and

slipstitch it to the binding. Tuck in the ends of the strips, and slipstitch them together securely, inserting button loops in the top and bottom right-hand corners of squares 1–11.

Press all round the edges of the square, then work running stitch through all the layers, 3mm/⅛in from the bound edge. Remove the tacking.

Sew a button to the top and bottom left-hand corners of squares 2–12. If you wish, you can place the loops and buttons differently to make a hanging in two or more rows (fig. r).

Stained Glass Window

This large round cushion is designed to be made in reverse appliqué, a form of cutwork in which the largest piece of fabric lies on top of all the others, rather than under them.

Hawaiian appliqué artists have developed their own particular style in this technique, but perhaps the best-known examples of reverse appliqué are the intricately patterned multicoloured blouses, or *molas*, produced by Cuna Indians on the San Blas Islands off the coast of Panama. An unusual example of what has come to be known as mola work is illustrated on page 10.

Reverse appliqué is usually produced by superimposing several layers of fabric and cutting through one or more to reveal different colours. For this cushion, made entirely of Indian dupion silks, I have used a simpler technique but more colours. I have cut quite simple shapes out of an emerald green circle and then placed beneath the holes brilliantly coloured scraps in pinks, purples, blues and turquoise, with strips of contrasting colours placed at angles across them. I have frayed the edges of the strips, which in the case of shot silks produces yet another colour, since the weft threads are a different colour from the warp. The final effect resembles a shining stained glass window.

For the piping, I have used short strips of all the appliqué colours, plus a patterned silk of which I had only one small scrap but which matches beautifully for colour.

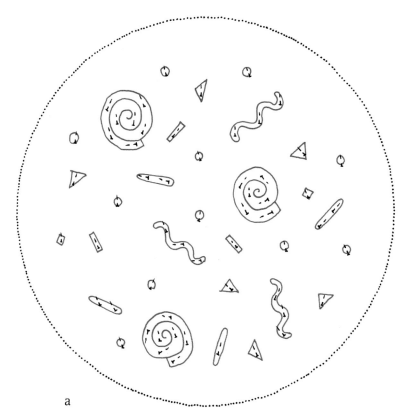

a

Materials
I have used 11 colours for the appliqué, apart from the green silk used for the main part of the cushion. You can, of course, make the cushion up with fewer colours than this. You will need about a metre/yard of fabric in total for the appliqué, so divide this amount by the number of colours you choose.

Emerald green silk – for cushion cover, 112cm/44in wide: 80cm/⁷⁄₈yd
Contrasting fabrics – for appliqué, 112cm/44in wide: a total of about 1m/1yd
Calico – for backing fabric: 50cm/½yd
Silk or cotton sewing threads in a colour contrasting with main fabric and in colours to contrast with and match appliqué fabrics
Circular boxed cushion pad 45cm/18in diameter
Medium-sized pre-shrunk piping cord: 3m/3³⁄₈yd
5 buttons
Fabric marking pen or dressmaker's pencil
Tracing paper

1 Cut out the fabric pieces as instructed on page 181. (See also the general instructions on pages 12–16.)

2 To prepare the top cover, first cut out the tracing paper shapes and arrange them randomly on the silk circle, spacing them as evenly as you can. None of the shapes should be closer than 4cm/1½in to the edge of the circle at any point. When you are satisfied with their distribution, pin them in place (fig. a). Draw carefully round them with a fabric marking pen or dressmaker's pencil, then remove the paper shapes.

3 Cut out the shapes along the marked lines, using small sharp-pointed scissors. Snip all the concave curves, circles and corners.

Take the large silk circle, now full of holes, and place it on the calico circle, aligning the raw edges. Pin the two layers together 1cm/³⁄₈in from the edge (fig. b).

4 Now position the backing pieces. Take one of your pieces of backing fabric and slip it behind a hole of the correct shape, so that it lies sandwiched between the two layers of the circle. Make sure that it is centred beneath the hole (holding the circle up to the light will enable you to check this easily). Pin, then tack the piece in place (fig. c), keeping the tacking a scant 1cm/³⁄₈in from the raw edges. In the case of the spirals, tack only round the outside of the shape (fig. d), so that you will be able to insert the strips under the coils.

Repeat to position all the backing pieces in the corresponding cut-out shapes (fig. e).

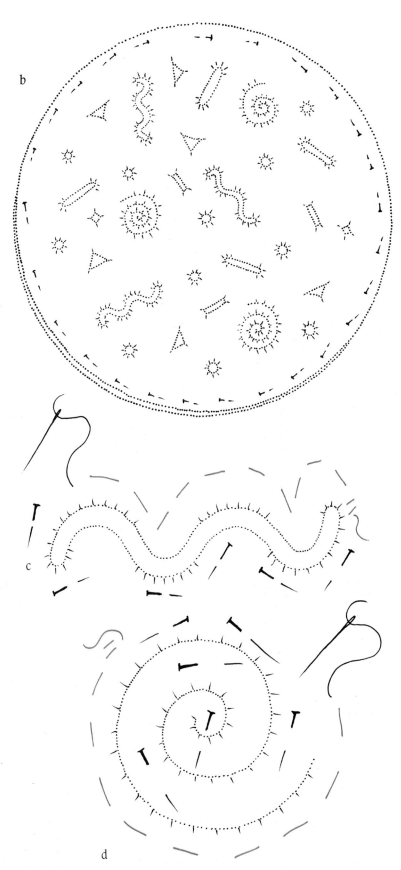

b

c

d

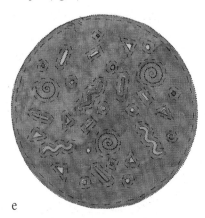

e

5 Add the contrasting strips,
cutting them from the remaining
scraps of silk. Cut short strips of
varying width – between 1.2 and
4cm/½–1½in, then cut these into
short lengths to fit across the shapes
as desired (long enough so that they
will not escape when you later turn
under 3mm/⅛in along these edges).

Choose contrasting colours and
arrange them in a way that pleases
you. I have used silks that fray very
easily for my cushion, and I have
deliberately frayed the edges of the
strips. But do not fray strips too
much before placing them in the
cuts, because they will continue to
fray while in place.

Tuck their ends under the raw
edges of the cuts and pin and tack
them in place (fig. f).

**6 Slipstitch round the cut-out
shapes** (see page 15). Turn under
3mm/⅛in as you go and work
through all layers, thus catching in
the contrasting strips too. Leaving
the tacking stitches in place, give the
work a careful press under a cloth.

Using contrasting thread, work
small running stitches (see page 16)
3mm/⅛in from the edge of each
shape.

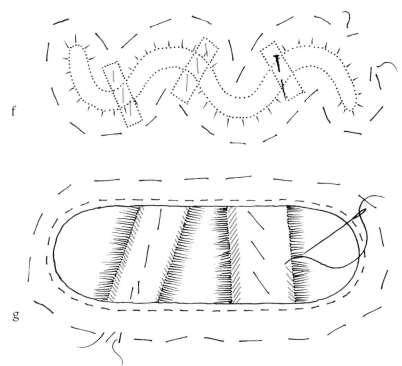

f

g

Now you can fray the edges of the
small strips to the amount you want.
Work slanted oversewing stitches
along them to prevent further
fraying and provide extra decoration
(fig. g). On some of the wider strips
you may wish also to work running
stitch inside the frayed edges. Now
remove the tacking.

7 To complete the cushion, join
the bias strips to make two lengths
of 150cm/59in each. Make up the
piping as described on page 18.
Make up the cover as described for a
boxed cushion, page 18.

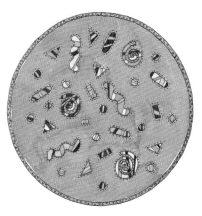

Left *Detail of a completed spiral*
Below *The cushion in an attractive
mix of 'Liquorice Allsort' colours*

Birds in the Trees

This quilt is a particular favourite of mine. I love the warm colours and the friendly-looking birds perched in different attitudes on their curving branches. There are six different birds (two of them are used twice), each using a different combination of colours. I have used a total of 18 colours on a natural calico background, but you could use fewer – or more – as you like. The important thing is to achieve a feeling of harmony within the variety. In the cutting-out instructions (page 186), precise fabrics for all the feathers are not specified; your choice for each bird will depend on your fabrics and how they relate to each other.

I have made the quilt in several soft yellows, with some peachy buffs and pinks. With these I have put a soft grey-green and a warm olive for the trees and leaves. Just one patterned bright yellow fabric among the others adds a bit of zest. The quilt is lined with pink and yellow stripes to echo the colours on the top, but in much hotter shades. I used cotton lawn – an excellent lining material, as it is very fine and smooth. A lightweight (2oz) wadding provides warmth without bulk.

Designed for a double bed, the quilt measures 220cm/87in long by 223cm/88in wide. Because of its size, it is made in two halves, which are joined when the appliqué is nearly complete.

Materials

Lightweight cottons, 90cm/36in wide, unless otherwise stated. A broad indication of the colours I used is given in the list below. For your own version of the quilt you may choose fewer, more or quite different colours.

A Lightweight calico – for base fabric, 114cm/45in wide: 4.5m/5yd

B Bright pink lawn – for lining: 4.5m/5yd

C Bright gold – for lining: 4.5m/5yd

D Grey-green – for trees, 114cm/45in wide: 2.4m/2⅝yd

E Gold – for edging on trees: 1.4m/1½yd

F Light peach pink – for top and bottom border, 3 birds' bodies: 40cm/½yd

G Sandy gold – for side borders, 2 birds' bodies: 40cm/½yd

H Pale apricot – for 2 birds' bodies: 20cm/¼yd

I Soft gold – for 2 birds' bodies: 20cm/¼yd

J Coral – for side border triangles, smaller tree circles: 30cm/⅜yd

K Mustard – for top and bottom triangles: 30cm/⅜yd

L Strawberry pink – for border edging, large tree circles: 40cm/⅜yd

M Bright gold – for corner motif: 10cm/⅛yd

N Olive green – for leaves: 20cm/¼yd

O Medium brown – for bird's head, feathers: 10cm/⅛yd

P Light rust – for bird's head, feathers: 10cm/⅛yd

Q Bright gold print – for some feathers: 20cm/¼yd

R Green-gold – for binding, 114cm/45in wide: 30cm/⅜yd

Lightweight (2oz) polyester wadding: enough to make up a piece the size of quilt (see page 14)

Cream sewing or quilting thread for topstitching

Cream stranded embroidery cotton for tying

1 Cut out the fabric pieces as instructed on page 186. (See also the general instructions on pages 12–16.)

2 Start by positioning the four wavy pieces of tree trunk on the background pieces. It will be easier to see what you are doing if you spread the two pieces of base fabric on the floor, right side up and side by side. The seam joining them eventually will run *across* the quilt. Where they meet, the edge of the lower piece should overlap that of the upper piece by 2cm/³⁄₄in. Now place the tree trunks on the fabric. At the point where they join, the left-hand tree should be 64cm/25in from the side edge of the base fabric (measured from the outer edges of the trunk), and the right-hand tree 61cm/24in from the edge (fig. a).

Bring the inner edges of the trunks right up to the centre edges of the base fabric. Check that the trunk sections will join correctly by overlapping the join edges by 2cm/³⁄₄in. Pin them temporarily in place, then fold under 1cm/³⁄₈in of the overlap (fig. b). When you are sure that the trunks will meet smoothly pin them to the base fabric. Tack them 1cm/³⁄₈in in from the edge.

3 To make the border strips, begin by joining the pieces. For the top and bottom strips (Fabric F), join lengths to make two strips, each 203cm/80in long. For the side strips (Fabric G), join lengths to make four strips, each 103cm/40½in long.

Turn under and press 5mm/¹⁄₄in along both edges of all the strips, and pin them to the two sections of base fabric, 12cm/4³⁄₄in from the raw edges, making sure that they

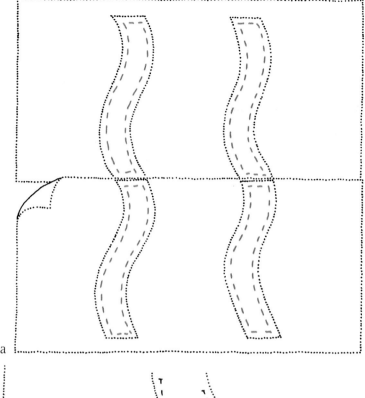

a

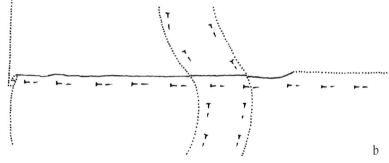

b

overlap the tree trunks. Just let the corners overlap at this stage. Check that the borders are straight, and tack them down the centre. Unpin the two halves of the quilt and continue working on the lower half.

4 Position four large branches and one small one on the two tree trunks as shown in fig. c. Tuck their wide ends 1.2cm/½in under the trunk pieces, then pin and tack them in place.

Place a bias strip along one edge of one tree trunk, tuck it 1.2cm/½in under the edge and pin it in place. Continue placing the other bias strips along both sides of the trunk pieces in the same way, overlapping and turning under the ends as required. Similarly, insert bias strips under the lower edges of the large branches, tapering each one towards the end until it disappears. The branch bias strips should overlap those of the trunks where they meet (fig. d).

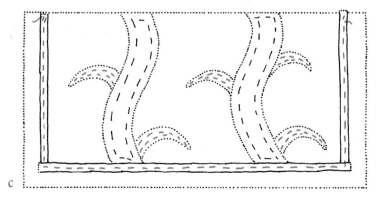

c

Tack the strips in place 1cm/³⁄₈in from the edges. Turn under and slipstitch the edges to the base fabric (see page 15).

5 The tree trunks can now be slipstitched in place. Turn under the edges as you go, and work through all fabric layers. Leave the top right edges of both tree trunks unstitched for 9cm/3½in to allow a branch to be inserted here after the two halves of the quilt are joined.

Slipstitch the branches and then press the work carefully. Now work running stitch (see page 16) along all the hemmed edges, as evenly as possible, making the stitches 3mm/⅛in long or slightly smaller, and keeping them 3mm/⅛in from the edge. Remove the tacking.

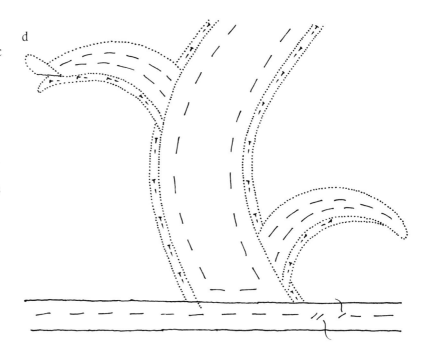

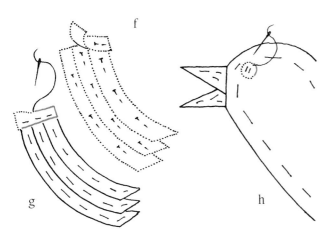

6 The pieces for the first bird (1) are now positioned on the top left-hand branch (fig. e). The body overlaps the legs, beak and tail feathers; the wing feathers overlap each other from the top down (fig. f); the tail feathers, from left to right. When you are pinning on the feathers, make sure that they overlap by a generous 5mm/¼in. Place the legs so they will just meet the branch when they are turned under by 3mm/⅛in and slipstitched. The wing on this bird is contained within the body. Pin and tack all the pieces in place.

Slipstitch the edges, beginning with the legs, then the beak, the tail feathers (beginning with the underneath one and working up to the top), the body, and finally the wing, again sewing the pieces on in ascending order, finishing with the little bar at the top of the wing (fig. g). Sew on a tiny circle for the eye (fig. h). Press the bird carefully before topstitching 3mm/⅛in from each edge. I have left the legs without any topstitching, as they are so thin. You can topstitch the beak or not, as you like. Remove the tacking after working each bird.

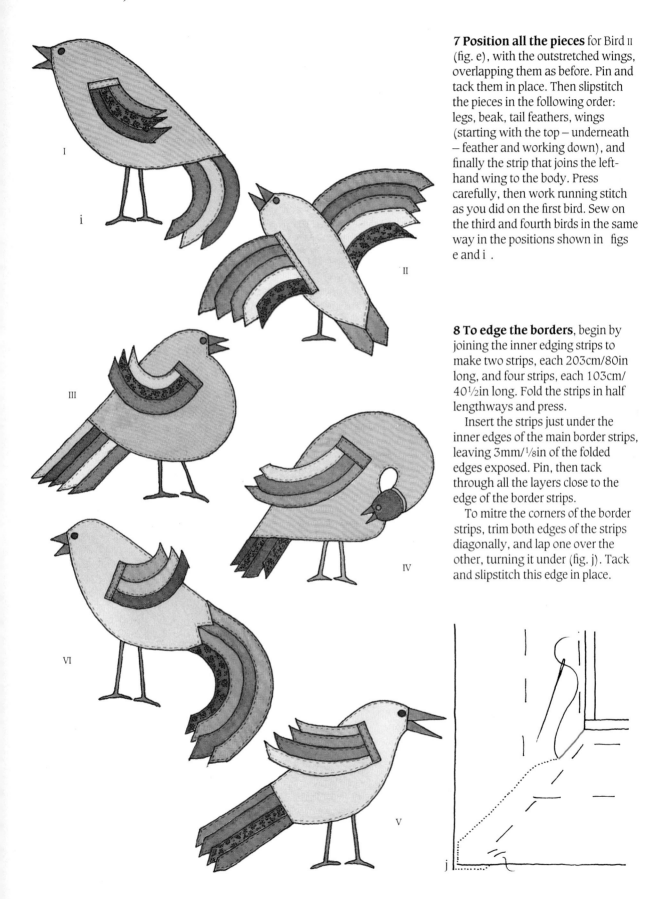

7 Position all the pieces for Bird II (fig. e), with the outstretched wings, overlapping them as before. Pin and tack them in place. Then slipstitch the pieces in the following order: legs, beak, tail feathers, wings (starting with the top – underneath – feather and working down), and finally the strip that joins the left-hand wing to the body. Press carefully, then work running stitch as you did on the first bird. Sew on the third and fourth birds in the same way in the positions shown in figs e and i .

8 To edge the borders, begin by joining the inner edging strips to make two strips, each 203cm/80in long, and four strips, each 103cm/40½in long. Fold the strips in half lengthways and press.

Insert the strips just under the inner edges of the main border strips, leaving 3mm/⅛in of the folded edges exposed. Pin, then tack through all the layers close to the edge of the border strips.

To mitre the corners of the border strips, trim both edges of the strips diagonally, and lap one over the other, turning it under (fig. j). Tack and slipstitch this edge in place.

9 To complete the border
decoration, position the triangles
evenly along the outer edges of the
border strips. Sixteen triangles fit
along the lower border and eight
along each short side. (You could
use Fabric K for the lower border, J
for the sides.) Pin and then tack
them in place. Tack along the outer
edge of the border strips.

The circles are then placed evenly
between the triangles, so that their
outermost edges are level with the
outer point of the triangles (Fabric J
circles along the bottom and Fabric K
circles on the sides). Pin and tack.

Position the leaf motifs at the
corners, so that their inner points,
when turned and stitched, will meet
the border corners. Pin and tack.

10 Slipstitch all the border pieces
in place. Begin with the triangles,
keeping their points as sharp as
possible. Next, slipstitch the outer
edges of the main border strip, then
the inner edge, taking the needle
through all layers to secure the inner
edging strips. Leave 5cm/2in at the
top ends unstitched; this will be
completed when the quilt halves are
joined. Slipstitch the corner leaf
shapes, then the circles, taking care
to keep the shape as smoothly
rounded as possible (fig. k). Press
the work carefully. Topstitch the
edges of the main border strip, the
triangles, the circles and the two leaf
shapes. Remove the tacking.

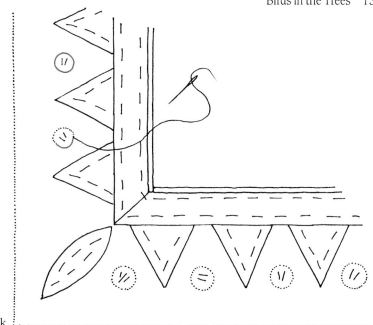

k

11 Next, **position the circle** motifs
on the tree trunks (fig. l). Begin by
placing a smaller circle centrally on
top of each larger one, then pinning
them as one onto the trunk. Place
the lowest circles 14cm/5½in from
the border strip and equidistant from

the tree trunk edges; the next three
should be approximately 17cm/
6½in apart. Tack and slipstitch the
circles in place, beginning with the
outer one and keeping them as
smooth as possible (fig. m). Press,
then topstitch round both edges.

l

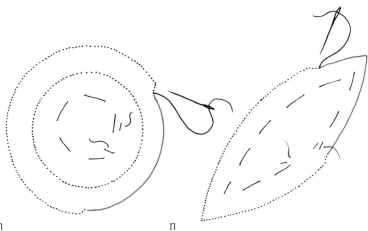

m   n

12 Apply the leaves, placing them
more or less randomly, clustered at
the ends of the branches and at
intervals along the trunk – wherever
you find a conspicuous gap (fig. l).
Pin and tack them in place, then
slipstitch round their edges (fig. n).
Press, then topstitch round each leaf.

The lower half of the quilt is now
complete.

13 Place the two halves of the
quilt together and check that the tree
trunks and borders meet exactly.

14 To apply the middle branches, begin by positioning two larger branches along the lower edge of the upper section so that they will join the trunk correctly when the two halves are joined. Pin and tack them in place (fig. o). Insert the bias strips and tack them in place, but do not slipstitch their outer edges.

Position the other branches as shown (fig. p), leaving the branch ends free. They will cross the join between the two halves.

15 For the upper half, apply the birds, border pieces and circular motifs as described for the lower half of the quilt, using the diagram as a guide for positioning (fig. p). Press all the pieces carefully before topstitching round the edges and removing tacking.

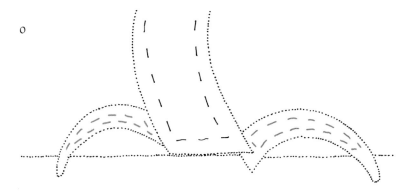

o

p

16 The two halves of the quilt are now ready to be joined. Lay the top half flat. Turn under 1cm/³⁄₈in along the upper edge of the lower half, and place it over the upper half, overlapping the edge by 1cm/³⁄₈in. Lift up the unsewn branch ends where they cross the join to enable you to do this. Pin, then tack through all the layers, matching the trunks and border strips carefully.

Slipstitch the folded edge in place. Press, then topstitch, working through all layers.

Similarly, join the border strips. Slipstitch them down, then complete the topstitching (fig. q). Sew on the last two circles, one on each side.

17 Complete the application of the middle branches, tucking them under the tree trunks and then slipstitching and topstitching round their edges. Slipstitch (fig. r) and topstitch the loose branch ends.

Extra leaves can then be sewn on at appropriate places around these branches.

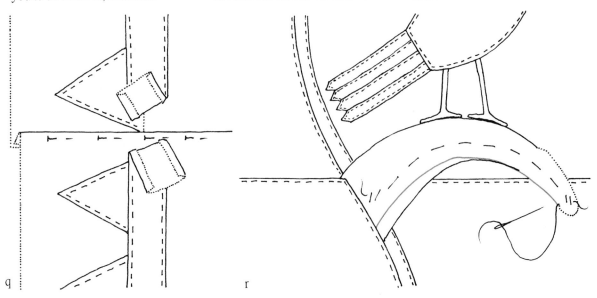

q

r

18 To make up the quilt begin by joining the strips of lining fabric to make up a piece the same size as the quilt top. Press the seams open. Join the wadding, if necessary (see page 14), and trim it to the same size.

Place the three layers of the quilt together, then pin and tack through all layers. Work round the edges, through the centre in both directions, across the width in two or three more places and 1.2cm/½in inside the border.

Quilt through the layers, working running stitch just inside the border strip (fig. s). Then tie the layers together at intervals of about 28cm/11in, making large loops of stranded cotton, cutting them and tying the ends tightly to make little tufts. Make these tufts all over the quilt, avoiding the birds and branches, and put one in the centre of each of the trunk circles (figs t, u and v).

s

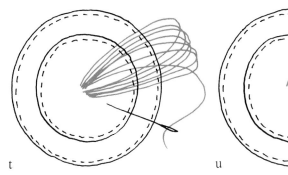

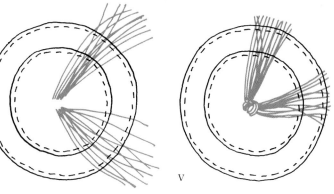

t   u   v

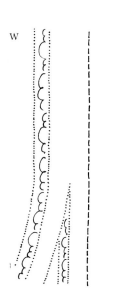

w

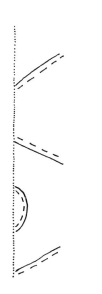

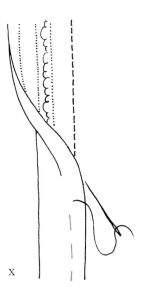

x

19 Join the outer edging strips to make one length of 915cm/360in, and press the seams open. Place the strip along the top of the quilt with right sides facing and edges matching. Tack, then machine stitch 1cm/³⁄₈in from the edge, overlapping the ends neatly. Trim the seam to 5mm/¼in (fig. w). Turn the strip over to the underside of the quilt, leaving an edge about 1cm/³⁄₈in wide. Pin and tack it in place, turning under the raw edge and making sure the machine stitches are covered (fig. x). Slipstitch the edges; remove tacking and press lightly, if necessary.

Chintamani

The twin wavy stripes and triple balls that adorn this kimono-shaped waistcoat are taken from a design known as 'chintamani'. I first saw it on the painted seat of an inlaid Turkish daybed, dating from about 1570, and have had it in mind for years as an idea for appliqué. According to Mimi Lipton's marvellous book *The Tiger Rugs of Tibet*, this motif is 'one of the great unexplained mysteries of classical Ottoman art', though it has been suggested that the three balls are derived from the Buddhist chintamani motif – the 'flaming pearl', which is the symbol of wisdom. It appears in varying conformations on textiles – including carpets, rugs and Imperial caftans – and also on pottery, bookbindings and other artefacts from the fifteenth century onwards.

As Mimi Lipton points out, the design bears a strong resemblance to the stripes of the Tibetan tiger rugs, and I have made the waistcoat in the rust and black of many of these rugs as homage to them and to the tigers that inspired them.

It is a simple and very strong motif, and I have used it in its plainest form here, slightly rounding the ends of the two wavy shapes and keeping the three balls plain. (The three balls often have other balls within them, placed off-centre to create a sort of fat crescent shape.)

The shape of the waistcoat is also very simple. It is easy to make, and if it needs to be enlarged or reduced in size, this can be done very easily by adding or subtracting at the long side edge. It consists basically of two rectangles, with a space cut out for the neck and front opening, and a third, folded rectangle which forms the slightly padded neck and front edges.

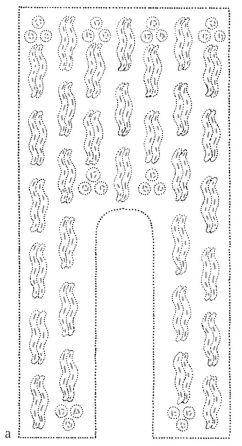

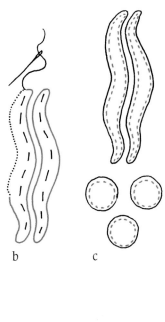

a
b
c

Materials

Cotton fabrics, at least 90cm/36in wide, in the following colours (or colours of your choice).
A Rust: 1.7m/1⅞yd
B Black: 40cm/½yd
C Black and red print – for lining: 1.4m/1½yd
Curtain interlining or brushed cotton: 1.7m/1⅞yd; or 10cm/⅛yd if more than 165cm/65in wide
Sewing or quilting thread to contrast with Fabric B.

1 Cut out the fabric pieces as instructed on page 185. (See also the general instructions on pages 12–16.) Transfer the centre line of each wavy motif to the fabric (see page 14) and cut along it, but keep the parts together.

2 First join the two main pieces of the waistcoat. Pin and tack, then stitch the sections together along the centre back edges, right sides facing, taking 1.2cm/½in seam allowance. Press the seam open.

Repeat this step to join the two lining pieces.

3 To apply the motifs, arrange them as shown in fig. a, keeping the wavy shapes straight to the grain of the fabric. Pin, then tack all the pieces in place. The twin wavy shapes should lie close together, touching along their inner edges. When they are stitched down, there will be 5mm/¼in between them.

Slipstitch the motifs in place, turning under 3mm/⅛in as you go (fig. b). Keep the balls as circular as possible (see page 16). Topstitch (see page 16) all the applied shapes (fig. c). Remove the tacking.

4 To make up the waistcoat, first join the side seams. Turn under and press 5mm/¼in on the upper edge of each triangular gusset piece (waistcoat and lining).

Join the side seams and lining up to the *, and press the seams open (fig. d).

Insert a gusset at the top of each side seam, placing the right sides together. Pin, tack and stitch up as far as the pressed fold (fig. e), then fasten off securely.

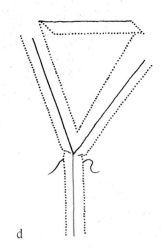

d

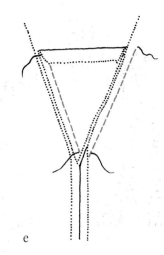

e

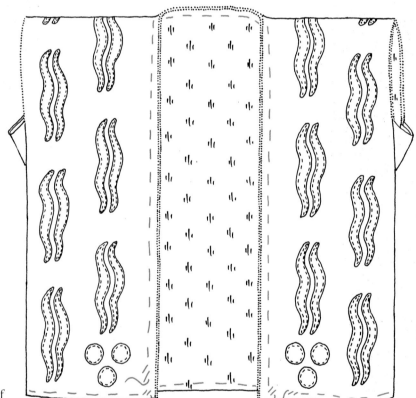

f

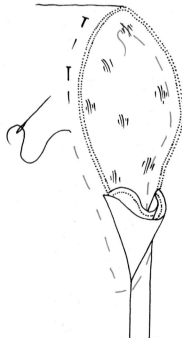

g

Place the waistcoat and lining together, right sides facing. Pin, tack and machine stitch them together along the lower edge. Now turn the waistcoat right side out, and press along this seam, pushing the lining very slightly upwards, so that it will not be visible. Pin, then tack these layers together along the stitched edge.

Pin the layers together up the front and round the neck, then tack about 1cm/⅜in from the edge (fig. f), and round the armholes, 2.5cm/1in from the edge (fig. g).

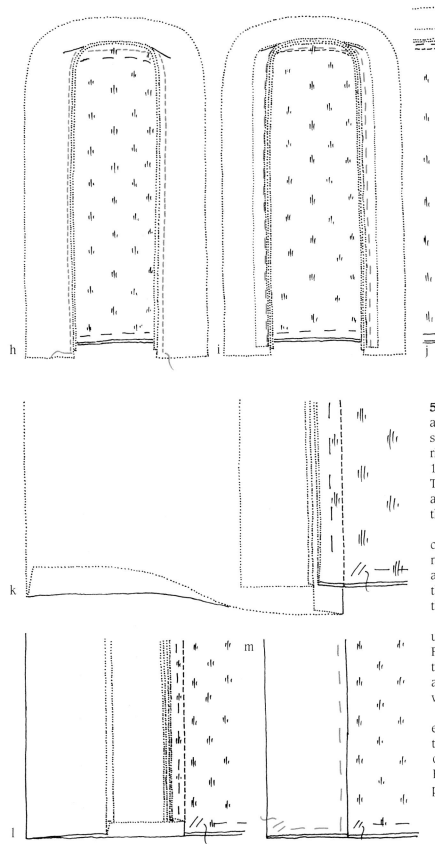

5 The neckband can now be attached. First pin, tack and machine stitch it to the neck edge, placing right sides together and taking 1.2cm/½in seam allowance (fig. h). Trim the ends, if necessary, leaving about 1.2cm/½in extending below the edge of the waistcoat.

Place the strip of interfacing on top of the neckband, matching the inner raw edges. Tack it firmly to the seam allowance (fig. i). Trim the ends so that they are slightly shorter than the waistcoat.

Now turn the neckband right side up, so that it extends flat (fig. j). Press. Turn under the lower ends of the neckband so that they are aligned with the finished edge of the waistcoat (fig. k). Press.

Fold back the raw edge to meet the edge of the interfacing (fig. l), press, then fold this edge over so that it just covers the machine stitching (fig. m). Pin and tack the neckband in place, then slipstitch it to the lining.

Slipstitch the ends to neaten them.

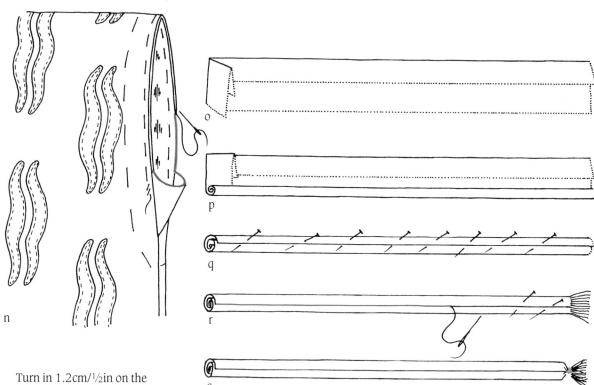

Turn in 1.2cm/½in on the armhole edge of both waistcoat and lining. Pin, tack and slipstitch them together (fig. n).

6 To make the ties, turn in 5mm/ ¼in on one long edge of each tie piece (fig. o). Press. Turn in and press the same amount on one end. Roll the strip up tightly, from the raw edges towards the folded edge (fig. p); pin the roll to hold it together (fig. q). Oversew the folded edge in place, working from the folded end. When you are about 1.2cm/½in from the end, pull threads from the free end to make a fringe (fig. r), then wrap the thread tightly around the end to make a tassel (fig. s).

Sew the two ties to the underside of the neckband, 30cm/12in from the lower edge.

The
Patterns

Some of the pattern pieces in the pages that follow can be traced directly from the page; most, however, need to be enlarged before they can be used. This can be done quite easily by scaling them up on graph paper, following the grid that is printed over them.

Alternatively, if you have access to a photocopier that does enlargements, you simply need to follow the degree of enlargement indicated on each individual pattern. A more detailed explanation of the process is given on pages 12–13.

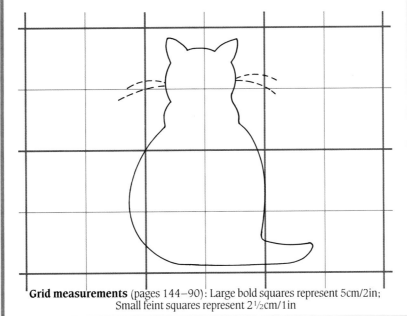

Grid measurements (pages 144–90): Large bold squares represent 5cm/2in; Small feint squares represent 2½cm/1in

Cat Family

Cutting-out instructions

See also the general instructions on pages 12 and 22.

For the main pieces and appliqué shapes use the patterns provided, cutting the specified number in the fabrics indicated.

Note Check to make sure that the cat fabric is sufficiently opaque so that the background and tablecloth fabrics will not show through. If they do, cut two pieces for each cat. Trim away 5mm/¼in from the edge of one piece. Pin and tack the two layers together, leaving an even margin all round. When slipstitching the edges in place, fold the top layer under the lower one.

For the tablecloth cut two pieces of Fabric C, each 36 × 9cm/14¼ × 3½in. Position the enlarged cat pattern over the fabric, with the cat's left-hand edge 10cm/4in from the fabric's left-hand edge and its lower edge 1cm/⅜in from the bottom. Insert pins just outside the pattern edge; remove the pattern, then cut away part of the tablecloth in a curve, about 2cm/¾in inside the pin line. Repeat with the other tablecloth piece.

For the binding cut enough 4cm/1½in-wide bias strips of Fabric E to make a total of 170cm/67in and enough 3cm/1¼in-wide to make a total of 230cm/90in.

For the cat's features and details trace the lines from the enlarged patterns.

Enlarge by 154%

Cut 8 in A

Cut 2 [or 4] in B
(1 [or 2] in reverse)

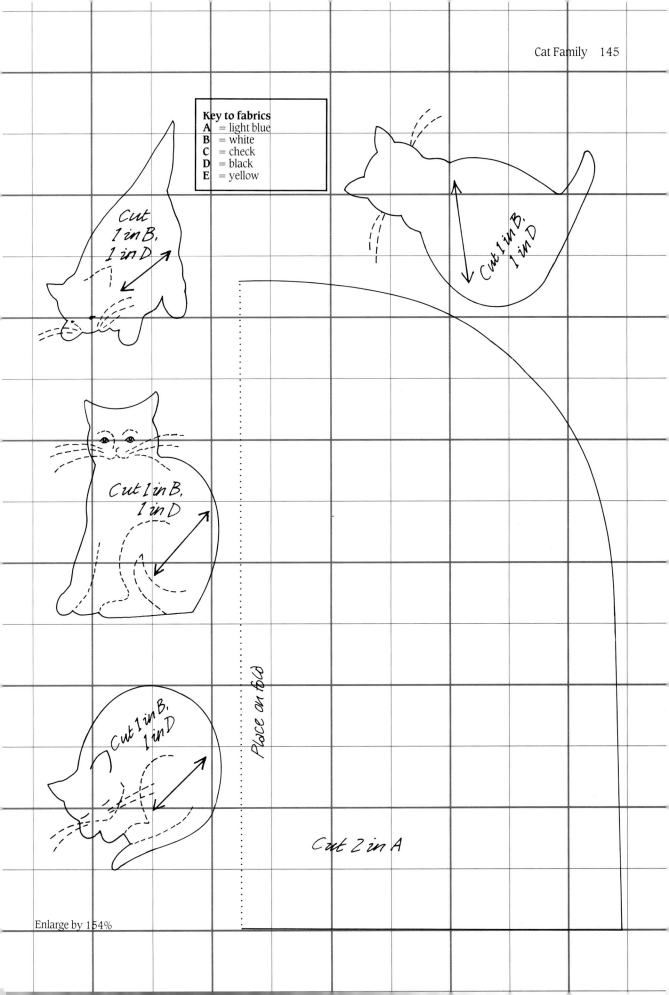

Key to fabrics
A = light blue
B = white
C = check
D = black
E = yellow

Cut 1 in B,
1 in D

Cut 1 in B,
1 in D

Cut 1 in B,
1 in D

Cut 1 in B,
1 in D

Place on fold

Cut 2 in A

Enlarge by 154%

Brilliant Blooms

Cutting-out instructions
See also the general instructions on pages 12 and 26.
For the cover cut one piece of Fabric A, 61cm/24in square, one piece 61 × 43cm/24 × 17in, one piece 61 × 20cm/24in × 8in and two pieces each 61 × 5cm/24in × 2in
For the edging cut enough strips of Fabric C, each 3.5cm/1½in wide, to make a total length, when joined, of 240cm/95in.
For the inner border cut four strips of Fabric B, each 43cm/17in long and 2.5cm/1in wide.
Also cut about twenty irregularly shaped pieces of Fabric J, about 1.5-2.5cm/½-1in overall, for scattering over the background.
For the remaining appliqué pieces use the patterns provided, cutting the specified number in the fabrics indicated. You may wish to trim some of the short strips to make them fit attractively

Key to fabrics
A = deep lavender
B = deep turquoise
C = coral pink
D = rose pink
E = fuchsia pink
F = golden yellow
G = mid yellow
H = pale yellow
I = bright green
J = black

together round the four sides.
For the edging strips on Side 3, cut three strips of Fabric J, each 10 × 1.5cm/4 × ⅝in.

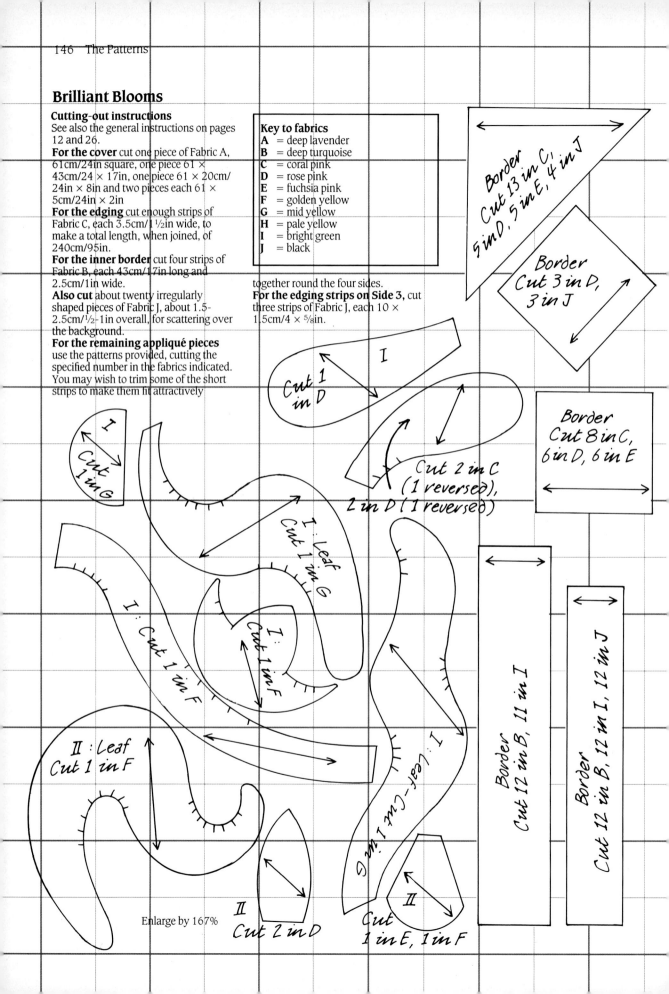

Border Cut 13 in C, 5 in D, 5 in E, 4 in J

Border Cut 3 in D, 3 in J

Border Cut 8 in C, 6 in D, 6 in E

Cut 1 in D

I

I Cut 1 in G

Cut 2 in C (1 reversed), 2 in D (1 reversed)

I Cut 1 in G

I Cut 1 in G

I Cut 1 in F

I : Leaf Cut 1 in G

I : Cut 1 in F

I : Leaf Cut 1 in G

II : Leaf Cut 1 in F

Border Cut 12 in B, 11 in I

Border Cut 12 in B, 12 in I, 12 in J

Enlarge by 167%

II Cut 2 in D

II Cut 1 in E, 1 in F

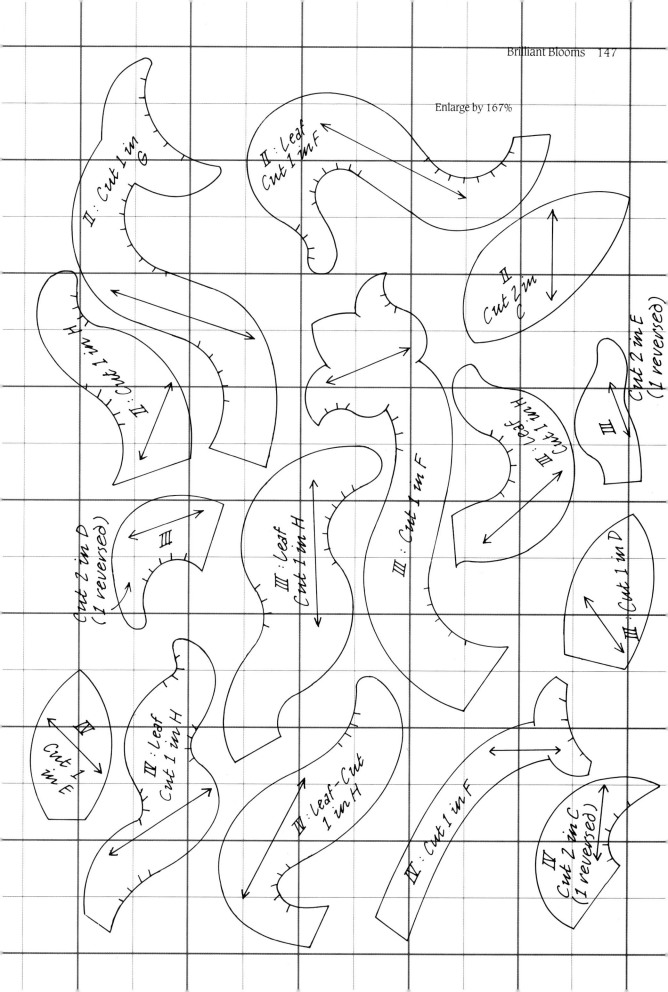

Enlarge by 167%

Swags and Diamonds

Cutting-out instructions

See also the general instructions on pages 12 and 30.

For the quilt top cut Fabric A in half crossways, then cut one of the pieces in half lengthways.

For the lining cut Fabric G in the same way.

For the binding cut eight strips of Fabric B, along the length of the fabric, making them 4cm/1 ½in wide.

For the appliqué pieces use the patterns provided, cutting the specified number in the fabrics indicated. Leave the cutting of the small circles until you have decided on the colours for the diamonds, then choose the colours that best complement those you have chosen for the diamonds.

Key to fabrics
A = dark blue
B = apple green
C = turquoise
D = kingfisher blue
E = emerald green
F = deep sea-green
G = plain or print

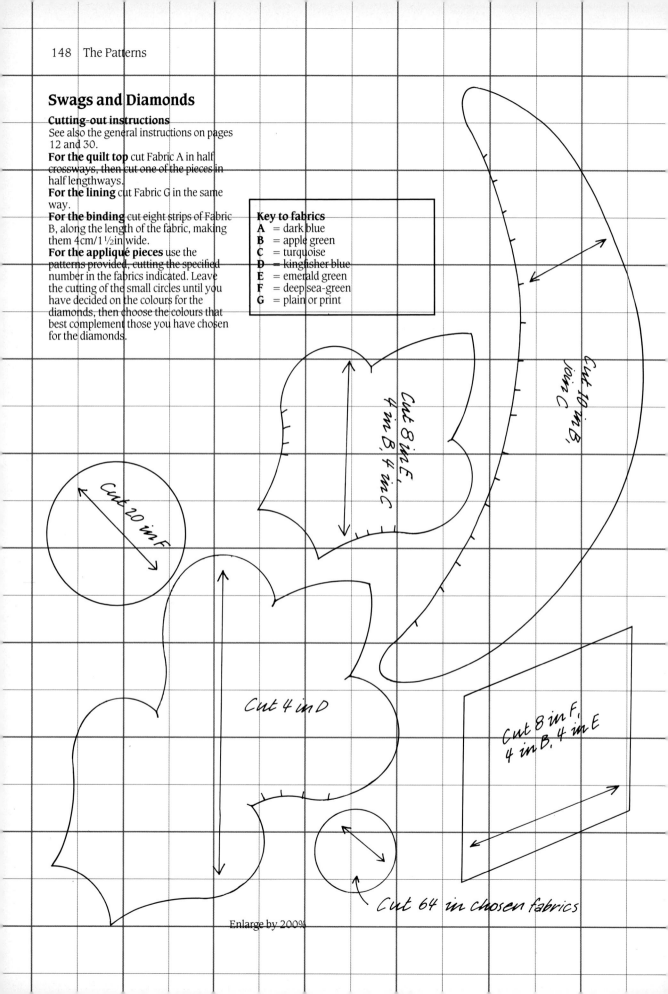

Cut 20 in F

Cut 8 in E, 4 in B, 4 in C

Cut 10 in B, join C

Cut 4 in D

Cut 8 in F, 4 in B, 4 in E

Cut 64 in chosen fabrics

Enlarge by 200%

Animal Parade

Cutting-out instructions
See also the general instructions on pages 12 and 40.

For the panel backgrounds cut six rectangles – three of Fabric A and three of Fabric B, each measuring 71 × 25.5cm/ 28 × 10in.

For the frieze backing cut six rectangles of calico, each measuring 73 × 25.5cm/28¾ × 10in.

For the straight edging strips cut twelve strips of Fabric C, each measuring 71 × 2cm/28 × ¾in.

For the long wavy edging strips trace the partial pattern twice, joining the ends to make a piece measuring 71cm/28in in length (straight across). Cut the tracing along the *lower edge only*, and use it as a template to mark the curved lower edge of all six panels and the calico backing pieces. Then cut completely round the tracing and use it as a pattern to cut twelve wavy strips of Fabric C.

For the appliqué pieces, use the patterns provided and cut them from the fabrics indicated. You may find it easier, in the case of detailed shapes, to use dressmaker's carbon (see page 14) to mark the fabric, rather than attempting to cut round the pattern, which might produce a cruder result or cause some distortion of the fabric.

Key to fabrics
A	=	dark blue
B	=	medium blue
C	=	red
D	=	white
E	=	buff
F	=	bright green
G	=	dark pink
H	=	light pink
I	=	mint green
J	=	deep turquoise
K	=	black
L	=	yellow

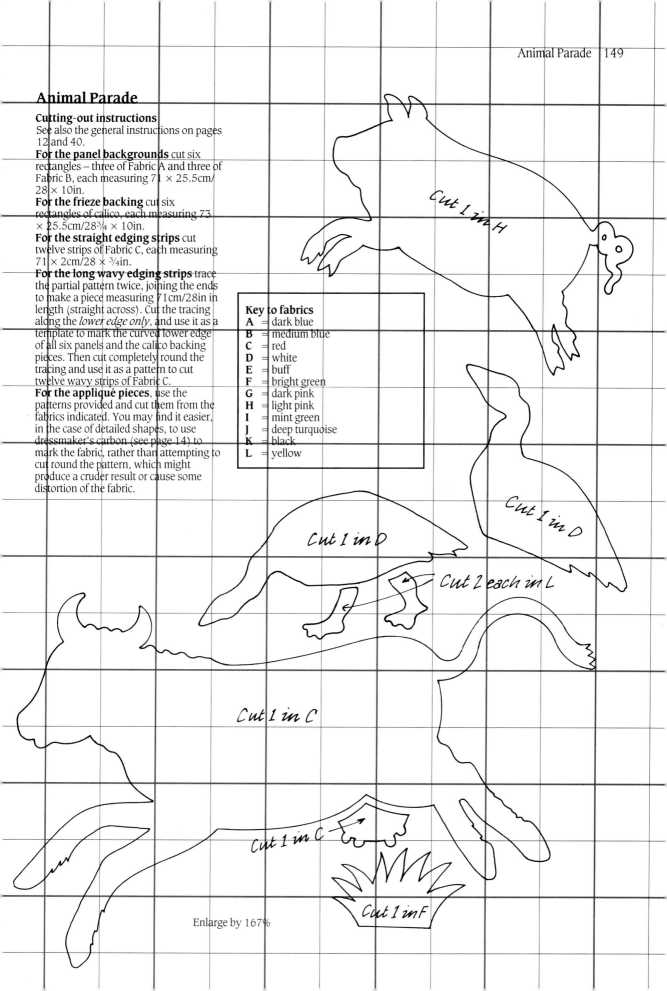

Cut 1 in H

Cut 1 in D

Cut 2 each in L

Cut 1 in D

Cut 1 in C

Cut 1 in C

Cut 1 in F

Enlarge by 167%

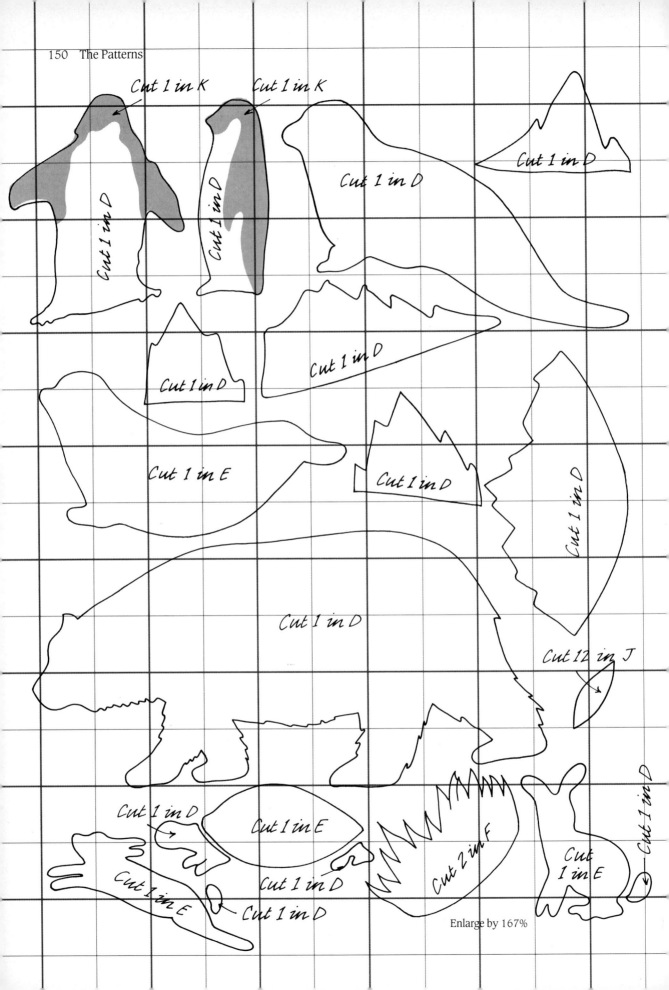

Cut 1 in K

Cut 1 in K

Cut 1 in D

Cut 1 in D

Cut 1 in D

Cut 1 in D

Cut 1 in D

Cut 1 in D

Cut 1 in E

Cut 1 in D

Cut 1 in D

Cut 1 in D

Cut 12 in J

Cut 1 in D

Cut 1 in E

Cut 1 in D

Cut 1 in E

Cut 2 in F

Cut 1 in E

Cut 1 in E

Cut 1 in D

Cut 1 in D

Enlarge by 167%

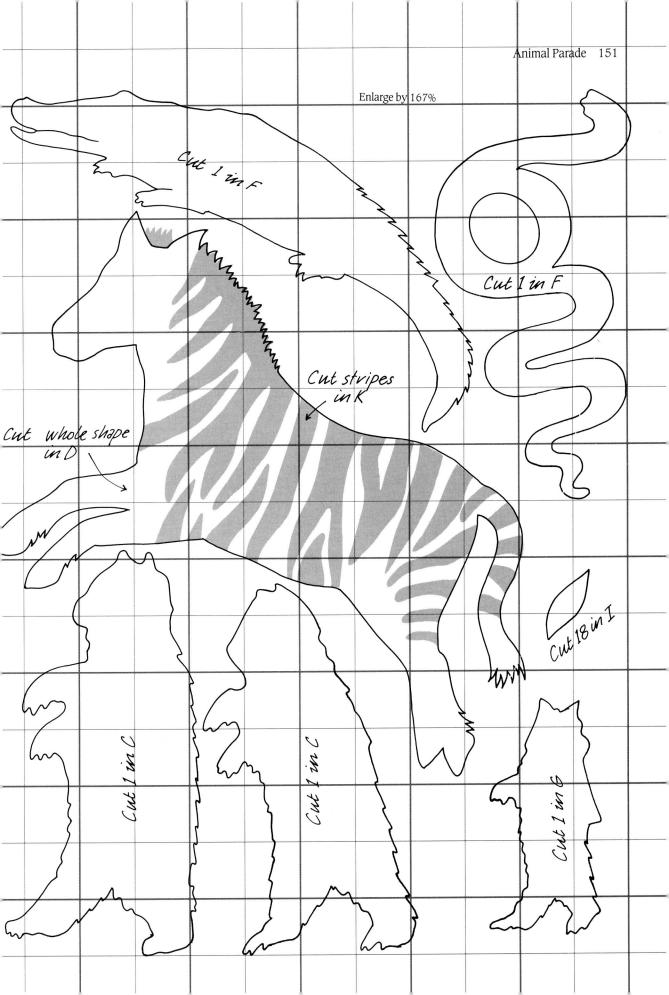

Enlarge by 167%

Cut 1 in F

Cut 1 in F

Cut stripes in K

Cut whole shape in D

Cut 18 in I

Cut 1 in C

Cut 1 in C

Cut 1 in G

152

Cut 36 in C

Trace for border – Cut 12 in C
See cutting-out instructions

Cut 1 in E

Cut 1 in F

Cut 1 in F

Cut 1 in D

Cut 5 in D

Cut 1 in E

Enlarge by 167%

Cut 1 in E

Cut 1 in E

Cut 1 in G, 1 in H

Cut 2 in E

Cut 2 in D

Cut 2 in D

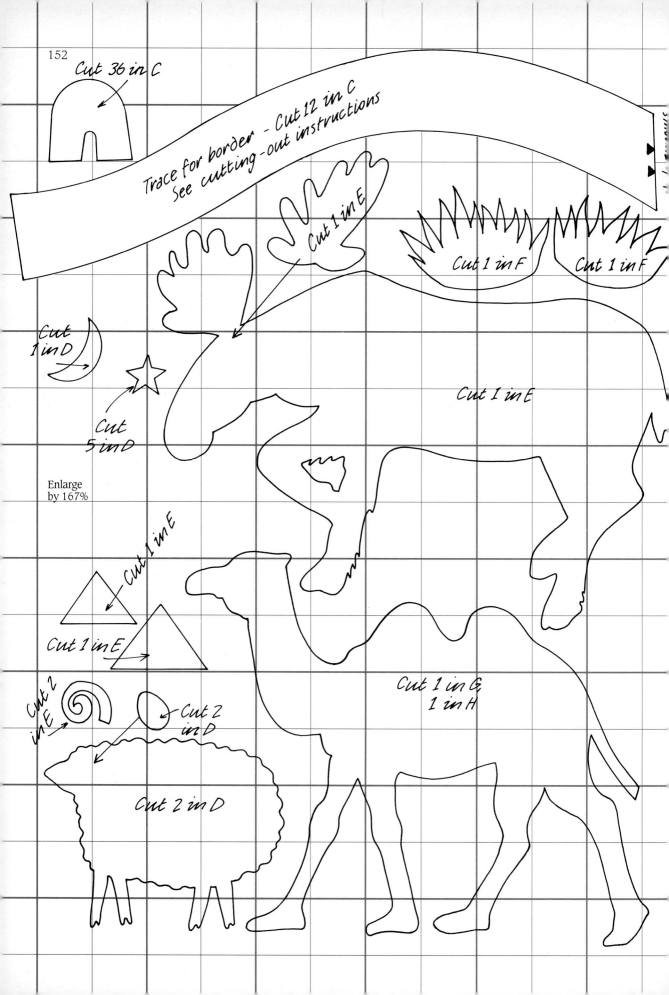

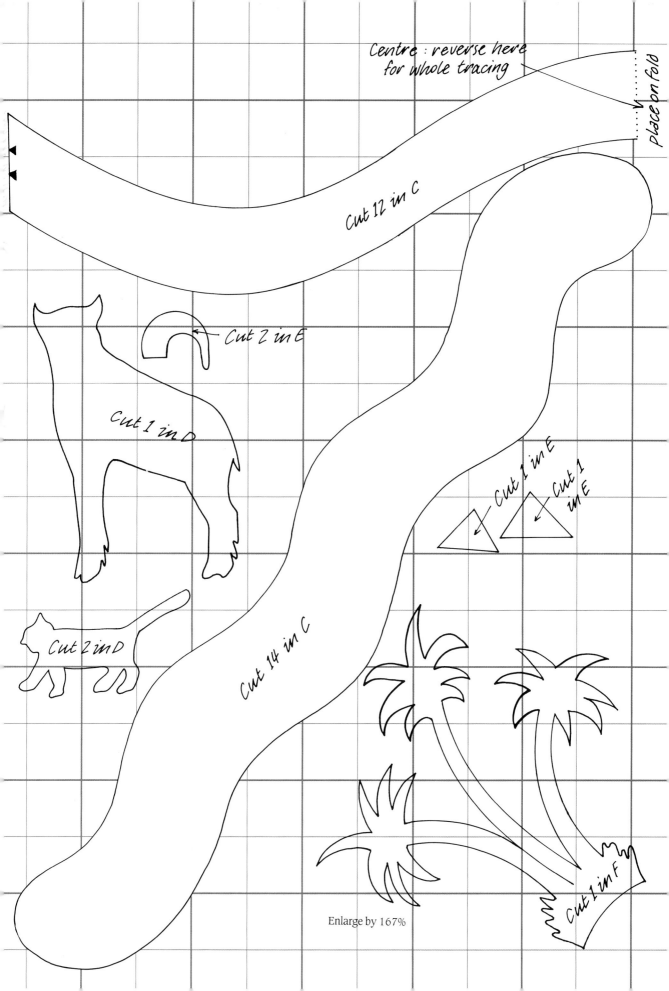

Centre: reverse here
for whole tracing

Place on fold

Cut 12 in C

Cut 2 in E

Cut 1 in D

Cut 2 in D

Cut 14 in C

Cut 1 in E

Cut 1 in E

Cut 1 in F

Enlarge by 167%

Buds in Spring

Cutting-out instructions

See also the general instructions on pages 12 and 44.

For the bedspread cut two lengths of Fabric A, each 2.23m/89in long. Cut one of these pieces in half lengthways.

For the lining cut two pieces the same size, but do not cut one of them in half. If you are using sheeting, simply cut the length to measure 2.23m/89in.

For the binding cut enough 3cm/1¼-wide bias strips of Fabric C to make up a strip 135cm/53in long; also cut two strips, the same width, 28cm/11in long and thirty-four strips, the same width, 24cm/9½in long.

For the appliqué pieces use the patterns provided, cutting the specified number in the fabrics indicated.

For the scalloped edge trace the circle, and use this pattern to cut a template from thin cardboard.

Key to fabrics
A = white linen
B = lining
C = light blue
D = turquoise

Cut 37 in D

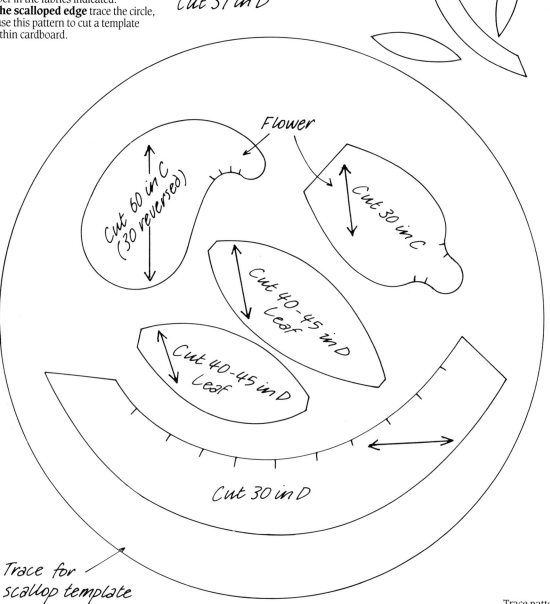

Flower

Cut 60 in C (30 reversed)

Cut 30 in C

Cut 40-45 in D Leaf

Cut 40-45 in D Leaf

Cut 30 in D

Trace for scallop template

Trace pattern

Provençal Garden

Cutting-out instructions

See also the general instructions on pages 12 and 50.

For the main sections cut four pieces of Fabric A, each 30 × 42cm/12 × 16½in (on the bag shown these are cut lengthways across the fabric, so that the ribbed weave runs vertically) and one piece 30cm/12in square.

For the lining cut the same pieces of Fabric B.

For the padding cut the same pieces from the wadding.

For the columns cut eight pieces of Fabric E, each 22 × 5.5cm/9 × 2¼in.

For the binding cut enough bias strips of Fabric C (see page 13) to make a total length of 7.6m/8⅝yd.

For the remaining appliqué pieces use the patterns provided, cutting the specified number in the fabrics indicated. Cut the printed leaves for Sides III and IV from appropriate fabrics.

For covering the cord cut (and join, if necessary) a strip of Fabric C 2cm/¾in wide and 120cm/47in long.

Key to fabrics

A = deep blue
B = blue and red print
C = red
D = bright turquoise
E = cream print
F = bright yellow
G = dull gold
H = dark green
I = emerald green
J = beige
K = leaf-printed chintz
L = faded turquoise leaf print

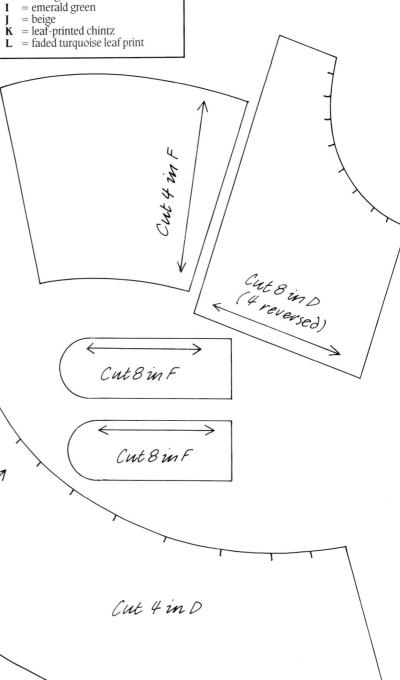

Cut 4 in F

Cut 8 in D
(4 reversed)

Cut 8 in F

Cut 8 in F

place on fold

Cut 4 in D

Trace pattern

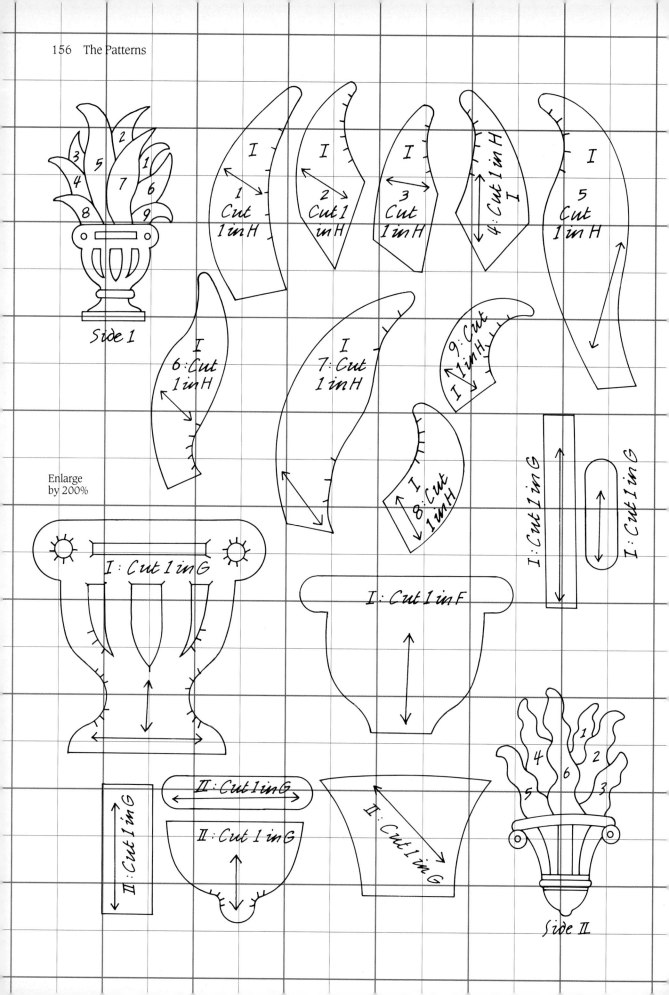

Side 1

I
1
Cut
1 in H

I
2
Cut 1
in H

I
3
Cut
1 in H

I
4: Cut 1 in H

I
5
Cut
1 in H

I
6: Cut
1 in H

I
7: Cut
1 in H

I
8: Cut
1 in H

I
9: Cut
1 in H

Enlarge
by 200%

I : Cut 1 in G

I: Cut 1 in F

I: Cut 1 in G

I: Cut 1 in G

II : Cut 1 in G

II: Cut 1 in G

II: Cut 1 in G

II: Cut 1 in G

Side II

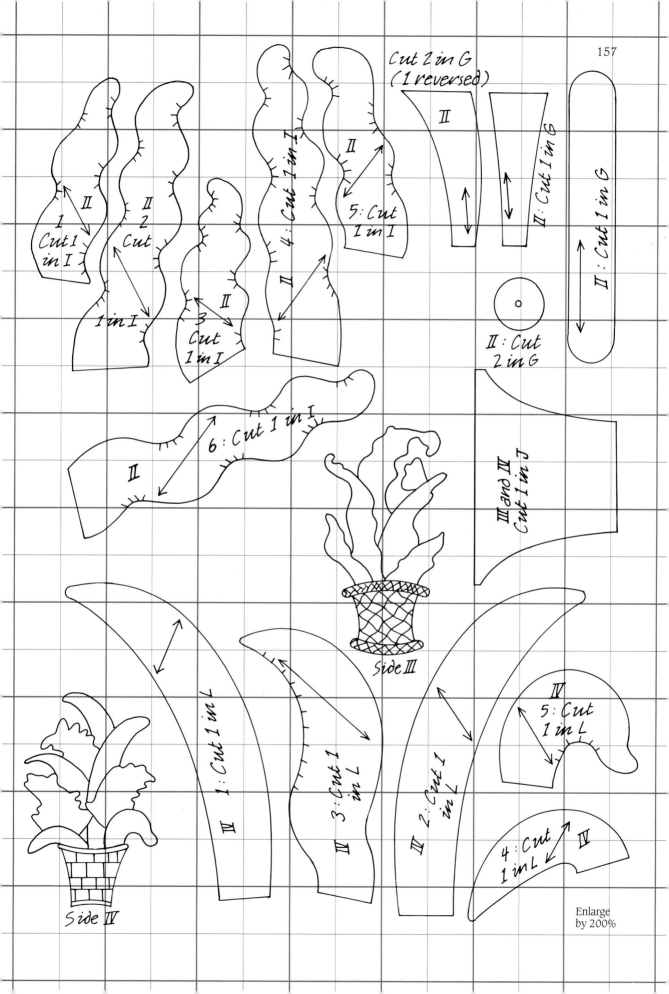

Cut 2 in G
(1 reversed)

II

II : Cut 1 in G

II : Cut 1 in G

II

1
Cut 1
in I

II
2
Cut

1 in I

II
3
Cut
1 in I

II : 4 : Cut 1 in I

II
5 : Cut
1 in I

II : Cut
2 in G

II : 6 : Cut 1 in I

III and II
Cut 1 in J

Side III

Side IV

IV : 1 : Cut 1 in L

II : 3 : Cut 1
in L

II : 2 : Cut 1
in L

IV
5 : Cut
1 in L

4 : Cut
1 in L   IV

Enlarge
by 200%

'Home Sweet Home'

Cutting-out instructions

See also the general instructions on pages 12 and 64.

For the base cut a piece of calico 41cm/16in square. Also cut pieces the same size from the wadding and Fabric K.

For the foreground cut a piece of Fabric D 10cm/4in deep and approx. 30–33cm/12–13in wide.

For the side garden cut two pieces of Fabric E, each about 12cm/5in deep and 6cm/2½in wide.

For the sky cut a piece of Fabric C, 10cm/4in deep and approx. 30–33cm/12–13in wide.

For the border strips cut four lengths of Fabric J, each 42cm/16½in long and 4–5cm/1½–2in wide, depending on whether you are using a decorative selvedge.

For the hanging loops cut four rectangles of Fabric K, each 9 × 7cm/3½ × 2¾in.

For the chimneys cut two 2cm/¾in squares of the chosen fabric.

For the house, simply trace the (enlarged) outline given; do not cut out the tracing. If you wish to make the house of fabric, rather than binding strips, use the outline as a pattern, adding 5mm/¼in to the outer edges only.

For the remaining appliqué pieces, use the patterns provided, cutting the specified number in the fabrics indicated.

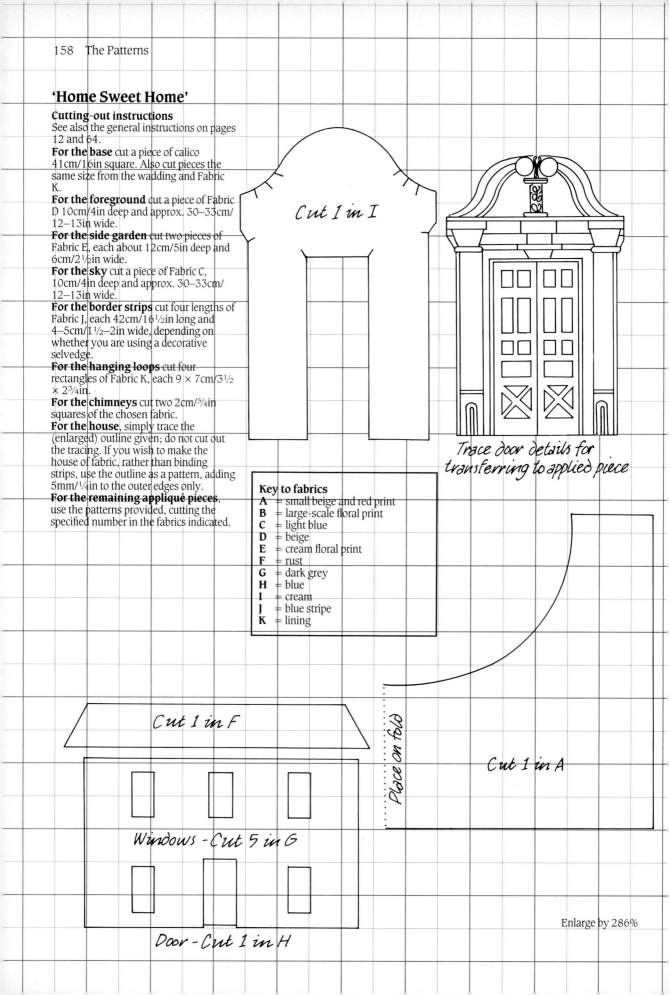

Cut 1 in I

Trace door details for transferring to applied piece

Key to fabrics
A = small beige and red print
B = large-scale floral print
C = light blue
D = beige
E = cream floral print
F = rust
G = dark grey
H = blue
I = cream
J = blue stripe
K = lining

Cut 1 in F

Place on fold

Cut 1 in A

Windows - Cut 5 in G

Door - Cut 1 in H

Enlarge by 286%

Beautiful Balloons

Cutting-out instructions

See also the general instructions on pages 12 and 90.

For the curtain panels cut Fabric A in half crossways to get two lengths, each measuring about 180cm/72in long.

For the lining cut Fabric B to the same measurements.

For the straight border strips cut a total of 6m/6⅝yds of 3cm/1¼in-wide strips of Fabric C.

Important Before working the appliqué, make sure that all the curtain lengths are perfectly straight (see page 12).

For the remaining appliqué pieces use the patterns provided, cutting the specified number in the fabrics indicated.

Key to fabrics

A	=	pale blue
B	=	lining
C	=	yellow
D	=	white
E	=	red
F	=	blue
G	=	bright green
H	=	pale green
I	=	assorted prints

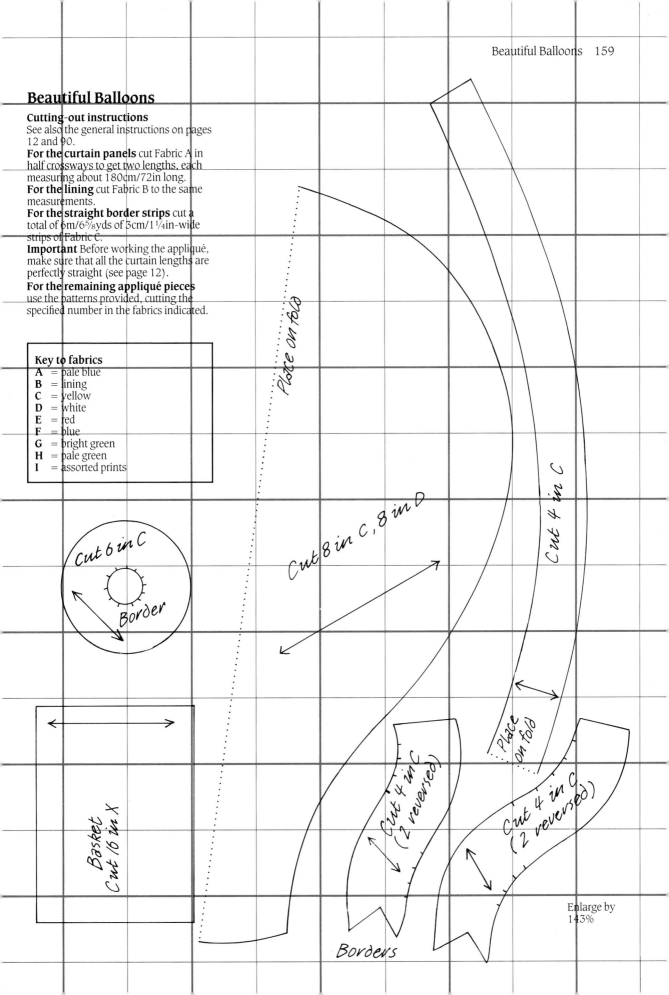

Place on fold

Cut 6 in C

Border

Cut 8 in C, 8 in D

Cut 4 in C

Place on fold

Basket
Cut 16 in X

Cut 4 in C
(2 reversed)

Cut 4 in C
(2 reversed)

Borders

Enlarge by 143%

Vertical stripes

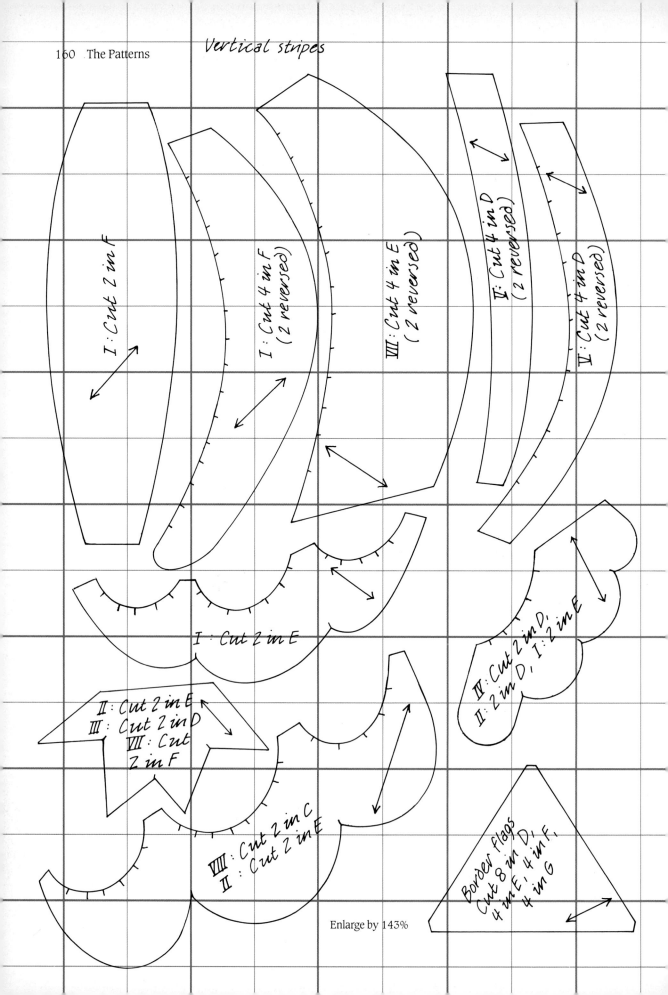

I : Cut 2 in F

I : Cut 4 in F
(2 reversed)

VII : Cut 4 in E
(2 reversed)

V : Cut 4 in D
(2 reversed)

V : Cut 4 in D
(2 reversed)

I : Cut 2 in E

IV : Cut 2 in D,
II : 2 in D, I : 2 in E

II : Cut 2 in E
III : Cut 2 in D
VII : Cut
2 in F

VIII : Cut 2 in C
II : Cut 2 in E

Border flags
Cut 8 in D,
4 in E, 4 in F,
4 in G

Enlarge by 143%

I: Cut
2 in C

III: Cut
2 in E

: Cut
in F

Horizontal stripes

VI: Cut 2 in D
IV: Cut 2 in E
III: Cut 2 in G

II: Cut 2 in C, IV: 2 in E,
V: 2 in F

IV: Cut 2 in D
VIII: Cut 2 in E

III: Cut 2 in D, 2 in G V: Cut 2 in F
VII: Cut 2 in F VI: Cut 4 in G

IV: Cut 2 in E
V: Cut 2 in F

I: Cut 4 in C
II: Cut 14 in C
III: Cut 6 in H,
    4 in D
IV: Cut 20 in D
V: Cut 8 in H
VII: Cut 6 in C
VIII: Cut 16 in E

Enlarge by 143%

Stars and Hearts

Cutting-out instructions
See also the general instructions on pages 12 and 60.

For the background piece cut Fabric A to measure 93 × 65cm/36 × 25½in.

For the lining cut Fabric B to the same size.

For the lattice strips cut four strips of Fabric C, each 65 × 11cm/25½ × 4¼in, and three strips, each 93 × 11cm/36 × 4¼in.

For the binding cut two 5cm/2in-wide strips of Fabric D, each 93cm/36in long, and two of the same width, each 70cm/27½in long.

For the rosettes cut twelve strips of Fabric D, each 30 × 7.5cm/12 × 31in.

For the inner edging strips cut twenty-four 2.5cm/1in-wide strips of Fabric F, each 20cm/8in long; two strips 93cm/36in long; and two strips 67cm/26½in long.

For the remaining appliqué pieces use the patterns provided, cutting the specified number in the fabrics indicated.

Key to fabrics
A = cream
B = red check
C = soft gold
D = coral red
E = dark red
F = pink
G = cream-yellow

Cut 3 in E

Enlarge by 143%

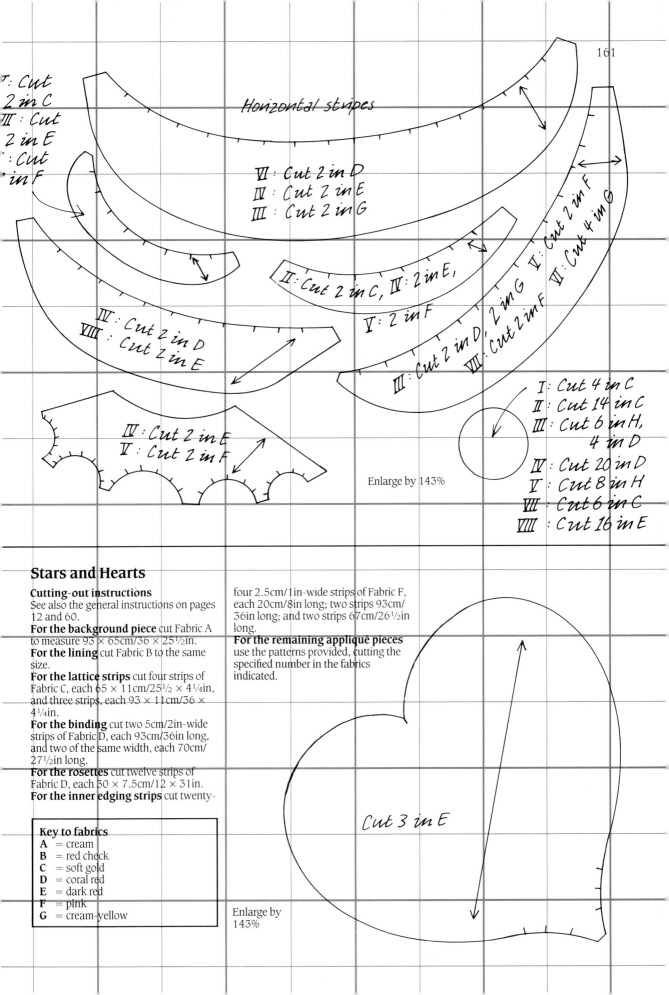

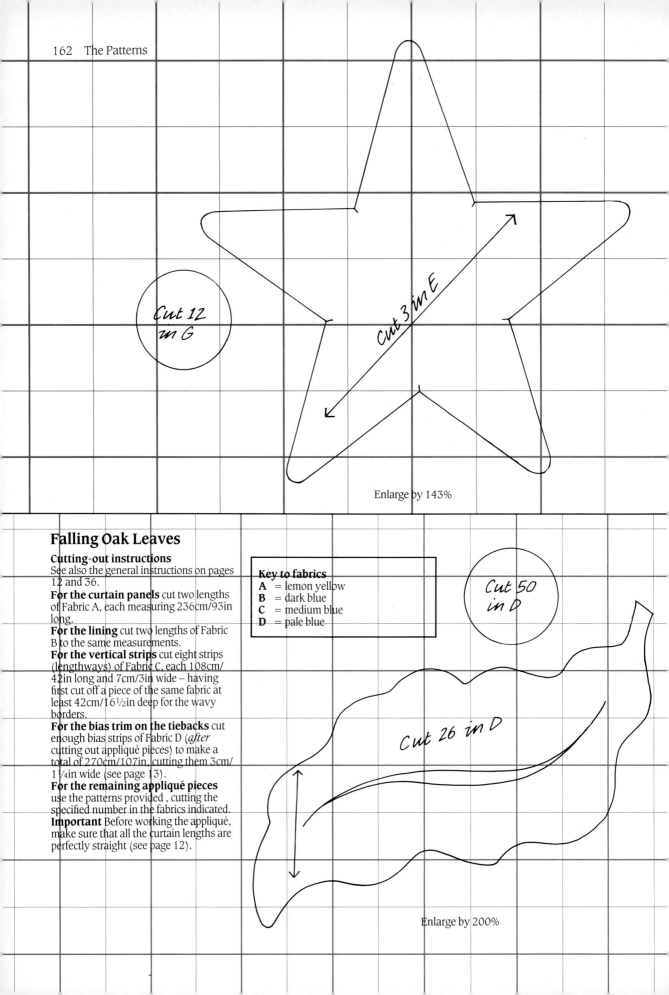

Cut 12 in G

Cut 3 in E

Enlarge by 143%

Falling Oak Leaves

Cutting-out instructions

See also the general instructions on pages 12 and 36.

For the curtain panels cut two lengths of Fabric A, each measuring 236cm/93in long.

For the lining cut two lengths of Fabric B to the same measurements.

For the vertical strips cut eight strips (lengthways) of Fabric C, each 108cm/ 42in long and 7cm/3in wide – having first cut off a piece of the same fabric at least 42cm/16½in deep for the wavy borders.

For the bias trim on the tiebacks cut enough bias strips of Fabric D (*after cutting out appliqué pieces*) to make a total of 270cm/107in, cutting them 3cm/ 1¼in wide (see page 13).

For the remaining appliqué pieces use the patterns provided , cutting the specified number in the fabrics indicated.

Important Before working the appliqué, make sure that all the curtain lengths are perfectly straight (see page 12).

Key to fabrics
A = lemon yellow
B = dark blue
C = medium blue
D = pale blue

Cut 50 in D

Cut 26 in D

Enlarge by 200%

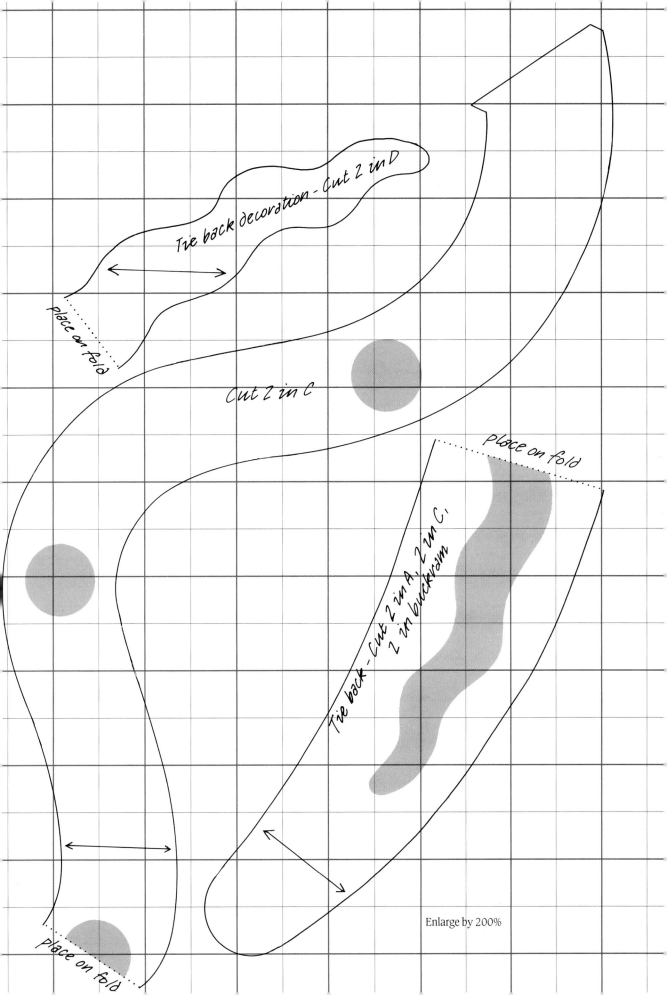

Tie back decoration - Cut 2 in D

place on fold

Cut 2 in C

place on fold

Tie back - Cut 2 in A, 2 in C, 2 in buckram

place on fold

place on fold

Enlarge by 200%

Fleur-de-Lys Variations

Cutting-out instructions

See also the general instructions on pages 12 and 72.

For each cushion cover cut four pieces of Fabric A, each 11.5 × 44cm/4½ × 17½in; one piece of Fabric A, 44 × 195cm/17½ × 7½in; one piece of Fabric A, 44 × 34cm/17½ × 13¼in; one piece of Fabric B, 24cm/9½in square.

For the piping cut enough 4cm/1½in-wide bias strips of Fabric E (see page 13) to make a total length of 10m/11yd.

For the appliqué pieces, use the patterns provided, cutting all except the wavy strip from Fabric C.

Note If the fabric you are using for the wavy strips tends to fray, add 3mm/⅛in around the edges, which will then need to be turned under and slipstitched.

Enlarge by 167%

Key to fabrics
A = blue
B = yellow
C = terracotta
D = print
E = small print (piping)

I : Cut 1 in C

II : Inner leaf
Cut 1 in C

I. Cut 1 in C

Cut 4 per cushion in D, with pinking shears

Cut 4 in C,
per cushion

Corner
Leaf shape

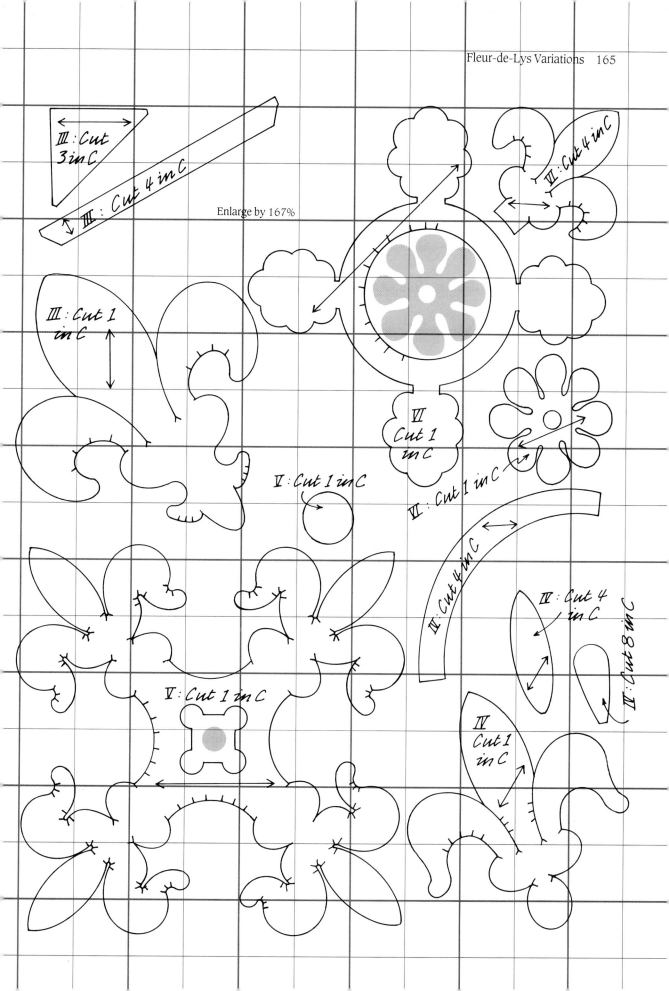

III : Cut 3 in C

III : Cut 4 in C

VI : Cut 4 in C

Enlarge by 167%

III : Cut 1 in C

VI Cut 1 in C

VI : Cut 1 in C

V : Cut 1 in C

VI : Cut 1 in C

II : Cut 4 in C

IV : Cut 4 in C

II : Cut 8 in C

IV Cut 1 in C

V : Cut 1 in C

Coral Reef with Mermaid

Cutting-out instructions

See also the general instructions on pages 12 and 76.

For the border cut two pieces of Fabric A, each 236 × 38cm/93 × 15in, and two pieces 87 × 38cm/34 × 15in.

For the centre panel cut one piece of Fabric B, 158 × 84cm/62 × 33in.

For the zigzag edging cut 112 5cm/2in squares of Fabric C.

For the serpents' teeth cut sixteen 2.5cm/1in squares of Fabric B.

For the narrow inner edging cut two strips of Fabric A, 160 × 2cm/63 × ¾in, and two strips 86 × 2cm/34 × ¾in.

For the narrow borders on the big fish and the mermaid's scales cut four strips of Fabric K on the bias, 26cm/10½in long and 1.2cm/½in wide.

For the outer binding cut enough 5cm/2in-wide strips of Fabric S to make up a strip 7.8m/8⅝yd long. This can be cut on the bias or on the crossways grain.

For the lining Cut Fabric T in half crossways.

For the remaining appliqué pieces use the patterns provided, cutting the specified number in the fabrics indicated.

For the multicoloured border cut strips of assorted fabrics (those used on the quilt shown are fabrics H, I , M and N), about 15cm/6in long and 4cm/1½in wide, enough to make up two strips 162cm/64in long and two 87cm/34in long.

Enlarge by 200%

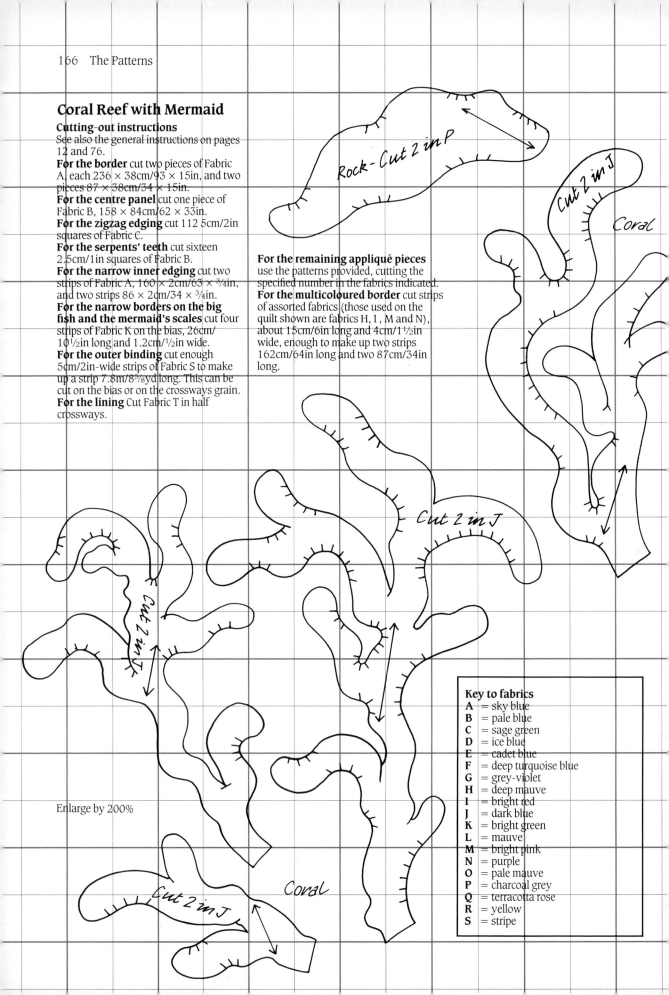

Rock - Cut 2 in P

Cut 2 in J

Coral

Cut 2 in J

Cut 2 in K

Cut 2 in J

Coral

Key to fabrics

A = sky blue
B = pale blue
C = sage green
D = ice blue
E = cadet blue
F = deep turquoise blue
G = grey-violet
H = deep mauve
I = bright red
J = dark blue
K = bright green
L = mauve
M = bright pink
N = purple
O = pale mauve
P = charcoal grey
Q = terracotta rose
R = yellow
S = stripe

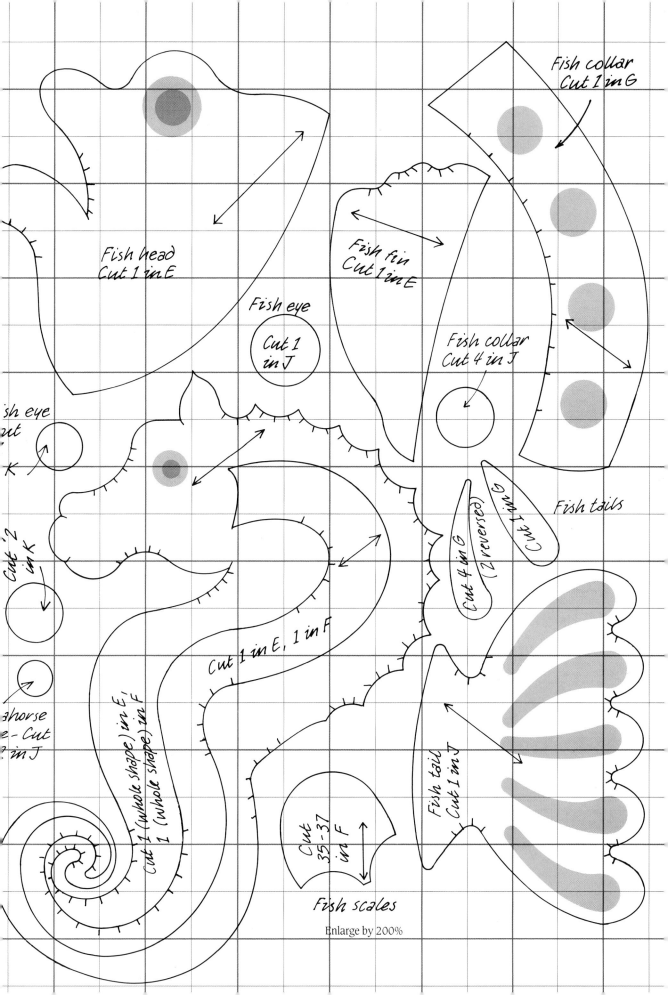

Fish collar
Cut 1 in G

Fish head
Cut 1 in E

Fish fin
Cut 1 in E

Fish eye

Cut 1
in J

Fish collar
Cut 4 in J

sh eye
ut

K

Fish tails

Cut 4 in G
(2 reversed)

Cut 1 in G

Cut 2
in K

Cut 1 in E, 1 in F

ahorse
e - Cut
? in J

Cut 1 (whole shape) in E,
1 (whole shape) in F

Fish tail
Cut 1 in J

Cut
35 - 37
in F

Fish scales

Enlarge by 200%

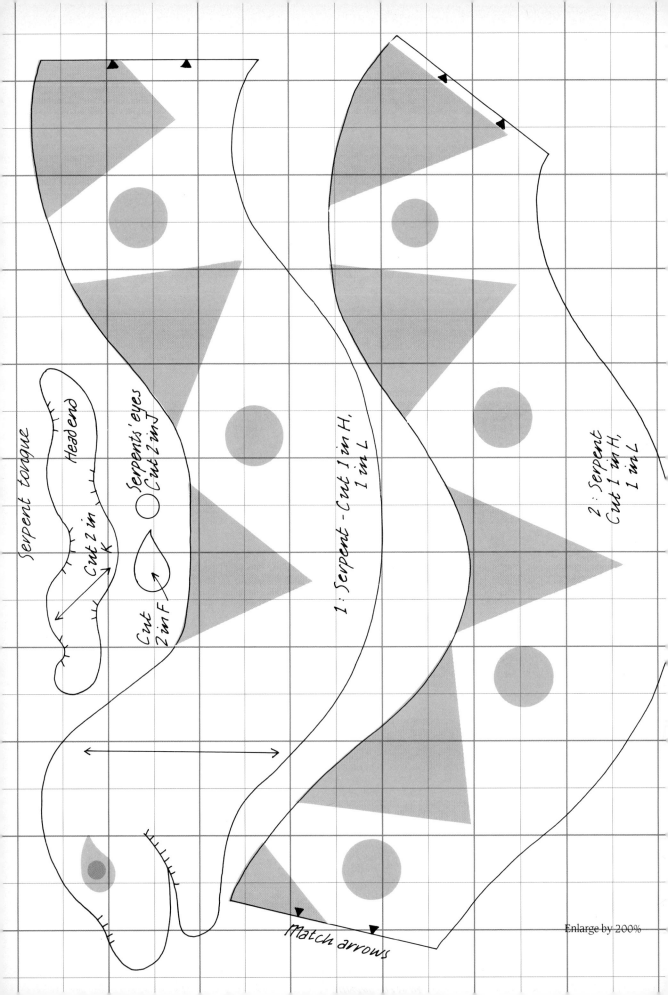

Serpent tongue

Head end

Cut 2 in K

Serpent's eyes
Cut 2 in J

Cut 2 in F

1: Serpent - Cut 1 in H,
1 in L

2: Serpent
Cut 1 in H,
1 in L

Match arrows

Enlarge by 200%

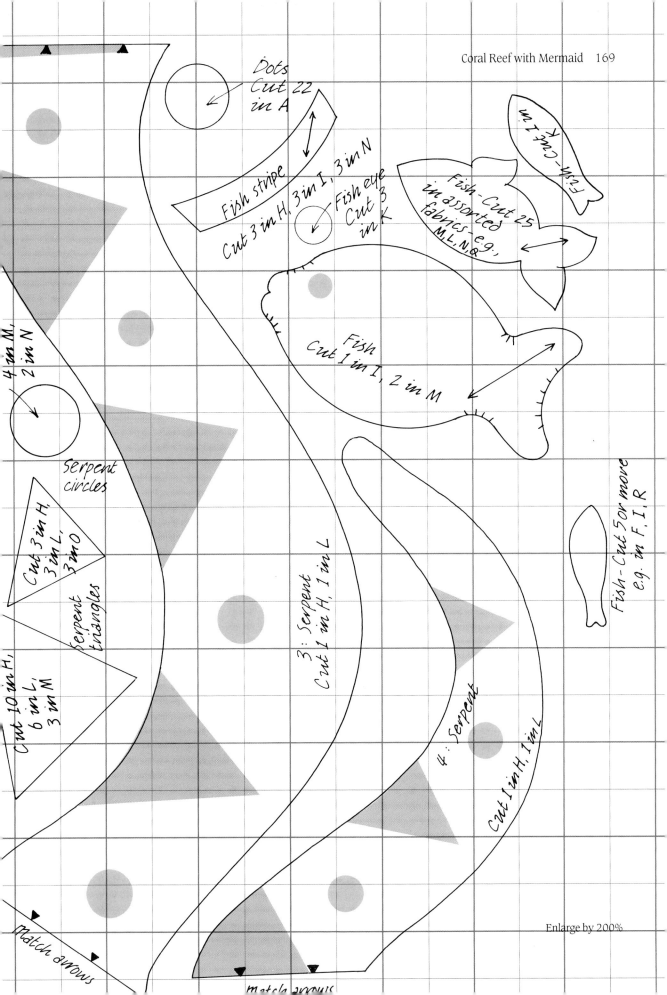

Dots
Cut 22
in A

Fish stripe.
Cut 3 in H, 3 in I, 3 in N

Fish eye
Cut 3
in K

Fish – Cut in K

Fish – Cut 25
in assorted
fabrics – e.g.,
M, L, N, &

Fish
Cut 1 in I, 2 in M

Fish – Cut 5 or more
e.g. in F, I, R

4 in M,
2 in N

Serpent
circles

Cut 3 in H,
3 in L,
3 in O

Serpent
triangles

Cut 10 in H,
6 in L,
3 in M

3: Serpent
Cut 1 in H, 1 in L

4: Serpent
Cut 1 in H, 1 in L

Match arrows

match arrows

Enlarge by 200%

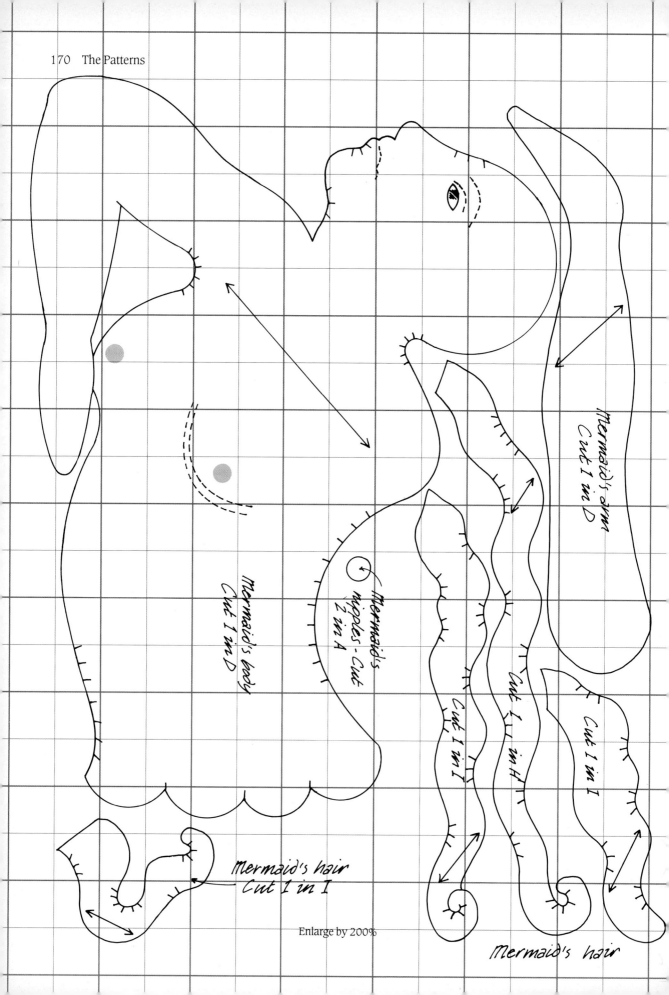

Mermaid's arm
Cut 1 in D

Mermaid's body
Cut 1 in D

Mermaid's
nipples - Cut
2 in A

Cut 1 in I

Cut 1 in H

Cut 1 in I

Mermaid's hair
Cut 1 in I

Enlarge by 200%

Mermaid's hair

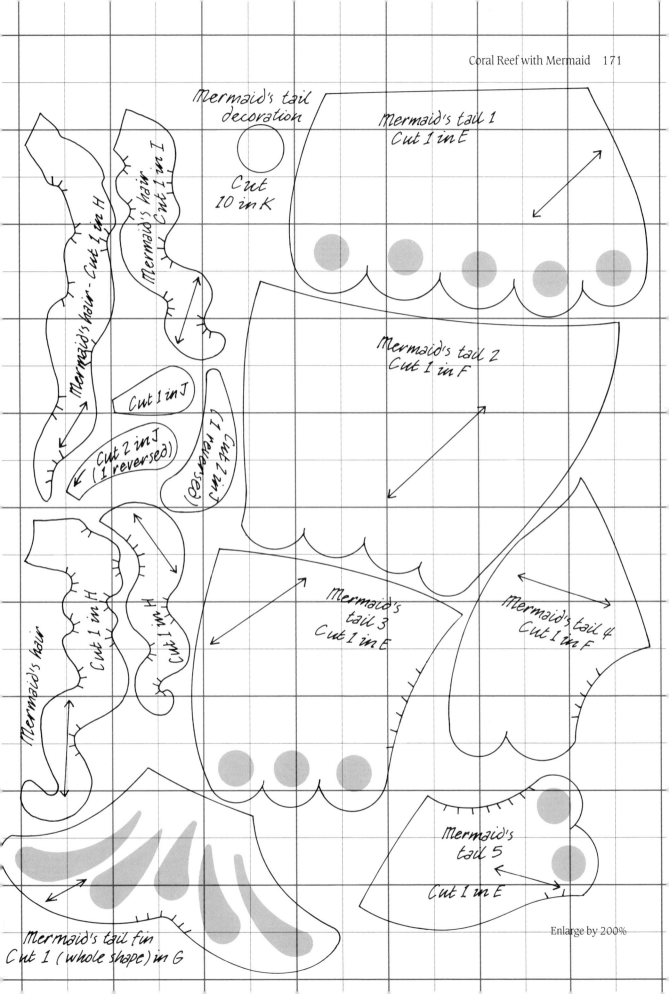

Mermaid's tail
decoration

Cut
10 in K

Mermaid's tail 1
Cut 1 in E

Mermaid's hair - Cut 1 in H

Mermaid's hair
Cut 1 in I

Cut 1 in J

Cut 2 in J
(1 reversed)

Cut 1 in J
(1 reversed)

Mermaid's tail 2
Cut 1 in F

Cut 1 in H

Cut 1 in H

Mermaid's hair

Mermaid's
tail 3
Cut 1 in E

Mermaid's tail 4
Cut 1 in F

Mermaid's
tail 5

Cut 1 in E

Mermaid's tail fin
Cut 1 (whole shape) in G

Venetian Gothic

Cutting-out instructions

See also the general instructions on pages 12 and 84.

For the main pieces and appliqué shapes use the patterns provided, cutting the specified number in the fabrics indicated.

For binding the lower edges cut three bias strips of Fabric C, each 38 × 15cm/ 15 × 6in (so that the section containing the full width is 27cm/10½in long).

For binding the joined sections cut enough 4cm/1½in-wide strips of Fabric D to make a total length of 135cm/53in.

For the bias appliqué strips (to enclose the motifs) cut enough 2cm/¾in-wide strips of fabrics E, G and I to make a total of 95cm/37½in in each colour.

For the inner edging strips (for arches and columns) cut enough 1.5cm/⅝in-wide strips of fabrics E, G and I (on the straight grain) to make a total of 45cm/ 18in in each colour.

For the columns cut three rectangles, 12.5 × 4.5cm/4¾ × 1¾in, from each of fabrics F, H and K, cutting them horizontally, diagonally and vertically, respectively.

From the wadding cut three rectangles, each 24 × 9cm/9½ × 3½in.

Cut 3 in K,
3 in B,
3 in wadding

Place on fold

Key to fabrics

A	= black
B	= lining
C	= red and gold stripe
D	= black and gold stripe
E	= bright gold
F	= woven stripe (side 1)
G	= silver grey
H	= woven stripe (side 2)
I	= copper brown
J	= red
K	= woven stripe (side 3)

Enlarge by 134%

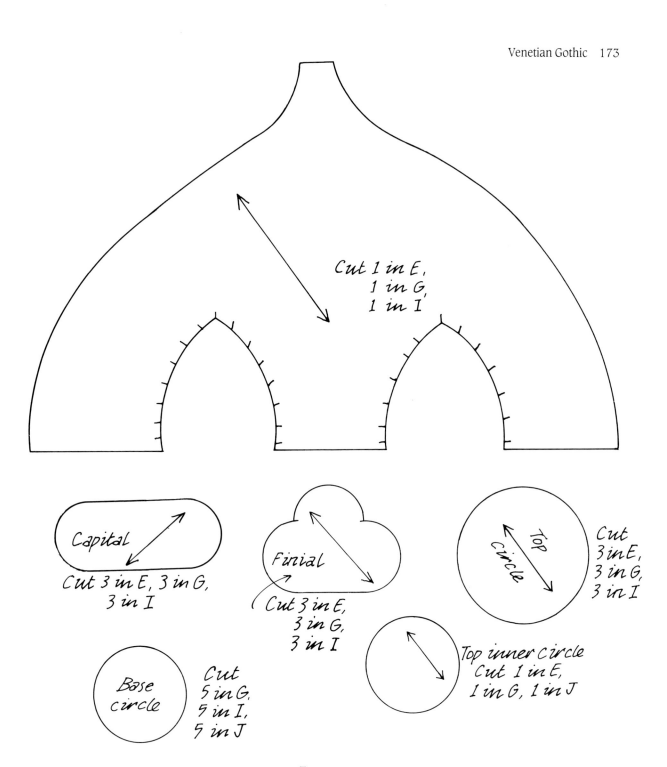

Cut 1 in E,
1 in G,
1 in I

Capital
Cut 3 in E, 3 in G,
3 in I

Finial
Cut 3 in E,
3 in G,
3 in I

Top circle
Cut
3 in E,
3 in G,
3 in I

Base circle
Cut
5 in G,
5 in I,
5 in J

Top inner circle
Cut 1 in E,
1 in G, 1 in J

Trace pattern

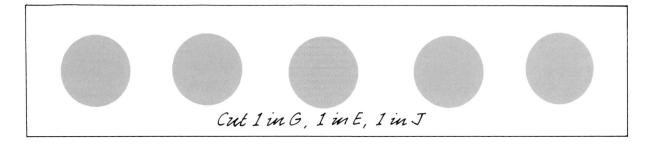

Cut 1 in G, 1 in E, 1 in J

Bowl of Fruit

Cutting-out instructions

See also the general instructions on pages 12 and 96.

For the main cushion pieces cut one piece of Fabric A, 44cm/17in square; one piece 44 × 11cm/17 × 4¼in; and one piece 44 × 43cm/17 × 16¼in.

For the piping cut enough 6cm/2½in-wide bias strips of Fabric E to make a total length of 180cm/71in.

For the appliqué pieces use the patterns provided, cutting the specified number in the fabrics indicated.

Key to fabrics	
A	= light blue
B	= gold
C	= ice blue
D	= dark turquoise
E	= mid blue-green
F	= dark blue

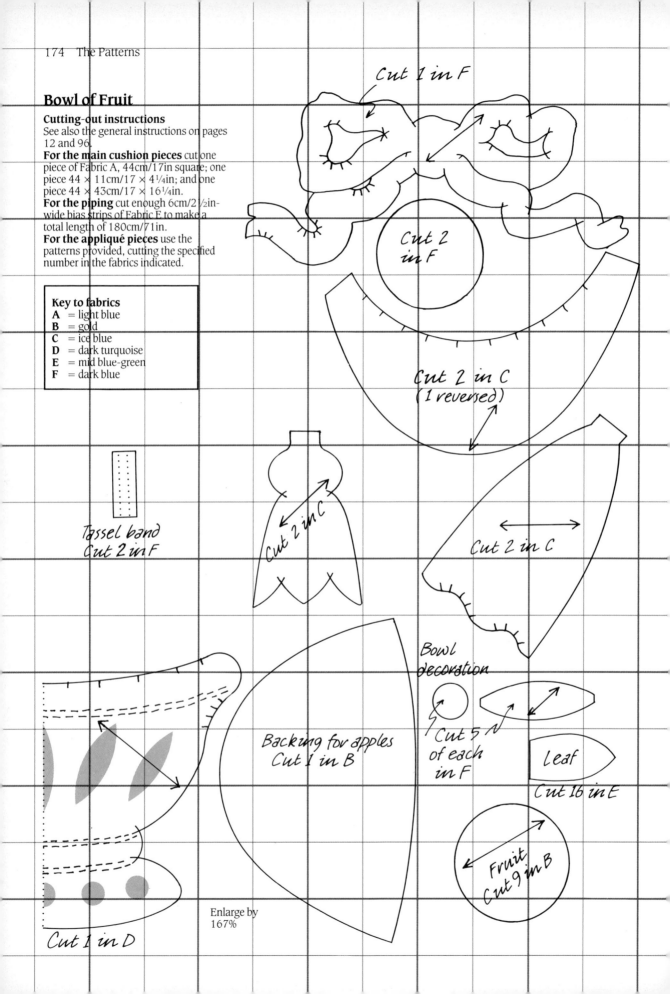

Cut 1 in F

Cut 2 in F

Cut 2 in C
(1 reversed)

Tassel band
Cut 2 in F

Cut 2 in C

Cut 2 in C

Bowl
decoration

Backing for apples
Cut 1 in B

Cut 5
of each
in F

Leaf

Cut 16 in E

Fruit
Cut 9 in B

Cut 1 in D

Enlarge by
167%

Trompe l'Oeil

Cutting-out instructions

See also the general instructions on pages 12 and 102.

For the circular undercloth cut Fabric A in half crossways, then cut one of the halves in half again lengthways.

For the background shape (red) make a pattern from the main tablecloth piece, after cutting the circle, as described in Step 2, page 104. Place the cloth on a large piece of paper, and trace the edge for a distance of 60cm/24in. Draw a perpendicular line from the centre of the curve to a point about 25cm/10in above it. Join the ends of the curve and the straight line, forming another curve. Cut out the pattern and use it to cut one background shape in Fabric C and one in D.

For the overcloth cut a piece of Fabric B measuring 65cm/26in square.

For the knitting bag cut a piece of Fabric F measuring 39 × 37cm/15½ × 14½in.

For the remaining appliqué pieces use the patterns provided, cutting the specified number in the fabrics indicated. If using ordinary – unquilted – fabric for the footstool pad, cut an additional piece from thin wadding, and trim off a scant 5mm/¼in all around it.

For the spectacles trace the outline provided. Set this aside for use later.

Enlarge by 167%

Key to fabrics

A = black and white plaid
B = white
C = red
D = calico lining
E = black cotton velvet
F = black and white check
G = black glazed cotton
H = grey
I = quilted print
J = soft black velvet
K = small print (for largest jar)
L = larger check
M = charcoal grey
N = pearl grey
X = assorted small prints

Cut 1 in H

Cut 1 in J

Cut 2 in G

Cut 2 in G

Place on fold

Place on fold

Cut 1 in I

Cut 1 in G

Cut 2 in M

Cut 2 in G

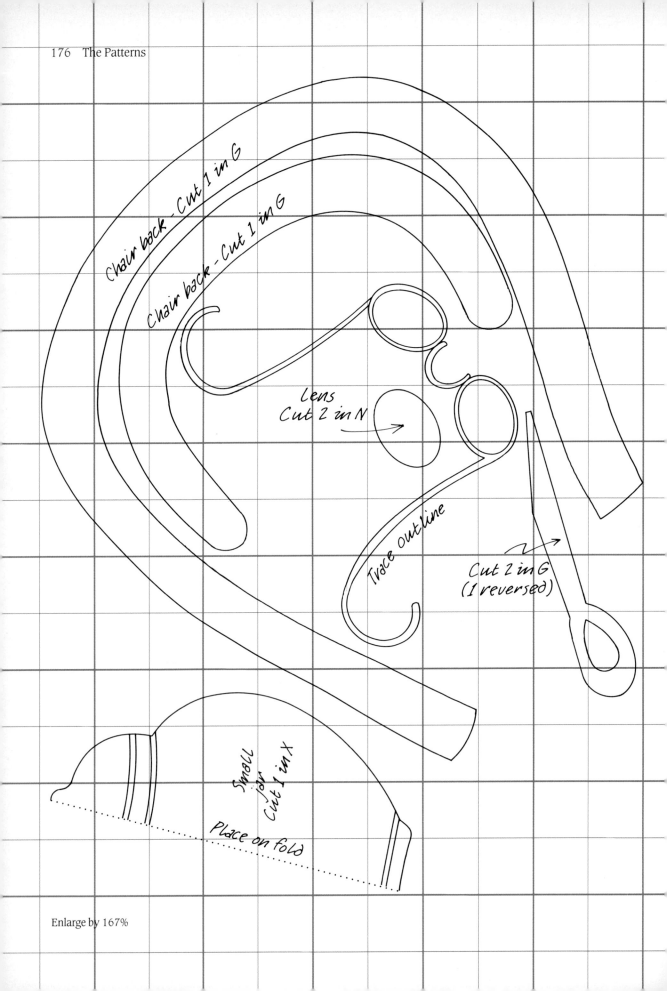

Chair back – Cut 1 in G

Chair back – Cut 1 in G

Lens
Cut 2 in N

Trace outline

Cut 2 in G
(1 reversed)

Small
for
Cut 1 in X

Place on fold

Enlarge by 167%

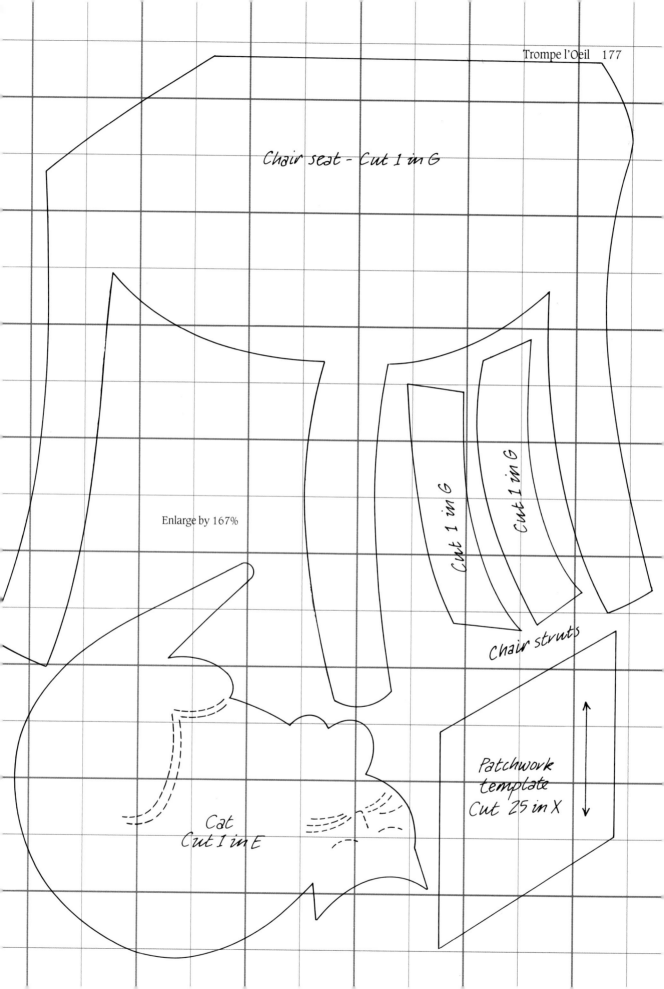

Chair seat - Cut 1 in G

Enlarge by 167%

Cut 1 in G

Cut 1 in G

Chair struts

Cat
Cut 1 in E

Patchwork
template
Cut 25 in X

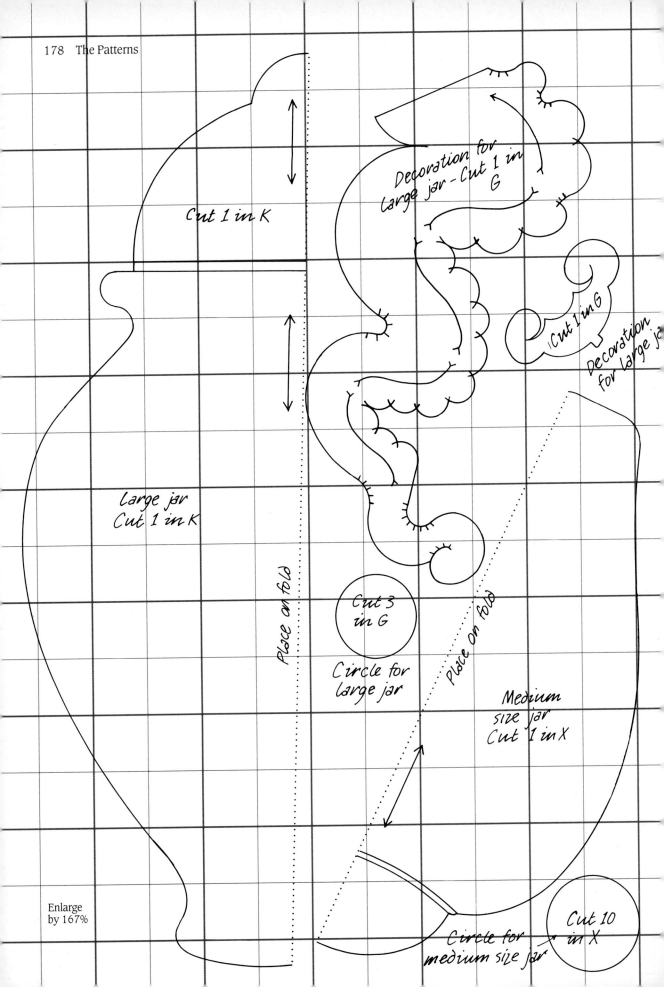

Cut 1 in K

Decoration for
Large jar - Cut 1 in
G

Cut 1 in G

Decoration
for large jar

Large jar
Cut 1 in K

Place on fold

Cut 3
in G

Circle for
large jar

Place on fold

Medium
size jar
Cut 1 in X

Enlarge
by 167%

Cut 10
in X

Circle for
medium size jar

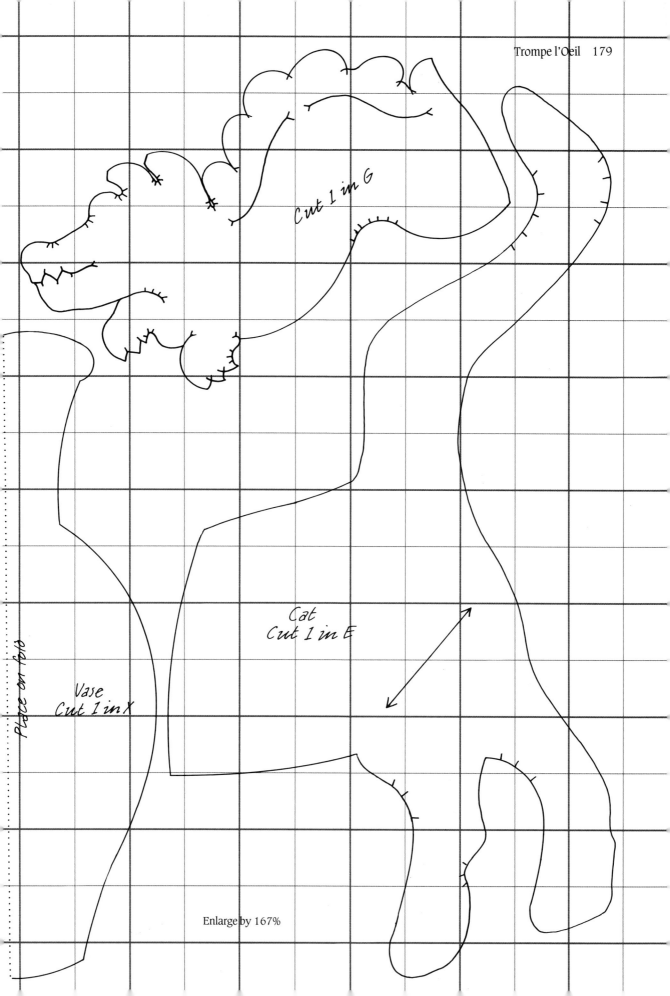

Cut 1 in G

Cat
Cut 1 in E

Vase
Cut 1 in X

Place on fold

Enlarge by 167%

Carrot Patch

Cutting-out instructions

See also the general instructions on pages 12 and 114.

For the patchwork cut eight squares of Fabric A and nine of Fabric B, each 18 × 18cm/7 × 7in, plus four squares of Fabric A and three squares of Fabric B, all 20 × 20cm/8 × 8in. Cut each of the larger squares in half diagonally to make eight and six triangles of fabrics A and B respectively.

For the binding cut four strips of Fabric F, each 6.5cm/2½in wide: make two 90cm/36in long and two 71cm/28in long

For the inner edging strips cut four strips of Fabric C, each 1.5cm/½in wide: make two 87cm/34in long and two 65cm/26in long.

For the appliqué pieces use the patterns provided, cutting the specified number in the fabrics indicated.

For the embroidered details trace the lines from the enlarged patterns.

Enlarge by 134%

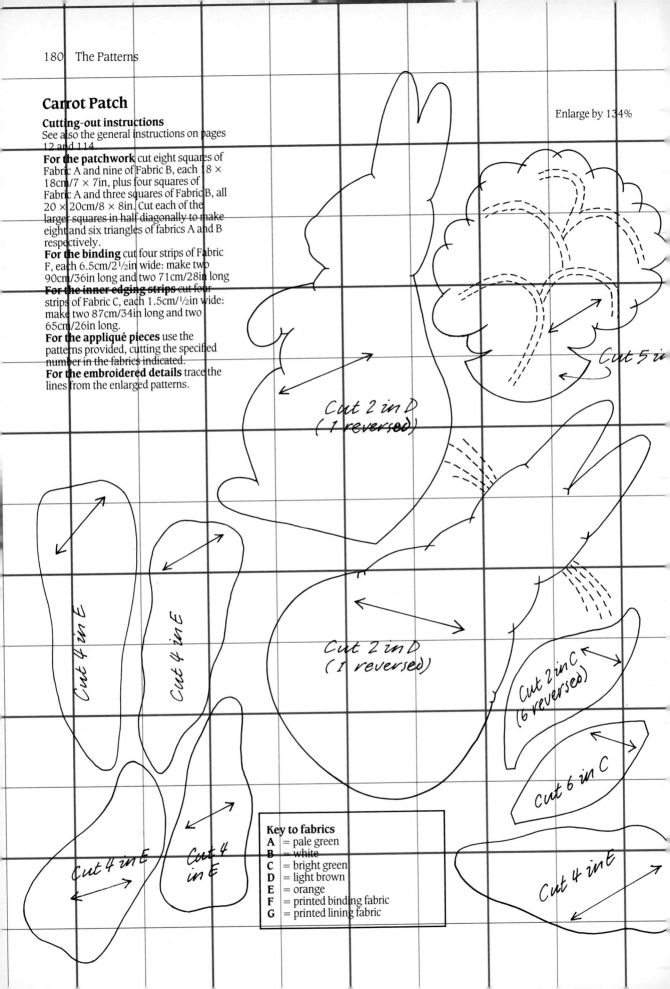

Cut 5 in C

Cut 2 in D
(1 reversed)

Cut 2 in D
(1 reversed)

Cut 2 in C
(6 reversed)

Cut 6 in C

Cut 4 in E

Cut 4 in E

Cut 4 in E

Cut 4 in E

Cut 4 in E

Key to fabrics	
A	= pale green
B	= white
C	= bright green
D	= light brown
E	= orange
F	= printed binding fabric
G	= printed lining fabric

Stained Glass Window

Cutting-out instructions
See also the general instructions on pages 12 and 126.
For the cover first make a pattern for a circle 50cm/19½in in diameter, using one of the methods described on page 14. Use this pattern to cut one circle of the main fabric and one of calico. Then cut the pattern in half. Use the two pieces to cut two semicircles of the main fabric, adding 6cm/2½in to the straight edges: 2cm/1in for the overlap and 4cm/1½in for turning under. Also cut and join 13cm/5in-wide strips of the main fabric to make a strip 150cm/59in long; this will make the side of the cushion.

For the piping cut enough 5cm/2in-wide bias strips (see page 13) of the various contrasting fabrics to make a total of 3m/3⅜yd when joined. The individual strips should measure about 15–18cm/6–7in long.
For the appliqué first trace the outlined shapes the number of times specified. Then, for each traced shape cut a corresponding piece of backing fabric, using the shaded patterns provided.

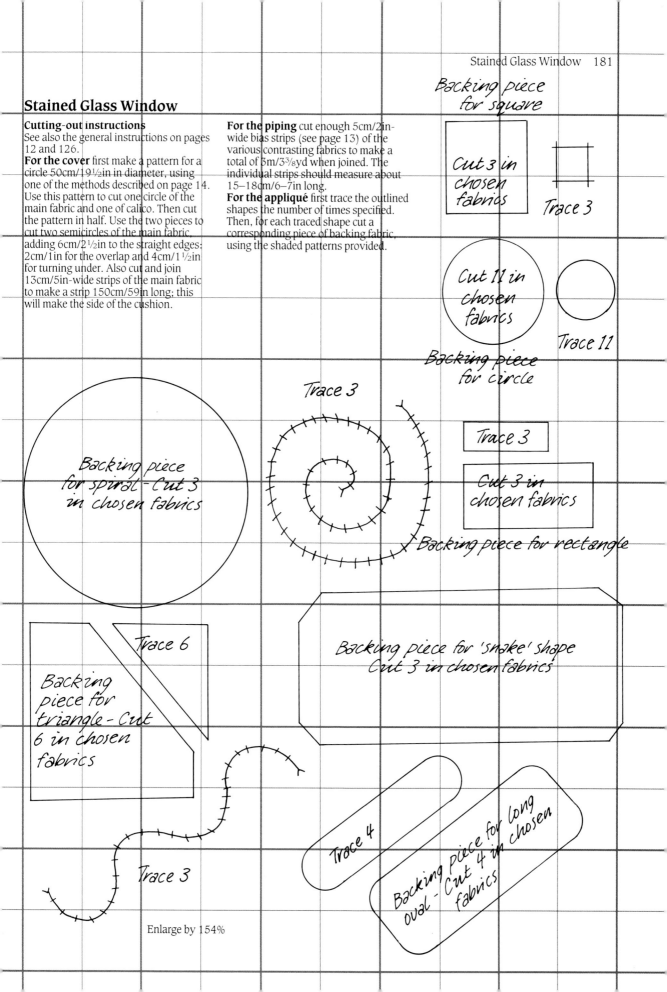

Backing piece for square

Cut 3 in chosen fabrics

Trace 3

Cut 11 in chosen fabrics

Trace 11

Backing piece for circle

Trace 3

Backing piece for spiral - Cut 3 in chosen fabrics

Trace 3

Cut 3 in chosen fabrics

Backing piece for rectangle

Backing piece for 'snake' shape Cut 3 in chosen fabrics

Trace 6

Backing piece for triangle - Cut 6 in chosen fabrics

Trace 4

Backing piece for long oval - Cut 4 in chosen fabrics

Trace 3

Enlarge by 154%

Fun with Numbers

Cutting-out instructions

See also the general instructions on pages 12 and 120.

For the squares cut twelve pieces of Fabric A, twelve of Fabric D and twelve of the wadding, each 24cm/9½in square.

For the binding and loops cut the following strips from Fabric C: forty-eight strips each 26 × 4cm/10¼ × 1½in; twenty-four strips, each 6 × 2cm/2¼ × ¾in; twelve strips, each 10 × 4cm/4 × 1½in.

For the appliqué pieces use the patterns provided, cutting the specified number in the chosen or specified fabrics.

Additional pieces: pyjama legs – cut two pieces, 17 and 19cm/6½ × 7½in long and 8cm/3¼in wide; crayons – cut binding into 10cm/4in lengths and trim as required.

For the lady's features and the clock numerals, trace the lines from the patterns after enlarging them.

Key to fabrics
A = calico
B = red print
C = blue print
D = lining

Enlarge by 143%

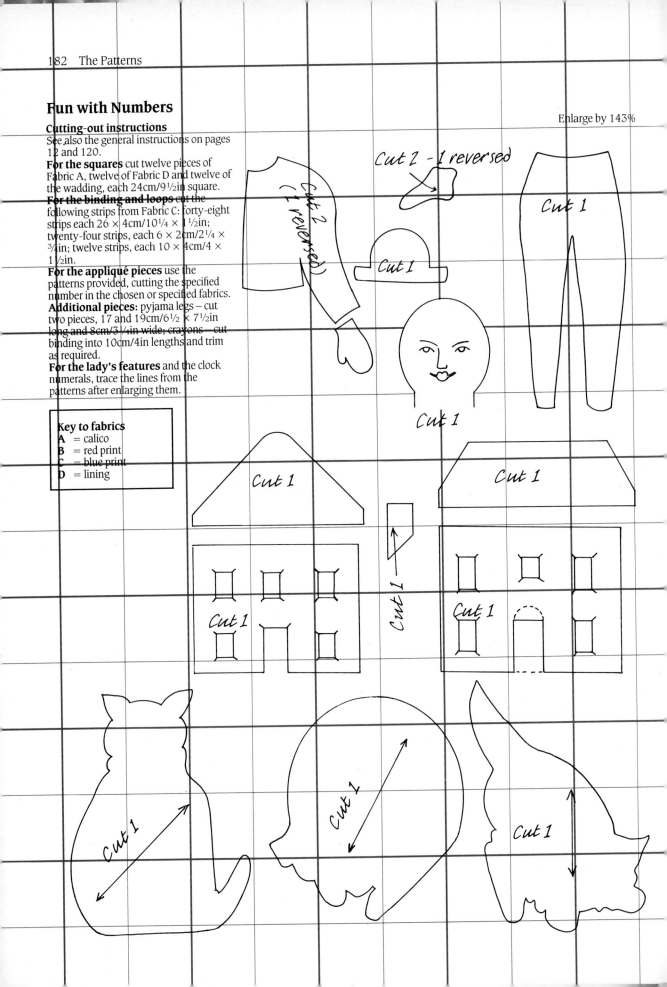

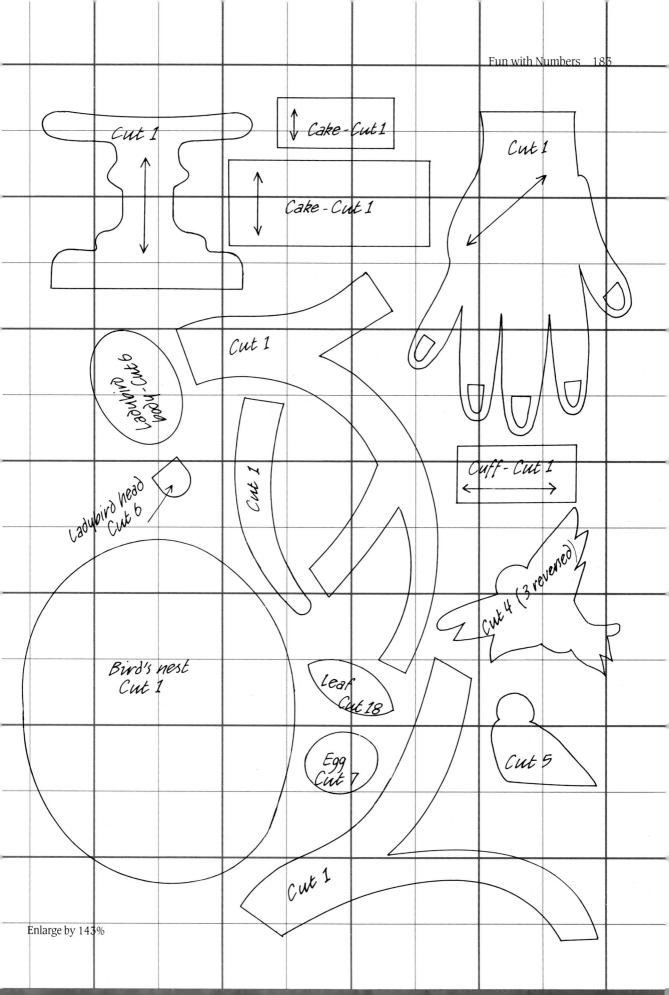

Cut 1

Cake-Cut 1

Cake - Cut 1

Cut 1

Cut 1

Ladybird body - Cut 6

Ladybird head
Cut 6

Cut 1

Cuff - Cut 1

Cut 4 (3 reversed)

Bird's nest
Cut 1

Leaf
Cut 18

Egg
Cut 7

Cut 5

Cut 1

Enlarge by 143%

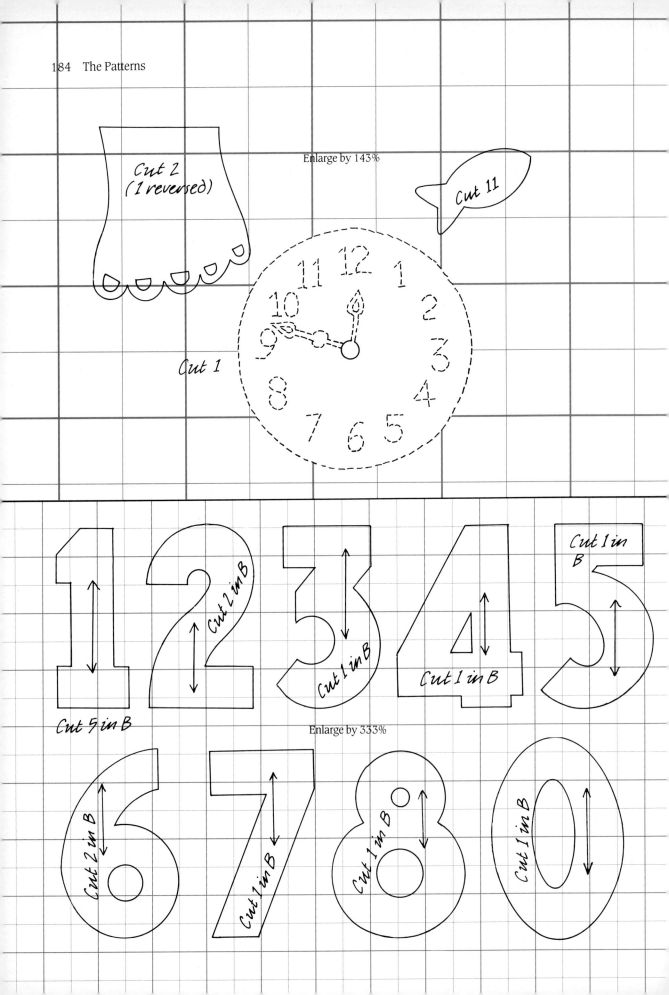

Chintamani

Cutting-out instructions

See also the general instructions on pages 12 and 138.

For the waistcoat first cut a 15cm/6in-wide strip from one long edge of Fabric A. This will serve as the neckband. Fold the remaining fabric in half lengthways, and cut the main pattern piece from this double thickness. Also cut the gusset piece.

For the lining cut the main piece and the gusset from a double thickness of Fabric C.

From the interfacing cut a strip 167cm/66in long and 5cm/2in wide.

For the appliqué use the patterns provided, cutting them the specified number of times from Fabric B.

Key to fabrics
A = rust
B = black
C = black and red lining

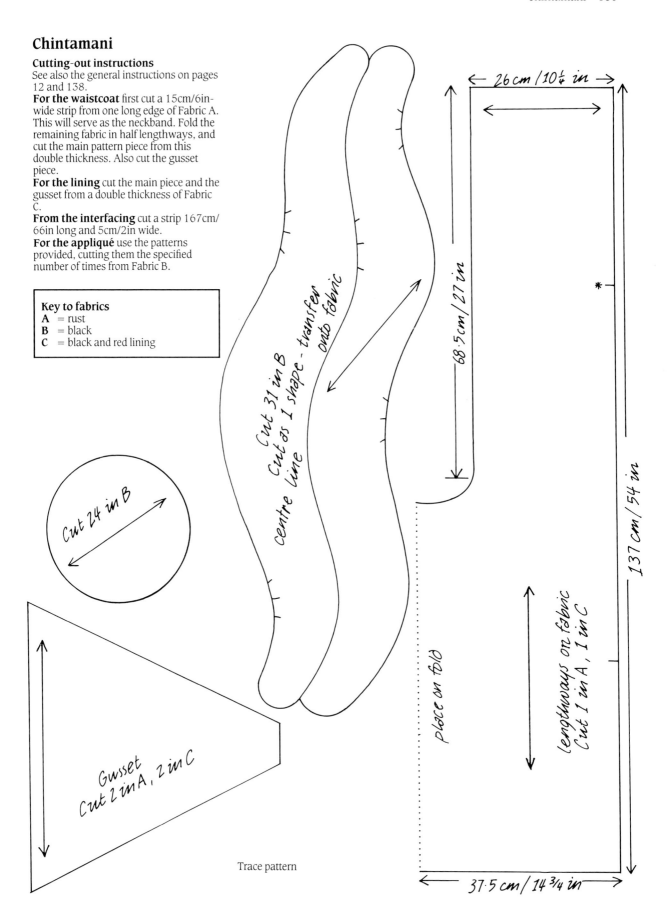

Cut 24 in B

Cut 31 in B
Cut as 1 shape – transfer onto fabric
centre line

place on fold

26 cm / 10¼ in

68·5 cm / 27 in

137 cm / 54 in

*

lengthways on fabric
Cut 1 in A, 1 in C

Gusset
Cut 2 in A, 2 in C

Trace pattern

37·5 cm / 14¾ in

Birds in the Trees

Cutting-out instructions

See also the general instructions on pages 12 and 130.

For the background cut Fabric A into two lengths, each 228cm/90in long.

For the lining cut five 28cm/11in-wide strips from the full length of Fabric B and four of the same width from Fabric C.

For the edging on the trees cut a total of 11.2m/12¼yd of 3.5cm/1¼in-wide bias strips (see page 13) from Fabric E. Turn under and press 5mm/¼in on one edge of all strips.

For the main border strips cut enough 5cm/2in-wide strips of Fabric F – on the straight grain – to make a total length of 4.1m/4½yd. Cut strips of the same width from Fabric G to make a total of 4.2m/4½ yd.

For the inner edging strips cut enough 2cm/¾in-wide strips of Fabric L – on the straight grain – to make a total length of 7.8m/8½ yd.

For the binding strips cut enough 3cm/1¼in-wide strips of Fabric R to make a total of 8.9m/9¾yd.

For the remaining appliqué pieces use the patterns provided, cutting the specified number in the fabrics indicated. Note that birds II and IV are used twice (once in reverse). Cut the body shapes first, then select appropriate colours for the wing and tail feathers for each bird.

For legs choose two from the four patterns shown to suit the position of each bird.

For beaks cut rectangles of approximately the size shown – two for each bird.

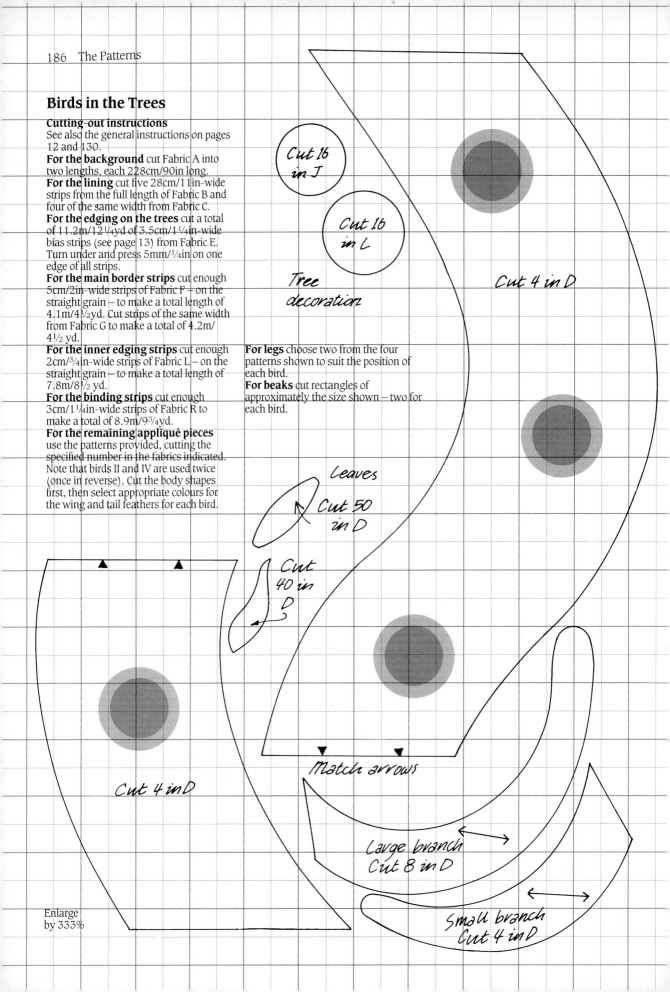

Cut 16 in J

Cut 16 in L

Tree decoration

Cut 4 in D

Leaves
Cut 50 in D

Cut 40 in D

Match arrows

Cut 4 in D

Large branch
Cut 8 in D

Small branch
Cut 4 in D

Enlarge by 333%

Enlarge by 200%

Key to fabrics
A = calico
B = bright pink (lining)
C = bright gold (lining)
D = grey-green
E = gold
F = light peach pink
G = sandy gold
H = pale apricot
I = soft gold
J = coral
K = mustard
L = strawberry pink
M = bright gold
N = olive green
O = medium brown
P = light rust
Q = bright gold print
R = green-gold

Border
Cut 32 in K,
32 in J

Corner leaf
Cut 4 in E

Border
Circle

Cut 68 in
assorted colours

Legs

I: Wing feather
Cut 1 in chosen fabric

I: Wing bar: Cut 1 in
chosen fabric

Birds' eyes - Cut
8 in chosen
fabrics

Wing feathers

I: Cut
chosen
1 in
fabric

I: Cut
chosen
1 in
fabric

I: Body
Cut 1 in I

I: Tail
feather

Cut 3 in
chosen fabrics

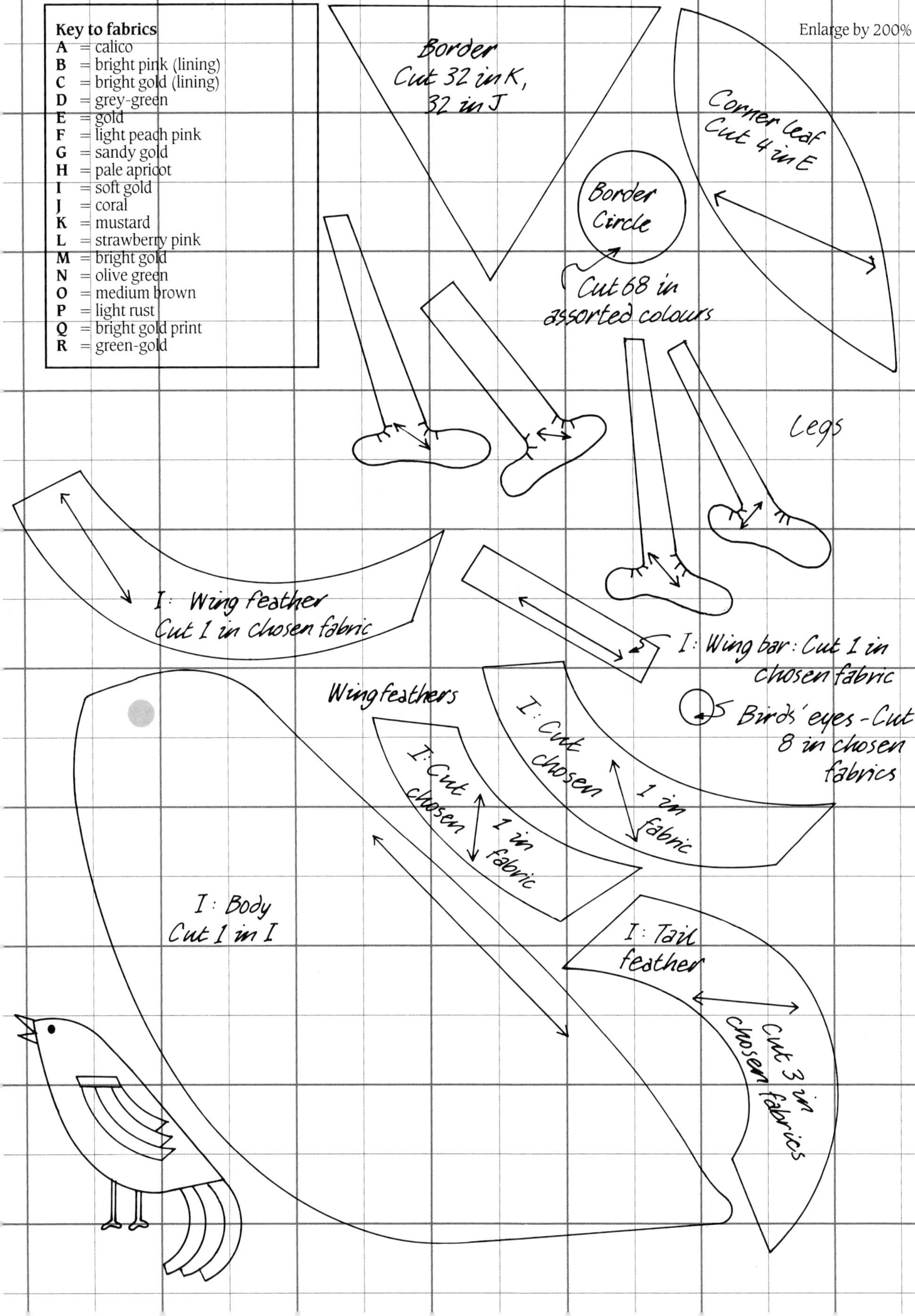

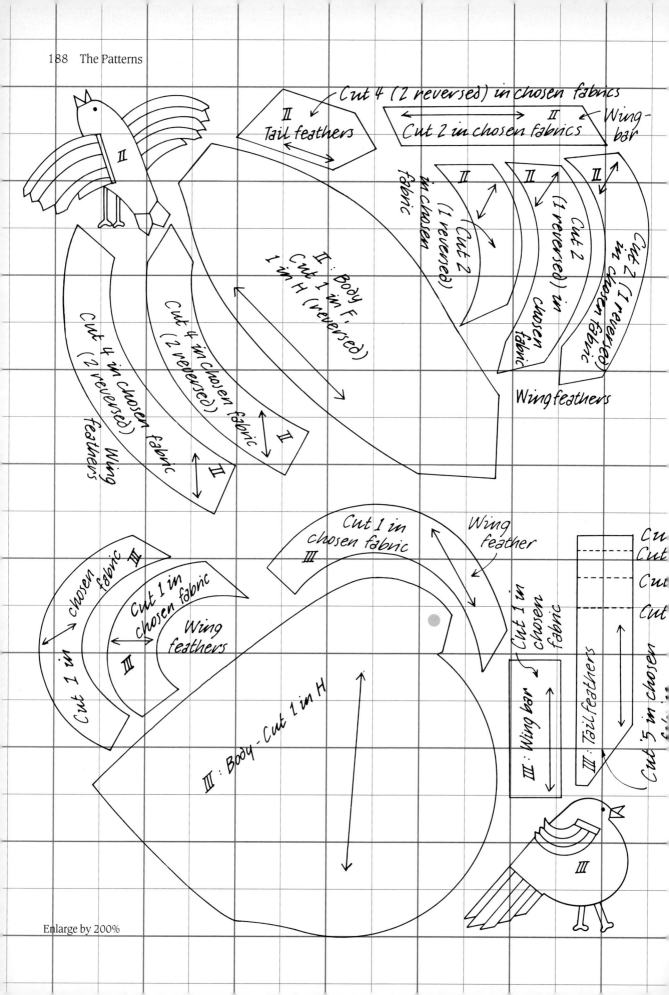

Cut 4 (2 reversed) in chosen fabrics

II Tail feathers

Cut 2 in chosen fabrics

Wing-bar

II

II

II

II Cut 2 (1 reversed) in chosen fabric

II Cut 2 (1 reversed) in chosen fabric

Cut 2 (1 reversed) in chosen fabric

II : Body Cut 1 in F, 1 in H (reversed)

Wing feathers

Cut 4 in chosen fabric (2 reversed) Wing feathers

Cut 4 in chosen fabric (2 reversed)

I

II

Cut 1 in chosen fabric III

Wing feather

Cut 1 in chosen fabric

III

III Cut 1 in chosen fabric

Cut 1 in chosen fabric III

Cut 1 in chosen fabric III Wing feathers

II : Body - Cut 1 in H

III : Wing bar

III : Tail feathers

Cut 5 in chosen fabric

Cut

Cut

Cut

Cut

III

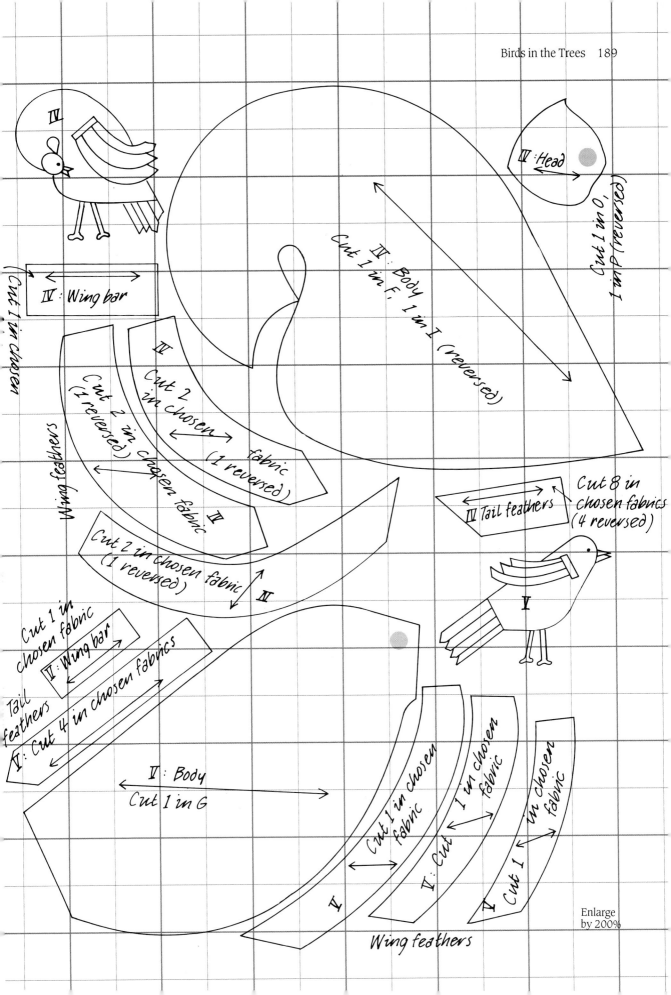

IV

IV : Head

Cut 1 in O,
1 in P (reversed)

IV : Wing bar

(Cut 1 in chosen

IV : Body
Cut 1 in f, 1 in I (reversed)

IV
Cut 2
in chosen   fabric
(1 reversed)

Cut 2 in chosen fabric
(1 reversed)   IV

Wing feathers

Cut 2 in chosen fabric
(1 reversed)   II

IV Tail feathers

Cut 8 in
chosen fabrics
(4 reversed)

Cut 1 in
chosen fabric

V : Wing bar

Tail
feathers

V : Cut 4 in chosen fabrics

V : Body
Cut 1 in G

V

Cut 1 in chosen
fabric

V : Cut 1 in chosen
fabric

V   Cut 1
in chosen
fabric

V

Wing feathers

Enlarge
by 200%

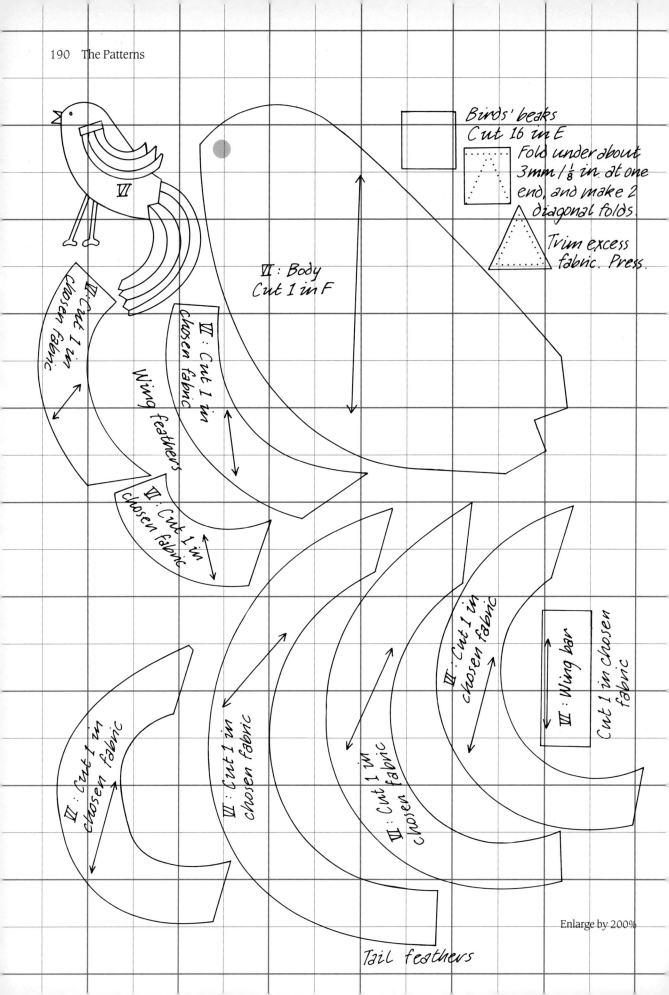

VI

VI : Body
Cut 1 in F

Birds' beaks
Cut 16 in E
Fold under about
3mm / ⅛ in. at one
end, and make 2
diagonal folds.
Trim excess
fabric. Press.

VI : Cut 1 in chosen fabric

VI : Cut 1 in chosen fabric

Wing feathers

VI : Cut 1 in chosen fabric

VI : Cut 1 in chosen fabric

VI : Cut 1 in chosen fabric

VI : Cut 1 in chosen fabric

VI : Cut 1 in chosen fabric

VI : Cut 1 in chosen fabric

VI : Wing bar
Cut 1 in chosen fabric

Enlarge by 200%

Tail feathers

Index

Acknowledgments

AUTHOR'S ACKNOWLEDGMENTS

First of all I would like to thank Olga, Kitty and Nell for being so encouraging and patient, and for their good ideas. Many thanks, also, to Rita Keskecs and Julie Shipp for looking after them.

Janis Clarke and Betty Groenevelt were both a terrific help with the sewing, I couldn't possibly have managed without them. Very many thanks to them and also to Ursula Simon, Christine Jay and Jacqui Watkins.

I would like to thank Rachel Campbell and Anne Fraser, whose idea it was in the first place, and, finally, all those at Frances Lincoln Limited who have worked on this book and have been such a help to me in different ways: Sallie Coolidge, Susanne Haines, Caroline Hillier, Anne Kilborn and Louise Tucker. Grateful thanks to Eleanor Van Zandt for her meticulous editing.

The white and yellow collage on page 131 is by Sebastian Verney.

PUBLISHER'S ACKNOWLEDGMENTS

The publisher would like to thank the following individuals for their help in the preparation of this book: Sylvia Ayton, Michael Dunne, Erica Hunningher, Debbie MacKinnon and Crispin Rose-Innes who kindly allowed us to use their homes for photography; Eleanor Van Zandt for her expertise and enthusiasm.

For their kind permission to reproduce the appliqué works illustrated in the Introduction to this book, the publishers would like to thank the following: The Augustinermuseum, Freiburg , page 6 (*right*); James W. Reid and Dover Publications, New York, page 6 (*left*); Henry Ford Museum, Dearborn, Mich., page 7; Schwenkfelder Museum, Pennsburg, Pa., page 8 (*left*); Strangers Hall, Norfolk Museum Service, page 8 (*right*); Victoria & Albert Museum, page 9; Liz Nunez-Perez, *Textile Arts,* M. Singer and M. Spyrou and A & C Black (Publishers) Limited, page 10 (*above*); Chile Solidarity Campaign, page 10 (*below*).

Illustrators

Sarah-Jayne Stafford pages 144–90;
Rose Verney pages 12–142

Hand lettering

Richard Bird

Photographers

Michael Dunne pages 23, 27, 29, 45, 49, 51, 54, 59, 61, 63, 85, 89, 97, 115, 130, 131
Tim Imrie pages 31, 33, 37, 39, 40–1, 42–3, 65, 68, 73, 77, 81, 91, 95, 102, 103, 113, 120–1, 122–3, 125, 127, 129, 139

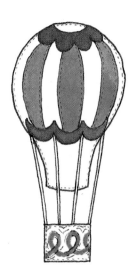

Editors Eleanor Van Zandt, Anne Kilborn
Art Editor Louise Tucker
Designers Clare Finlaison, Claudine Meissner, Karen Stafford
Production Controller Maureen Hegarty   **Picture Researcher** Sue Gladstone
Art Director Caroline Hillier   **Editorial Director** Erica Hunningher
Picture Editor Anne Fraser